Culture, Place, and Nature Studies in Anthropology and Environment K. SIVARAMAKRISHNAN, SERIES EDITOR

Centered in anthropology, the Culture, Place, and Nature series encompasses new interdisciplinary social science research on environmental issues, focusing on the intersection of culture, ecology, and politics in global, national, and local contexts. Contributors to the series view environmental knowledge and issues from the multiple and often conflicting perspectives of various cultural systems.

The Camphor Tree

FAIZAH ZAKARIA

and the Elephant

RELIGION AND

ECOLOGICAL CHANGE

IN MARITIME

SOUTHEAST ASIA

University of Washington Press *Seattle*

The Camphor Tree and the Elephant *was made possible in part by a grant from the Association for Asian Studies First Book Subvention Program.*

Additional support was provided by the Charles and Jane Keyes Endowment for Books on Southeast Asia, established through the generosity of Charles and Jane Keyes.

UNIVERSITY OF WASHINGTON PRESS | *uwapress.uw.edu*

LIBRARY OF CONGRESS CATALOGING-IN-PUBLICATION DATA
Names: Zakaria, Faizah, author.
Title: The camphor tree and the elephant : religion and ecological change in maritime
    Southeast Asia / Faizah Zakaria.
Description: Seattle : University of Washington Press, [2023] | Series: Culture, place, and
    nature | Includes bibliographical references and index.
Identifiers: LCCN 2022034418 (print) | LCCN 2022034419 (ebook) | ISBN 9780295751191
    (hardcover) | ISBN 9780295751184 (paperback) | ISBN 9780295751177 (ebook)
Subjects: LCSH: Human ecology—Religious aspects—History—19th century. | Human
    ecology—Indonesia—Sumatera Utara—History—19th century. | Human ecology—
    Malay Peninsula—History—19th century. | Environmental degradation—Religious
    aspects—History—19th century. | Environmental degradation—Indonesia—Sumatera
    Utara—History—19th century. | Environmental degradation—Malay Peninsula—
    History—19th century. | Sumatera Utara (Indonesia)—Environmental conditions—19th
    century. | Malay Peninsula—Environmental conditions—19th century. | Sumatera Utara
    (Indonesia)—Religion—19th century. | Malay Peninsula—Religion—19th century.
Classification: LCC GF80 .Z34 2023 (print) | LCC GF80 (ebook) |
    DDC 201/.77—dc23/eng20221209
LC record available at https://lccn.loc.gov/2022034418
LC ebook record available at https://lccn.loc.gov/2022034419

♾ This paper meets the requirements of ANSI/NISO Z39.48-1992
    (Permanence of Paper).

To my nephews   Rehan, Amir, Zarif, and Zayn

CONTENTS

FOREWORD

In this gripping study, Faizah Zakaria provides an original account of the North Sumatran Highlands and Malay Peninsula during the nineteenth century. She is interested in the role played by religion in environmental change across these areas. While under the grip of colonial rule, various communities were reconstituted by both migrations and religious conversions as many of the forest people turned to monotheistic Islam and Christianity. This change occurred even as they adopted new forms of agriculture and as older social and political relations between forest uplands and riverine polities were curtailed.

As Zakaria shows in direct and elegant prose, by about 1800 CE several processes had begun to converge and interact in this region. One process was the spread of commercial agriculture, which brought with it migrations between lowlands and uplands accelerated by agrarian investments and associated displacements. Another was what she perceptively discusses as the entrenchment in North Sumatra of modern Islam, with its reformist zeal and bureaucratic forms. This shift in religious values and the practice of religion in the everyday contexts of North Sumatrans also reshaped the relationship of Islam and Christianity with animist faith to alter early-modern hybrid religious practices in which upland Islam had forged an accommodative relation with other religions, especially local forms of animist and spiritual practice and belief.

The consequence of these changes for the environment, forests, wild animals, and human life in the region is examined in a framework that Zakaria ably develops. She calls it the "spiritual Anthropocene." It is not her intent to relitigate the extensive debate on the origins and intensity of the Anthropocene in different historical periods. She wishes to insert into discussions of the Anthropocene a consideration of religion and thereby of concern with life other than that of humans. She argues that gods, spirits, and animals, as well as varied forest denizens, must enter these debates on human impact on the planet if we are to understand how religion—including spirituality, ritual, and conversion as its chief manifestations—is integral to profound and irreversible changes that have fundamentally altered the ecology of North Sumatra since the colonial period.

In her work, Zakaria alternates between finding common threads among the Batak people of the region and noting their differences in relation to subgroups in which they more readily locate themselves. Historical analysis of such upland peoples, who left a scanty historical record in their own terms, is challenging. She is creative, therefore, in using ethnographies, genealogies, and oral traditions along with colonial archives. She looks for insight into how various Batak groups thought about faith, agriculture, nonhuman life, and mobility or settlement across the uplands and returns with a carefully crafted account of how religious change and environmental change shaped each other. She provides a valuable historical and process-oriented analysis that charts new directions for fields such as spiritual ecology and for the study of religion and environment.[1] Too often in these kinds of research, ahistorical treatments of faith and its relation to nature have been more prevalent.

Zakaria maintains a resolute focus on everyday religious practices in the North Sumatran highlands and how they are enmeshed in broader changes in customs, farming, relations with forests and animals, trade, and migration. In this way she is also connecting this area to wider circuits from China to mainland Malaysia, South Asia, and the Middle East, providing a truly inter-Asia examination of the movement of faith and extractive economies across maritime Southeast Asia and its outer islands. Such an approach also avoids easy assumptions about premodern religions and practices and how they might have held the world of plants in esteem or served as a fount of native environmental ethics. Equally, the conversions to Islam and Christianity do not provide robust spiritual resources, Zakaria argues, for upland people like the Batak to form healthy, mutually respectful relations with the nonhuman world around them, itself under considerable stress from various extractive economies.

Having established the cultural and ecological patterns associated with intensive colonization of North Sumatra and rapid changes brought by modern faith and modern government, Zakaria considers the wars of the early nineteenth century and their impact on nature. She brings this valuable perspective from an out-of-the-way place, as did Anna Tsing in the context of South Kalimantan, Indonesia, to the historiography of a burgeoning field of study that considers the relation between war and the environment.[2] It was wars that brought the Dutch, commercial coffee cultivation, Christianity, and modern Islam to the region. Consequently, there were adverse consequences for spirits and their role in mediating human relations with the nonhuman world in the region of North Sumatra.

The second and third sections of the book range ambitiously and successfully across the Straits of Malacca, connecting lowlands to the uplands, considering both the impact of Dutch colonists in Indonesia and the British imperium in Malaysia. This sweep across the nineteenth century, the migrations and displacements experienced in that period, and the role modern monotheism played in severing enchanted connections among humans, plants, and animals all track the fate of many species that are now endangered. Notably, the camphor tree became mere timber to be cut, and the elephant was ruthlessly hunted, confined, and captured to facilitate agriculture and incorporate various animal products into a forest commodities trade.

This wonderful book leaves us with much to ponder in this moment of rising environmental concerns, which have left their imprint on modern monotheisms. The book emerges as a discussion of how conversion, commerce, and forced relocations deeply transformed human relations with nature in places like Sumatra, with implications for the rest of the world. It quite convincingly makes the case that a discussion of the Anthropocene is not complete without attention to the religious and spiritual dimensions of human life on a planet being irreversibly altered by human depredation. As Zakaria shows, spiritual beliefs and practices served as important wellsprings of human ethics and values in relations with the nonhuman universe. Like much else that was deeply transformed in their landscapes and lives, upland North Sumatrans found new forms of faith, trusted their salvation to new gods and saints, and layered modern beliefs about the place of the human in the wider universe onto older ideas of spiritual relations with nature. In this way she integrates land-use changes into everyday religion to show how a struggle over nature and environmental values was always also a struggle over moral values, spiritual beliefs, and the cultivation of pious selves.

K. Sivaramakrishnan
YALE UNIVERSITY

ACKNOWLEDGMENTS

I have always felt uneasy with the claims of individual expertise and even more so at the culmination of a project haunted by so many voices—past and present—from around the world. I am grateful to mentors, colleagues, and friends who have supported my research over the years. Much of this monograph was developed at Yale University with the guidance of faculty in the History Department, the Agrarian Studies Program, and the Southeast Asian Studies Program; my deepest gratitude to Ben Kiernan, Peter Perdue, Alan Mikhail, James C. Scott, and Michael Dove. This project's focus on conversion, ecology, and everyday religion would not have come into view without the prior work and generosity of scholars and friends in Indonesia and Malaysia who made personal worlds accessible. I especially thank Abdur-Razzaq Lubis, Salma Nasution, Razali Nasution, Apriani Harahap, Fadly Rahman, Martina Safitry, Prima Nurahmi, Hendra Sihite, and Liyana Taha for pointing me toward inspiring sources. As much of my research is archival, I am indebted to the librarians and archivists who made their collections legible for me even at early stages of my research, when ideas were at their fuzziest; many thanks to Rich Richie at the Yale University Library, Jeff Petersen at the Cornell University Library, Annabel Teh Gallop at the British Library, Doris Jedamski and Lam Ngo at the Leiden University Library Special Collections, Tan Hui Sim at the National Library Board in Singapore, Zaini Mohamed at the Perak branch of the National Archives of Malaysia, and the staff of the Rare Books and Newspapers Collection at the National Library of Indonesia.

Institutional support in the form of grants, fellowships, and language training has made this book possible, and for that support I am heartily grateful to the following: the Association for Asian Studies First Book Subvention program, Yale University's Charles Kao Fund Research Grant and Council for

Southeast Asian Studies summer grants, the Henry Luce Macmillan Center International Dissertation Grant, the Tan Kah Kee Foundation, the American Historical Association's Bernadotte E. Schmitt Grant program, and the School of Oriental and African Studies for their tuition waiver on a Jawi manuscript summer course. Special thanks to Chrissy Hosea, Mulaika Hijjas, and Ben Murtagh for their help with language training. Atma Jaya Catholic University hosted my stay in Indonesia, facilitated by Regina Yanti and Johan Purnama at the American Institute for Indonesian Studies (AIFIS). Cornell University's Southeast Asian Studies Program (SEAP) and the International Institute of Asian Studies (IIAS) at Leiden University have supported my postdoctoral research and provided me with a stimulating academic environment in which to write; I heartily thank Eric Tagliacozzo, Thamora Fishel, Paul van der Velde, and Philippe Peycam for making these stays possible. This book could not have been completed without material support from Nanyang Technological University through their International Postdoctoral Scholarship and Faculty Start-Up Grant. I am deeply thankful to NTU COHASS leaders Joseph Liow and Alan Chan, as well as my faculty mentors, Miles Powell and Goh Geok Yian, for their encouragement for this project.

This work has benefited tremendously from the insights gleaned from many fellow scholars in various forums. A 2018 workshop, Southeast Asian Natures, organized by David Biggs, enabled me to think through the theoretical framework of the book. I am truly indebted to all the interlocutors in this workshop whose sharp probing has been invaluable, in particular Anthony Medrano, Juno Salazar Parreñas, Celia Lowe, and Michele Thompson. My heartfelt thanks as well to scholars who were generous with their thoughts when my ideas were at their most nebulous: Julia Stephens, Clara Brakel-Papenhuyzen, Anthony Reid, Nur Amali Ibrahim, Sandra Manickam, Stuart Earl Strange, Ian M. Miller, Bradley C. Davis, Alder Kelemen, Seng Guo Quan, Daniel Birchok, and Ismail Fajrie Al-Atas. Indeed, there have been so many serendipitous conversations in workshops, conferences, and seminars that have stayed on my mind and guided my thinking that any list cannot be exhaustive.

Likewise, the emotional support and uplift from colleagues and friends cannot be enumerated, though I do wish to heartily acknowledge friends who have been tremendous cheerleaders and sounding boards even when the subject of this work might not be of particular interest to them: Yiwen Li, Mark Baker, Chan Cheow Thia, Matt Reeder, Emiko Stock, Colum Graham, Anissa Rahadingtyas, Genie Yoo, Humairah Zainal, Ngoei Wen Qing, Ervyna Sani, Afrianny

Adlan, Lin Hongxuan, Kevin Fogg, Veronika Kusumaryati, Nurul Huda Razif, Carmel Christy, Mitchell Tan, Koh Choon Hwee, and Masnidah Masnawi. I offer a special shout-out to the wonderful humanities and social sciences community at NTU, especially Zhou Taomo, Tapsi Mathur, Monamie Bhadra Haines, Katherine Hindley, Michael Stanley-Baker, and Scott Anthony, all of whom have encouraged and/or read my writing. Loh Shi Lin read through the entire manuscript and streamlined the prose; I truly appreciate her thoughtful input and unerring attention to detail.

Huge thanks to the awesome team at the University of Washington Press for facilitating the production of this book with much care. K. Sivaramakrishnan's encouragement of my work has been invaluable, and it is wonderful to be part of this amazing book series that he is helming. Many thanks to Lorri Hagman for her patience, kindness, and helpful editorial suggestions; to Chad Attenborough for his support in production; and to Kait Heacock for her work on the publicity. Independent of the press, Lee Li Kheng produced the maps in this volume in short order, for which I am very grateful. Two anonymous reviewers provided important feedback that was instrumental in improving this book's framing, content, and scholarly engagement. I have been told that it is often possible to guess the identities of the reviewers, but I confess myself unable to do so and simply wish to record my appreciation and awe at their brilliant engagement with the material. Thank you so much.

I count my blessings twice when it comes to my family—having two sisters who love me enough to read more about camphor trees, elephants, and graveyards than they ever wanted to; two brothers-in-law whose support never wavered; four joyful and rambunctious nephews; and, most of all, two parents whose love and sacrifices have been the mainstay of my life.

The Camphor Tree and the Elephant

INTRODUCTION Spirits of the Anthropocene

In early 2018, several residents in the village of Hatupangan, North Sumatra, stabbed to death a tiger that was sleeping under a stilt house. They then hung its disemboweled body from the ceiling of the village's public hall (*sopo*). Media reported that the villagers had thought the critically endangered tiger to be a shapeshifter (*siluman*) and painted such beliefs as an obstacle to conservation efforts. A government official for the conservation arm of Indonesia's Ministry for the Environment and Forestry asserted that they had tried to prevent the killing, stating, "We had talked to them [the residents], even involving the National Army [TNI] officers, but they still won't listen to us."[1] Several easy dichotomies are embedded in these prevalent media narratives about the conservation of tigers—villagers versus environmentalists, animals versus humans, superstition versus rationality.

In a different part of North Sumatra, another conservation narrative has emerged from a disparate set of binaries no less facile. At the end of 2016, Indonesian president Joko Widodo took the historically unprecedented step of returning thirteen thousand hectares of customary land (*tanah adat*) to nine Indigenous communities in the archipelago. One of them was a North Sumatran traditionally ordered (*adat*) community known as Pandumaan-Sipatihuta, which over the past decade had been locked in a contentious tussle with the pulp and paper company PT Toba Lestari over the latter's encroachment on their benzoin forests (*tombak haminjon*) by cutting down local trees to plant monocrops of fast-growing pine and eucalyptus for pulp.[2] Widodo's recognition of customary rights for Indigenous peoples was an indirect acknowledgment of belief systems that have long cherished a special relationship with nature, in part by maintaining a sustainable harvest of natural resources through customs that elude state structuring. Here, the categories are inverted—indigenes versus developmentalists, native trees versus imported monocrops, traditional ecological wisdom versus modern capitalistic avarice.

The complex positioning of small, dispersed communities currently living in Southeast Asia's forest frontiers often rests on polarizations in which one side is more highly developed than another. Depending on who is telling the story, these communities are either guardians or destroyers of the forest, or both at once.[3] North Sumatra presents a new terrain from which to explore these environmental narratives; it is a terrain that shows how religion is implicated in understanding and articulating relationships between the human and nonhuman in nature. However, the focus on remnants of traditional belief in these narratives, whether rendered as superstition or wisdom, means that Islam and Christianity are conspicuously absent from stories of conservation entanglements in North Sumatra, despite currently being the professed religions of the majority of its population. This raises several questions: What is the role of religion in shaping and structuring interactions between the human and nonhuman in nature? How do they change? And why are Muslim and Christian organizations generally not a potent force in the region's environmental movements? The answers not only complicate prevalent binaries but also suggest critical confrontations that need to take place in order for religious-based environmental efforts in the region to succeed.

This book brings these questions into the history of ecological change in Southeast Asia through the lens of conversions. Conversion provides a new entry point into historicizing static binaries that underpin present environmental narratives and movements in the region. Geographically, this study focuses on upland North Sumatra and the Malay Peninsula during the long nineteenth century. At the beginning of this era, the two were a unit distinguished by a common trade language, a preponderance of riverine polities linked to but distinct from stateless forest peoples, and connected waterways flowing into the Straits of Malacca. By the end of the period under study, movement by way of land rather than water, enforced by different empires on each side, not only severed both landmasses from each other but also created new frictions between the uplands and the coast. That one side became part of Malaysia and the other, of Indonesia, highlights the artificiality of boundaries established and enforced by colonial states. Concurrently, on the back of colonial conquest, many inhabitants of the North Sumatran uplands commonly grouped together as "Batak" turned toward monotheism, in the forms of Christianity and Islam. These waves of mass conversion were accompanied by shifts in productive ecology. Subsistence rice farming and forest foraging increasingly gave way to cash cropping and a plantation economy—a violent change that sent refugees and economic migrants down from the highlands toward the coasts and brought a mobile, educated elite in from the opposite direction. Rural-urban migrations fueled more conversions as the circulation of new ideas continuously transformed everyday religious life.

This focus on the long nineteenth century centers the roles of religion and colonialism in shaping the "human epoch," better known as the Anthropocene. Religion has been marginalized in most studies of this epoch; sociologist Bronislaw Szerszynski has recently argued that the Anthropocene needs to be "desecularized" to take into account how the earth was and remains "coeval with gods and spirits."[4] In Southeast Asia, environmentalism, in its broadest sense of preserving, restoring, and living in harmony with the natural world, cannot be fully understood without a sense of how animist religions have conditioned the political and social ecology of the region. However, as seen in the anecdotes at the beginning of this book, explanations for environmental problems and approaches based on those traditional beliefs are contradictory and inadequate. The study here considers a spiritual dimension in the transition to the Anthropocene, which occurred in tandem with the turn toward modernist monotheism in many of Southeast Asia's upland areas. To neglect this shift when thinking about religion and ecology in the region is to hark back to the economic historian J. C. Van Leur's infamous assertion that "both these world religions [Islam and Christianity] were only a thin, flaking glaze on the massive body of indigenous civilization."[5] Decolonizing and desecularizing, in this case, went hand in hand.

A core argument in this book is that modernist monotheistic religion has largely failed to cultivate the ethics and social will to protect the environment in the region under study because conversions became yoked to an imperial vision of progress during the long nineteenth century. Specifically, the process in which religious conversions occurred during this era helped to shape a sociopolitical ecology that voided the natural world of enchantment, ushered in a cash economy that emphasized transaction rather than kinship, and relocated power so as to put local landscapes into the hands of an elite estranged from these places. Religious conversions here do not refer merely to a change of allegiance from one system of belief to another that identifies itself as a distinct entity. Along the lines of previous work by the historians Anthony Reid and Merle Ricklefs, I take conversions to be long-term processes that also encompass discontinuous reform *within* a particular religious tradition.[6] In the period under study, the transition from a traditionalist Islam, which had been relatively accommodating to animist imaginaries, to a modernist Islam, which was not, formed a crucial locus of change that sparked and facilitated environmental transformation. Two modes of conversions are thus important here: a conscious repudiation of animism in favor of monotheism, as well as reforms that distinguished early modern Islam from its modern version.

Theological articles of faith in a specific religion did not affect environmental change as much as the ways in which these principles were discontinuously reconfigured when landscapes, like societies, were dislocated. Conversely, environmental change factored into the development of more anthropocentric interpretations that fused old and new in everyday praxis and emphasized human stewardship at the expense of a more-than-human religious imaginary. Everyday religion as practiced in the Anthropocene, not theology, was central to this process.

THE ANTHROPOCENE AND THE EVERYDAY

An account of God's creation of humans, found in the charm book of a Selangor shaman or healer (*pawang*) at the end of the nineteenth century, demonstrates unease with humankind's impact on the world. In this story, a god in the Abrahamic tradition seeks to fashion a man from earth, telling his angels to descend and obtain its "Heart." But Earth, while no recalcitrant devil, is a willful antagonist. When the angel Azrael explains his mission to it, he is met with point-blank refusal: "'I will not give it,' said the Earth (referring to its Heart), 'forasmuch as I was so created by God Almighty, and if you take away my Heart I shall assuredly die.'"[7] Azrael nevertheless extracts Earth's heart, and from it God makes Man. In this tale, Man's creation, and his advent in this world, is not one of triumph and hopeful beginnings but a harbinger for the death of Earth itself. This unusually bleak turn in a narrative derived from monotheistic world religions and localized into the magic book of an animist-influenced Muslim convert points toward a recognition of humanity's massive impact on the natural environment during this moment in the nineteenth century. In this imagining, it seems that the natural world has entered its Anthropocene from the moment of human creation.

The term "Anthropocene" was first formally defined by the geologists Paul Crutzen and Eugene Stoermer as a new era in which humans are the predominant force altering geological processes on the planet. Crutzen and Stoermer were part of a group proposing that this epoch could be divided into two periods: a start triggered by the Industrial Revolution and a great, ongoing acceleration since 1945, precipitated by nuclear power.[8] Since then, others have argued for earlier starting points, whether at the inception of agriculture, which left heightened traces of carbon dioxide in the soil, or with the discovery of fire, which allowed for more efficient consumption of animal protein and the evolution of large-brained species. Such expansive perspectives seemingly equate the Anthropocene with the decline of untouched wilderness and entail the depressing conclusion that nature is best served by human extinction. This dualistic view should arguably be supplanted by understanding the epoch as a nature-culture continuum.[9] Many scholars have found it more constructive to focus on the geological markers of the Anthropocene, thereby closely following the timeline of a start circa 1800 and an acceleration in 1945. This chronology is represented through graphs that show sharp increases in twelve earth system trends used as parameters of human impact from 1750 to 2000: levels of carbon dioxide, nitrous oxide, methane, stratospheric ozone, surface temperature, ocean acidification, marine fish capture, shrimp aquaculture, nitrogen intrusion into the coastal zone, tropical forest loss, domestication of land, and terrestrial biosphere degradation. Multiple socioeconomic trends accompanying these discernible changes to the earth system strongly indicate that they are human-induced changes as a result of concurrent sharp increases in world population, real gross domestic product (GDP), foreign direct investment, urban populations, large dams, water use, telecommunications, transportation, paper production, and fertilizer use.[10]

If we could graph the rate of conversions from a local religion to Christianity or Islam during this period, it is likely that we would also see a significant increase coinciding with the advent of the Anthropocene, as defined by Crutzen's timeline. Similarly, if we were to pinpoint the beginning of a decline for heterodox, syncretic, and localized practices of Islam in Southeast Asia, we would probably also arrive at the same period circa 1800. This was arguably a second phase in the Islamization and Christianization of the region, forming part of staggered processes that began in the sixteenth century and shaped the practice of these religions into forms recognizable today. Histories of religions have evaluated these changes as part of a modern phase of globalization or an epoch shaped and facilitated by intensified telecommunications, transportation, and the rise of print media. What can examining conversions through the lens of the Anthropocene offer us that extant analyses based on globalizing modernity cannot? Two critical factors come to the fore: timescales and nonhuman agency. As a concept, the Anthropocene evokes long-term processes even when used to study a discrete period of time, providing what the literary scholar Jeremy Davies calls "both a motive and a means for taking a very long view of the environmental crisis."[11] When applied to religious history, the Anthropocene blurs the impression of progress so often implicit in histories that emphasize modernity. Conversion narratives and environmental narratives frequently take inverse trajectories, with the former highlighting ascent while the latter stresses decline. Seen as part of the Anthropocene, both narratives take on a new complexion: environmental narratives grow more sensitive to how beliefs through which humans make meaning about nonhuman worlds can impact the material realm, and conversion narratives find themselves contending with a *longue durée* rather than a moment of enlightenment.

Second, the Anthropocene expands the space of inquiry relative to modernity by including nonhuman beings as active agents, collapsing distinctions between natural and human history in the process.[12] This is especially important for a study involving animism in Southeast Asia, as animism is an ontology that assigns agency and personhood to humans and nonhuman beings alike. Anthropologists Kaj Århem and Guido Sprenger's explication of the dimensions of animism in Southeast Asia identifies three distinguishing aspects of this ontology. First, human experiences, including illness and death, are seen as part of a constant cycle of predation: humans take the lives of other beings in nature, and those beings' spirits take human lives in return.[13] Second, the human form and that of other natural beings can be interchangeable, as illustrated in folklore from North Sumatra and the Malay Peninsula that describes ancestor weretigers, as well as elephant, fish, and bird shapeshifters.[14] In these tales, the fluidity of transformations from one form to another exemplifies the essential unity of living beings. Lastly, the hierarchy between humans and nonhumans is reversible. As Sprenger expresses it, "The status of plants and animals as food results from their subordination through superior ritual techniques. The hierarchy thus created is not permanent, but reversible."[15] The spirit in a rice stalk is capable of subduing humans even as the latter consumes the former.

These features distinguish Southeast Asian animism from Abrahamic monotheistic religions, as the latter tend to place humans apart from the natural world in conceptualizations of the soul, notions of the afterlife, and human stewardship. Christianity, Judaism, and Islam outline a hereafter in a realm separate from earth where humans are held to account for their temporal deeds or are judged for their faith in God. Humans are the only beings to be so assessed and deemed capable of vice-regency over the world since animals and plants are perceived as incapable of higher-level thought and agency. The animist afterlife, in contrast, posits that the spirits of the departed live among us on earth and should be venerated. Achieving harmony in coexistence is the moral thrust of animism, while accountability, justice, and faith underpin monotheism. Boundaries between humans and nonhumans are harder in the latter: the ram that replaces one of Abraham's sons in his sacrifice, for instance, was not perceived as the equivalent of a person in either faith or agency, even as it was harnessed for the same sacrificial purpose. Monotheistic religions view the world on earth as a temporary abode and place special stress on the agency of humans.

In practice, animism and monotheism need not be perceived as binaries. Such stark differentiation, while grounded in empirical thought adduced from scripture, misses how varied ideological underpinnings can collapse and merge in everyday existence. A rich literature on these everyday entanglements in religion has emerged, leading to categories of analysis such as "Islam *mondain*," "expert religion," "governed religion," "lived religion," "high/low religion," and "folk religion."[16] All these categories suggest fuzzy boundaries between sacred and profane spaces, each created through socializations that simultaneously respond to and resist power dynamics. This book accesses the quotidian experience of religion by hewing closely to the religious scholar Robert Orsi's approach of centering the individual work of social interlocutors who personally narrate their own histories and the stories they tell.[17] Opting for a lived religion approach, which disassociates personalized practice from class in a way that folk, vernacular, or popular religion does not, leaves room to attend to the power structures that define the Anthropocene. Instead of class hierarchy, everyday religion in this lived experience of economic life centers a sociality that operates through production and consumption networks, in line with the historian of religion Kathryn Lofton's framing of religion in the modern world.[18] The enmeshing of the sacred in banal socioeconomics illuminates the latter's organizing logics and its effects on the nonhuman environment, which are in turn impacted by religious change. Bringing lived religion to the field of ecology thus allows us to perceive an environmental optic within these self-articulated stories, and this optic interprets, exploits, and protects the nonhuman natural world within a broader personal understanding of faith, drawing on sociality as much as scripture, if not more so, in its workings.

For the purposes of this study, everyday religion is defined by its functions and practice. It is performed in mundane rather than sacral spaces; it is more preoccupied with the benefits of the present world than the next; it pays spotty attention to texts and scriptures; it enables embodied creativity from multiple traditions. Finally, it is entangled with concerns about production as well as reproduction. These aspects of everyday religion simultaneously distance it from theologically differentiated paths toward salvation while bringing theology and religious interventions closer to universal human concerns. Thus, as an analytical lens into religious life, the everyday brings us toward unexpected connections that can form in a space resistant to the control of formal religious institutions and/or the state, even while imbricated by the latter entities. The everyday indexes the entanglement of two modalities of conversion—embracing both a new religion and internal reform—as being religious responses to the same ruptures and dislocations in politics and environments. Everyday religion relates yet also disrupts the agency of human and nonhuman actors partly through the power of place. Here, I certainly take the point made by scholars of religion that modern religious lives and secularization unfolded in a nonlinear fashion, while also emphasizing how everyday religion underscored those complexities.[19]

In this book, the everyday boundaries between animism and monotheism evolve in fixity, hardening significantly by the end of the period under study. Earlier waves of conversion to Islam and Christianity in the sixteenth and seventeenth centuries had generated ebbs and flows in the surf of religious identities, occurring in response to rapid commercialization, direct contact between missionaries and Indigenous peoples, political competition, and sporadic colonial incursions. These earlier conversions were accompanied by new uses of writing that articulated a moral universe and the institutionalizing of early forms of the rule of law. Rigor in institutionalizing Islamic and Christian identities waxed in the long seventeenth century but waned over the next hundred years, such that by the beginning of the nineteenth century, enforcement of monotheistic law and public ritual had become neither visible nor effective.[20] I pick up the narrative during this period of ebb, demonstrating that anthropogenic environmental changes triggered a fresh round of conversions, all with longer reach and durability. Such changes were more intense because, unlike during the preceding period, they were accompanied by the displacement of enchanted ecologies and the repression of more-than-human charisma. In focusing on disenchantment and the charismatic, this book deeply engages with and revisits the ideas of Max Weber, not in the sense of resurrecting a German sociology of religion for a Southeast Asian context but in helping to articulate the dynamics of rationalization that formed part of the Anthropocene worldwide.[21] Here, the limits of a Weberian framework become clearer, as a Protestant ethic was not the sole or even main driver of change; similar turns toward bureaucratic rationality could also be found in modernist Muslim societies. Within this context, conflicts over land rights frequently became intertwined with evangelical pressure to convert everyday religions into a rationalized form of Christianity and Islam, which encouraged human stewardship in the absence of spirits that charmed the natural landscape.

In short, this book tells stories of evolving everyday religions in the Anthropocene. It does not aim to question the geological basis on which the epoch is theorized, other than to take the long nineteenth century as a starting point. "Spiritual Anthropocene" is not meant to add to a long list of alternative conceptualizations of the epoch but to highlight that the world of spirits is also part of its story. These intergenerational stories are attentive to place and stress the relative empowerment and disempowerment among different human groups. In this re-ordering, we may come to see conversion less as a personal decision than as the collective transformation of self-perception with respect to a physical environment, generated by a disequilibrium in the notion of how a higher power works on that environment. Here, I differ from Szerszynski, whose desecularization of the epoch leads him to posit that "what might once have been distinct territorialized 'cultures' or 'natures' in which humans engaged in particular situated patterns of interaction with animals, spirits and other beings are increasingly being convened into a global multi-natural system."[22] In writing these histories of conversions, I argue instead that it remains important to understand the situatedness of these changes, which could diverge into a rich multiplicity of new traditions that simultaneously included modernist Islam, localized Christianity, reformulated animism, and multiple customary norms (*adat*). In understanding how the political position of the former two became privileged over the latter, we begin to see why neither Islam nor Christianity has served as a potent check at the frontier of forest loss in the region.[23]

WRITING THE NORTH SUMATRAN UPLANDS

Only scattered scholarly attention has been paid to the North Sumatran highlands and their inhabitants, largely due to limited sources and the absence of state-like governance in the area's history. A history of the Batak, who inhabited the highlands as a "complex society without bureaucracy," remains a major gap in the literature.[24] The historian Leonard Andaya traces a brief genesis of this identity, connecting its emergence to the camphor trade within the context of a larger process of ethnicization along the Straits of Malacca in the early modern period.[25] Historical analyses were usually not linked explicitly to North Sumatra's landscape; soil composition and periodic volcanic eruptions were sparsely and separately studied by geologists and paleoanthropologists.[26] Moreover, the challenge in writing a Batak history is compounded by their division into subgroups with different dialects—Toba, Karo, Pakpak, Dairi, Angkola, Mandailing, and Simalungun—clustered in the upland areas. Some of these groups no longer wish to self-identify as Batak. Scholars of the region rightly tend to avoid this thorny issue by focusing on a specific subgroup rather than attempting to study the Batak as a cohesive people, which they are not. Some cultural phenomena and rituals that apply to one subgroup, such as the Toba, are not necessarily true of the Mandailing or the Karo. For this reason, when this project discusses Indigenous religion or common cultural traits, I usually note subgroup variants in practice in the endnotes while trusting readers to remain aware of intergroup diversity on the ground.

Most English-language scholarly work on the Batak has been done by anthropologists who have conducted in-depth studies of various aspects of their culture. This anthropological work took great care not to generalize about the Batak, resulting in rich and suggestive studies that are unevenly distributed throughout the cultural landscape. The cultural, legal, and religious life of the Toba has received particularly fruitful attention.[27] The Karo's religious life in the twentieth century has been significantly studied.[28] Batak history has also been embedded in subgroup studies of linguistics, literature, music, and textiles.[29] Few historians, however, have ventured into the historical terrain of Batak migration in the Malay Peninsula. The research of historians Abdur-Razzaq Lubis and Salma Nasution has been particularly fruitful in producing a body of work that serves as a provocative revision to Malaysia's national history. Their work, however, concerns only the Mandailing, which they hold to be distinct from the rest of the Batak, in accordance with the self-identification of many Mandailing today.[30]

Rather than purporting to be a comprehensive history of the Batak, this book aims to uncover parallel conversions of landscapes and peoples during the transition from a complex, stateless upland territory into an administrative division that was called the Tapanuli Residency during the Dutch East Indies

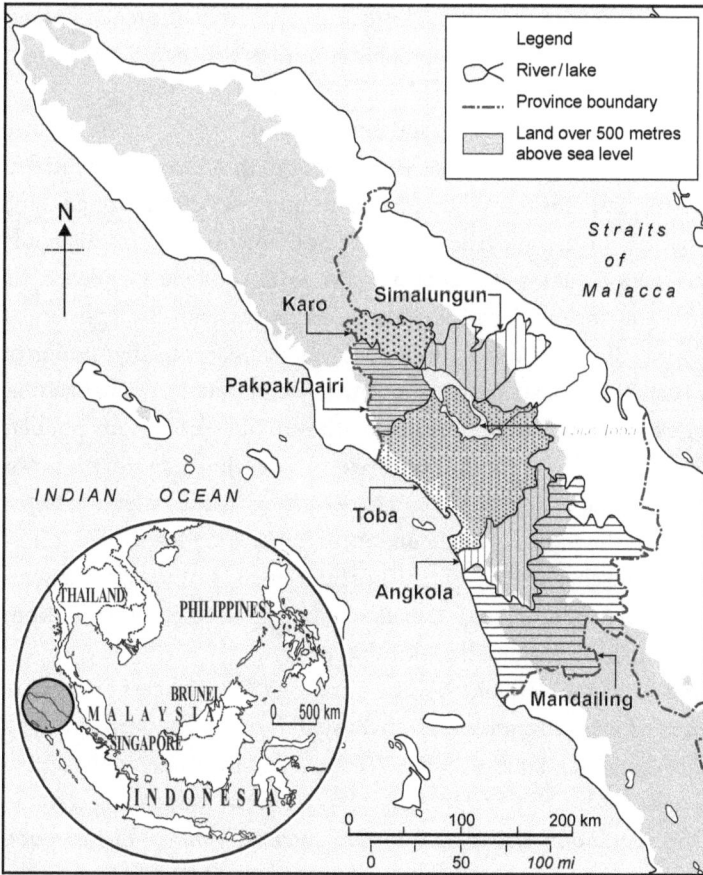

North Sumatran uplands and geographic distribution
of Batak subgroups. Map by Lee Li Kheng.

period. Due to their dominant presence in this locale, the subgroups of the
Toba, Pakpak/Dairi, Angkola, and Mandailing receive much more attention in
this project than the Karo and the Simalungun, who were eventually incorporated into the Sumatran East Coast Residency. That geography was nonetheless
hardly circumscribed. As we shall see, people of the North Sumatran highlands
had historically pursued interactions stretching beyond the uplands, across the
waterways to Malaya as well as China, South Asia, and what is now the Middle
East, the supple threads of adat interweaving this broad terrain.

Batak precolonial culture, or adat, as a set of local practices and customary
norms that governed a community, has undergone significant evolution. Due to

the scarcity of documentary sources, a historical approach to the region cannot hope to replicate the depth of ethnographic studies in this area. Recovering a Batak history requires getting around limitations posed by their geographic isolation, ahistorical recordkeeping, and limited use of writing. In the absence of history, there is, however, a great richness of stories that have the potential to shed light on the past. The most illuminating accounts of Batak life often came from biographical or literary renderings of family memories.[31] In this book, family stories, genealogies, and memories imbricate documentary evidence as a means of accessing the interiority of conversions, both spiritual and physical. I read these stories along the vein of the anthropologist Mary Steedly's notion of "memory artists"—as constructs of people who weave "public dramatizations of personal experience that become both stimuli and patterns for popular imagination."[32] As such, the specific narrative arc in each family story is not as crucial as the motif adorning them, and here I pay particular attention to the pattern of embellishments that occur and recur in these stories, as well as how they originated and changed over time. These stories and historical documents are also compared to ethnographic data that have generated models of various subgroups of Batak society and their kinship patterns.

Indigenous Batak scholars and descendants of key Batak leaders made these stories available for reading and research. Basyral Hamidy Harahap's work on the history of early Mandailing scholar Willem Iskander rendered the latter's writing more accessible by translating his texts from the Mandailing script to romanized Bahasa Indonesia.[33] Collections of patriclan (*marga*) histories and family stories presented in publicly accessible ways by Z. Pangaduan Lubis, Akhir Matua Harahap, Poernama Rea Sinambela, Adniel Lumbantobing, Batara Sangti Simanjuntak, and Mangaradja Onggang Parlindungan made possible a text-based excavation of everyday religion during a restless period.[34] In North Sumatra, scholar of religion W. B. Sidjabat's careful biography of the key Batak leader Si Singamangaradja XII was based on a family manuscript that has since been lost; this biography enabled a richer insight into the Singamangaradja dynasty's role in the community's religious life.[35] On the other side of the Straits of Malacca, the heritage work of Abdur-Razzaq Lubis and Salma Nasution has been instrumental in preserving migrant Sumatran family stories in the Malay Peninsula; part of my work is indebted to their sharing of a family manuscript before its publication as a local history in 2021.[36]

These human stories must be put in the context of geographic and mental structures that governed life in the North Sumatran uplands and the role that religion played in their mountain riverine ecology. The synergy between mountain and river meant that stateless uplands emerged with state-like riverine polities and that local spirits coexisted with universal gods. Moreover, in the context of everyday religion before the nineteenth century, animism and monotheism were not clearly bounded belief systems. Writing against the Braudelian notion of a geo-history in which human relations with the surrounding milieu remained largely immobile, the opening chapter of this book utilizes origin myths, folklore, travel accounts, and scientific studies to uncover both a landscape and the peoples that existed in dynamic equilibrium. The physical setting here is the Bukit Barisan, a mountain range bisecting the island of Sumatra, which lies within the restless seismic zone of the Ring of Fire and is crisscrossed by rivers flowing east and west. Taking readers through a cycle of birth, life, and death in Batak society, this chapter establishes the social organization that enabled humans, spirits, and nonhuman nature to acquire agency over the local environment, and it sets the scene for how they would be tested during the long nineteenth century.

The dynamic equilibrium of the uplands was disrupted by local religious and political change—changes worth studying despite taking place in a small, upland theater of action. Batak local politics have been marginalized in political histories of Indonesia, with the Batak characterized as a largely acquiescent minority who unhesitatingly joined the nationalist project. The nationalist turn in Indonesian-language historiography in the 1950s, 1960s, and 1970s produced some interest in several major Batak leaders who resisted the advent of colonialism, such as the priest-king Si Singamangaradja XII. However, these histories have tended to be hagiographic or in the mold of "great man" narratives that marginalize period and place. The religious history of the area is as limited as its political history. Missionary and church accounts have documented religious conversions through narratives of salvation that also foreground "great man" saviors such as the singular preacher Ludwig Ingwer Nommensen. While the priest-king and the preacher are important figures in this history, an inordinate focus on their agency obscures the context in which they were situated, the religious diversity of the region, and, most important, the socio-environmental impact of conversion. It is in moving beyond the hagiographic, nationalist, and evangelical bent of the existing historical literature on the Batak that this book makes its foremost contribution to Batak history.

Broadening the rubric of conversion to encompass internal reform and the embrace of a new religion, this book's second chapter examines the relationship between these two aspects of conversion through a pivotal conflict from 1793 to 1838 that deeply affected upland societies in West and North Sumatra, remembered by today's Indonesians as the Padri War. The civil war of this period provided an opportunity for the Dutch to intervene on the side of West Sumatran Minangkabau adat leaders when they were losing the fight against the Islamists. West Sumatra, along with a sizable chunk of adjacent Batak territory, subsequently became a Dutch colony. This chapter investigates the little-known North Sumatran theater of this conflict, using the confessional manuscripts of Padri War leaders and Batak family stories while paying attention to how these sources memorialize rupture and resilience during this period. The conflict's legacy induced changes to the local environment that reshaped the uplands, rendering them more accessible to the Dutch colonial state as well as the displacement of local spirits during attempts to impose coffee cash cropping by the Padri and then the Dutch.

As the uplands became more accessible in the mid-nineteenth century, new ways of articulating moral thinking about the nonhuman natural world through writing, print, and the modern biography emerged. Animism and monotheism became more sharply distinguished, as capitalist imperialism and technology—the two forces driving the Anthropocene—delinked mundane places of worship and sites of production from the natural world. In turn, the desacralization of nature led to an intergenerational amnesia of nonhuman personhood in the local environment. The second section in this book examines how these new forms and genres of writing brought out fresh ways of representing the natural world and human societies' spiritual positions within it. Centralizing Indigenous sources such as early biographies, school textbooks by Indigenous teachers, and family history, the two chapters in this section demonstrate that writing gained new potency as a means of articulating space and planning for what it could become. Biographical writing—a new genre in nineteenth-century maritime Southeast Asia—was particularly instructive in showing that the structure of such emerging narratives embeds an environmental optic that is less attuned to nonhuman agentive power. Projections of long-term damage stemming from economic exploitation of the nonhuman natural world, exemplified in this book by tin mining and camphor harvesting, were blinkered by this optic. The biographies depict humans' increasing power to conquer mountains and direct water while embracing a view of God that privileges the position of humankind. As histories written for future generations, they emphasize individual human agency and mute the landscape's potency.

Although this book's ambitions are modest in the direction of Batak historiography, its spotlight on conversions in the North Sumatran uplands demonstrates that the global turn toward modernist monotheism in many places around the world, especially those remote from imperial metropolises, indicated an important phase of globalization at the world's margins. The environmental historian Richard Grove has demonstrated that the intellectual thread of environmentalism in Europe emerged from scientists working in and on the metropole's Edenic tropical colonies, making these peripheral places centers of environmental concern and innovation.[37] If these colonies have deeply influenced environmentalist thought, it is perhaps not a coincidence that religious thought from the metropole became deeply embedded in these colonies: almost all the peoples on the islands in Grove's study now follow a monotheistic religion. Without belaboring the comparison, the juxtaposition of religious, environmental, and political changes in remote, politically anarchic societies during the eighteenth and nineteenth centuries appears to merit greater examination, not least because extant analyses still lack an Indigenous perspective.

The final section of this book seeks to provide such perspectives on the material impact of newfound faith in the duality of nature and humankind, as well as human stewardship. Incorporating sources such as prayer books and dream divination manuals, the final chapters follow the vicissitudes of the camphor tree and the elephant—potent symbols of nonhuman nature and endangered species—as charismatic traditional leadership on both sides of the Straits of Malacca lost political power. In Sumatra, the camphor trade gradually became irrelevant in a colonial economy shaped by Dutch rule. The decimation of the camphor forests occurred with the active acquiescence of new converts who were open to exploiting nonhuman nature and adopting confrontational approaches toward increased human conflicts with tigers and other wild animals. Disenchanted in tandem with the passing of traditional authority, this new socio-religious landscape favored gardens over wilderness, owing to encouragement by local Christian leaders. Cash crops such as benzoin produced in these small-scale Indigenous enterprises became new botanical affiliates of an Indigenous identity, resisting the plantation economy sprouting at the highlands' doorstep while simultaneously uprooting themselves from wild forests and their unpredictable inhabitants.

Similar trends were under way in the Malay Peninsula, a newly formed British colony across the Straits where charismatic authority under kings was being replaced by rational-legal authority, which was structured under the British and enacted through local collaborators. The ebb of elephants' status symbolized this change. Since the early modern period, elephants had played a significant role in confirming the authority of a human's claim to leadership. However, the charismatic status of elephants was reduced in tandem with their secularization and their gradual redundancy from the transport system. The religious aspect of this change is highlighted in the declining use of multireligious mantras to tame elephants and in pragmatic modifications to these charms that decentralized the elephant's personhood. Animist-inflected practices, which entailed an understanding of the world—humans and nonhumans—as a community of persons, all of whom deserved respect, were supplanted in favor of an Islamic modernist monotheism that placed humans at the apex while cutting shamanic power from the political structure. In light of this history, the final chapter suggests that the Muslim and Christian environmentalisms variously taking shape in the region today lack a radical edge. Without confronting this nineteenth-century precedent of antagonism toward traditional forest faiths, or the consequent estrangement from fragile ecological systems it has engendered, these movements cannot hope to enact fundamental reform.

Adat communities in Indonesia and Malaysia today remain marginal, despite the pendulum slowly swinging toward a recognition of their contributions to environmental sustainability. But the anthropologist Anna Tsing has astutely observed that a people's marginalization and exclusion accompany an active engagement with their own marginality by "protesting, reinterpreting and embellishing their own exclusion."[38] For the Batak during the long nineteenth century, engagement with marginality involved not only resistance but also remaking their landscape and identities, with conversion as an escape valve. The emphasis of this book on out-of-the-way marginality and its environmental impact distinguishes it from other new studies of the Indigenous in Sumatra and Malaya.[39] It is in this highly peripheral yet fluid position, reified by others, that we find the significance of the North Sumatran uplands and its people. Theirs is a history of perpetual conversion that uniquely positions them to shed light on the questions that drive this study: How do beliefs and identities change when the landscape changes? How does the environment change when beliefs change? These questions steer us toward understanding how religion, political economy, and the natural world have historically moved in synchrony within a small, upland, and remote place.

STRUCTURES

ONE A Time before Religion

The linguistic term for pre-monotheistic religion varies across Batak areas: in Karo, it is *pamena* ("the original religion"); while among the Toba, Simalungun, and Pakpak, it is often referred to as *parbegu* ("religion of the spirits"). In my early visits to Toba, however, one phrase repeatedly surfaced in conversations with Batak guides, friends, and informants when we discussed culture and religion in the past. This phrase was *sebelum ada agama*—"in the time before religion." At a replica village of the Siallagan patriclan (*marga*) on Samosir Island, for example, the guide spoke vividly about the trial and execution of treasonous prisoners whose prolonged death involved pouring the juice of limes over open wounds. This was, he hastened to add, in the time before religion.[1]

What *is* a time before religion? It has been argued that in antiquity there was no domain where the religious and the secular were clearly demarcated, and thus a separate religious life was a recent invention of history.[2] What this phrase gestures toward is perhaps not the *absence* of religion but its pervasive *presence*, a supernatural divine so ubiquitous and banal that it was fused into the texture of everyday life and landscapes. It was a religion that did not speak its name in terms of institutionalized ethics and norms but amplified the everyday human pursuits of production and reproduction with a spiritual dimension of the more-than-human. The nineteenth century was an inflection point for that religion, whose remnants are found today in practices considered to be nonorthodox, such as nature cults or persistent beliefs in local spirits and supernatural beings (*djinn*). In Indonesia and Malaysia, these practices are now sometimes forced into the category of adat and thus not considered to be elements of religion (*agama*).

"Before religion" is part of a historical time and place that Fernand Braudel has termed "structures": a stabilizing ground that enables historical chronology.[3]

How did the landscapes, peoples, and gods of the North Sumatran highlands historically interact with each other before the epoch of change in the long nineteenth century? In answering this question, it is important to bear in mind that while these interactions have coalesced around certain trends that distinguished upland and lowland culture in the Malay-Sumatran world, those trends were by no means static. The ordering of historical inquiry does not reify it. A dynamic equilibrium between upland and lowland operated through the earliest myths of the origins of the Batak peoples. Agriculture conditioned key features in their adat, and trade in camphor and enslaved persons connected maritime highlands with their coasts while providing an impetus for Batak societies to remain distinct from their state-like neighbors. Malay states were necessary to Batak statelessness. Movement across the two helped to define distinctions between animism and Islam as well as to stabilize ethnic identity.

There are two dominant models of the relationship between upland and lowland in Southeast Asia, both of which offer insights. The political anthropologist James C. Scott inverted the widely held view that the uplands were stagnant, isolated, self-sufficient entities and has shown instead that in mainland Southeast Asia, the region's political decentralization, agricultural strategies, and even illiteracy were actively molded as defensive moves against state-like neighbors.[4] In the maritime region, the anthropologist Tania Li concurs that the state had limited reach in the highlands up to the mid-twentieth century. However, unlike Scott, she argues that they did not resist state rule; instead, "desires for security and access to trade rule drew them into the orbit of coastal powers," where "attraction, threat, coercion, [and] the channeling of choice" resulted in the uplands being enmeshed in a "set of extractive relations on the coast."[5] The historian David Henley goes further by arguing that, far from being repelled by the state, the uplands of Sulawesi were attracted to the security it provided and had a history of accepting stranger-kings.[6]

The North Sumatran uplands did not perfectly fit models of isolationism, anarchism, or attracted orbiting. They were historically engaged with but aloof from their state-like neighbors in terms of geography and politics. For much of their known history up to the twentieth century, the interior highlands of Sumatra had a much higher population density than the coastal lowlands, leading some scholars to speculate that there had been a centuries-long trend of escaping coastal maritime empires like Srivijaya and later coastal Muslim polities by moving upland, much like Scott's model of the uplands as a shatter zone. However, there was also considerable movement downhill and downriver, as trade and cash crop cultivation attracted the Batak to the coast. A dynamic equilibrium existed between the statelike and the stateless, as well as between animism and Islam, through a cycle of birth, life, and death.

BIRTH: INSIDE-OUT AND OUTSIDE-IN

Sumatra is part of the most seismically active region in the world. Plate tectonics over thousands of years created not only the Bukit Barisan mountain range but also the thirty-five volcanoes that pockmark it. More than half of these are stratovolcanoes, or conical volcanoes, formed by sequential outflows of lava and volcanic ash pushed out by pressure exerted by mantle rock from the oceanic crust melting and pooling under the continental crust. How long the melting took and the amount of time between each lava outflow is unknown, but the stratovolcanic formations indicate some regularity in each outflow. Clearer are the violent punctuations of eruptions on the land. About seventy-five thousand years ago, a supervolcano in Toba erupted, spewing more than twenty-eight hundred square kilometers of sulfuric material and giving birth to a lake that is today known as Lake Toba, in which sits an island now called Samosir. The destructive force of the eruption was such that it seemed highly likely to have caused a volcanic winter and a subsequent period of global cooling.[7] Volcanic activity on land and in water continued to breathe new life into the soil by distributing a layer of tuff over generally acidic earth. When the highlands came to be peopled—the next epoch in the transformation of the land—soil fertility became a determinant of birth, eventually generating denser populations in the relatively fertile areas around Toba and Karo, while settlements were fewer in number in the less bountiful territories of Pakpak and Dairi.[8]

Early human conceptions of these changes to the land can be glimpsed through Batak folklore that tells of humans coming into the world. Most origin stories begin with the daughter of one of the gods, Si Boru Daeng Parudjar, who fled from the heavens to avoid marrying her cousin, whom she despised.[9] She let herself down onto the earthly realm in a rectangular iron basket harnessed to a rope of black silk tied to a heavenly tree. On earth, she found herself stranded on a rock amid the waters of a primordial sea that was roiled by a giant underworld serpent. She called out for help and, aided by the gods, shackled the serpent's head and stabbed a sword through it; after it was stilled, she was able to live on earth and cultivate the land. The Toba Batak trace their ethnic descent from one of her descendants, a mythical Si Raja Batak, who emerged from a mountain called Pusuk Buhit on the shores of Lake Toba.

The story of Si Boru Daeng Parudjar's spouse illustrates a long-standing tradition of human oneness with the natural world. In this story, a magical chicken called Hulumbujati laid three eggs the size of large cooking pots, from which male divinities emerged. These gods, named Batara Guru, Soripada, and Mangalabulan, were given wives by the creator god Mula Jadi Nabolon, and sons as well as daughters were born to them. Not all their descendants were human; among the sons was born one "shaped like a lizard . . . with four feet, and a tail like the point of the spindle."[10] This man was called Si Raja Endaenda, and it was to escape marriage to him that Si Boru Daeng Parudjar exiled herself on earth.[11] Si Raja Endaenda pursued and won her after he managed to shed his lizard appearance. In this story, then, the divine takes many forms, whether as human, flora, or fauna.

Folklore is neither historical evidence nor consistent across the uplands.[12] These tales would have likely undergone several transformations after the Toba Batak converted to Christianity, a conversion that possibly inspired the motif of a woman's fall from the heavens. There are nonetheless several suggestive images in this popular folk story that point toward an underlying pre-mono-theistic cosmology. Earth is conceptualized as the middle layer in a three-tiered universe that is animated by powers from above and below.[13] The arresting image of a serpent underground captures this animism; the body of the earth is represented by a reptile, which is physically an amalgam of fluid and flesh, just as water and soil make up the earth. The divine is externalized and sep-arated from the middle layer, a world predominantly human, while divinity is a restless, creative force both benevolent (the heavens) and destructive (the underworld). Gods in this universe have little personal interest in the affairs of humans but are enduring forces for creation. Embedded within this view of the gods, moreover, is a keen awareness of defining moments in the birth of peoples in the land as catalyzed by the divine. The first is the formation of a bridge that had enabled humans to enter the highlands, a metaphor for an upper world. Next, there is a period of unstable ground whose shaking had to be quieted before human and animal life could reproduce. And third, the coming of agriculture further heralds an explosive growth in human life. These transformations, taking place over many human lifespans, congeal in folklore neither as memory nor history but as a collective explanation for how the world came to be born.

Archaeological and geological evidence concurs with part of the mythologized explanation in folklore. Declining sea levels and temperatures during the last glacial period at the end of the Pleistocene uncovered land bridges connecting the islands of the Sunda shelf (Java, Sumatra, and Borneo) with what is now mainland Southeast Asia. Evidence of human remains suggests that the peopling of Sumatra began during this period in the early Holocene before sea levels rose and the land bridges disappeared about eleven thousand years ago. Artifacts from a so-called Hoabinhian culture—shell mounds, burial in karst hills, and rudimentary tools—surfaced in Sumatra as well as in parts of present-day Cambodia and Vietnam.[14] A second wave of migration to Sumatra about three thousand years ago from what is now southern China and Taiwan displaced or absorbed the first wave of settlers, who started occupying open sites rather than caves. Their choice of open sites during this period indicates an increased capability or technology to defend themselves against predators and a capacity to clear land for growing food.

There is some debate over the direction from which the initial migrants arrived and dispersed throughout what eventually became Batak territory, as well as the mechanism through which their ethnic identity gradually formed after Sumatra was separated from the mainland. One theory—which the Toba musicologist Julia Byl has dubbed an "inside-out" hypothesis—proposes that Toba was the cradle of Batak culture, which then dispersed over the uplands and even found its way down the coast.[15] From Toba, highland migrants replicated their patriarchal lineage system, clan structure, and secondary burial practices, all of which became distinguishing features of Batak culture. This thesis is partially supported by Malay manuscripts that begin with a king's emergence from the hills before eventual Islamization.[16]

It is not certain at which point in these early waves of migrations that highland peoples started to tell stories about their origins, nor is it clear when the myth of Si Boru Daeng Parudjar began. It is also not certain when group identity began to develop among the people in the North Sumatran highlands, and no scholar has thus far provided a satisfactory explanation for the origins of the term "Batak."[17] What is clear is that from the eleventh century, there are also indications of significant contact between the Batak and the peoples of South Asia and of China based on inscriptions left in scattered places in Tapanuli.[18] Ruins of temples apparently dedicated to Hindu and Buddhist gods, possibly of the Vajrayana tradition, have been found in Padang Lawas in Angkola.[19] The Batak had absorbed the concept of a pantheon of a divine creator, sustainer, and destroyer similar to Shaivite beliefs, translated in Batak cosmology as the autochthonous ancestor god called Mula Jadi Nabolon, who ruled the heavens with a triad of gods called Debata Na Tolu.

These Hindu influences likely entered the North Sumatran highlands from the Hindu-Buddhist empires of Srivijaya in South Sumatra and subsequently Majapahit in Java. There are also linguistic legacies that suggest direct contact between Tamils and the Sumatran highlanders. In Karo, for example, a few clan names, such as Sembiring—which means "dark-skinned" and is derived from the Tamil language—implied the absorption of a darker-skinned people into Batak clans.[20] The Chinese also appeared to have had significant contact with and some knowledge of the Batak. By the end of the thirteenth century, Chinese sources began to mention a people called the "Bata" as a dependency of the Srivijayan Empire.[21] "Batak" could have been a Malay appellation for peoples in Sumatra's interior that the Chinese had merely cited, or it might have been a term that the Batak self-identified with and used in their dealings with others. The intensive contact with "other" peoples through trade catalyzed a Batak group identity facilitated by a mobile group of priest-magicians known as *datu*, who brought local knowledge of magic from one settlement to another, thus creating a shared culture.[22]

It was also the datu who started using a writing system, and it is from this point that we can trace the documentation of a Batak cosmology with greater precision. Judging from the writing system, the idea that Toba was the authentic center of Batak civilization from which settlement patterns and subgroup formation radiated seems to fray. The Batak language most likely descended from a proto-Austronesian language of early migrants before the Common Era. It was distinct from the Western Malayo–Polynesian that developed into the Malay language in riverine and coastal settlements. The development of writing, however, occurred long after the initial dispersion of the highland peoples, and the similarity of Batak script to Sanskrit and Old Javanese as well as Bugis suggests that the script was derived from contact with Indian merchants who bought camphor at Sumatran ports from the tenth century onward.[23] Linguistic evidence from around that time shows that the script moved from south to north, suggesting that the Batak written language originated from Mandailing in the south rather than Toba in the north.[24] The existence of certain phonetically transcribed sounds in Simalungun that are absent in Toba and the heavier

Sanskrit influences in the former also indicate some independent development of language not accounted for by the inside-out thesis. These observations, together with the presence of both South Asian and Malay religious influences in the highlands, indicate a more dynamic, multidirectional movement: the inside-out must have been complemented by movements from the outside in.

Nonetheless, there was a certain unity underpinning group identity in the highlands amid the waves of multidirectional movements. The magic of the datu suggests that religion provided part of that unity. The datu documented their magic spells in *pustaha*, comprising a long strip of bark folded multiple times to form the pages of a book; it was then attached on two ends to a carved wooden cover. The serpent-dragon of the Batak underworld, glimpsed in origin myths, was a prominent feature in these books. Popularly known as the *naga padoha*, he was believed to move continuously around the center of the world in a clockwise direction, halting every three months.[25] At the spot where he stopped, he caused a new village to be founded. Therefore, each year there would be four new villages found at the points of a compass surrounding the original village. The founding of these villages came at a price: for each new village founded, the naga padoha took human lives through disease, accidents, or war. To minimize these losses, the datu needed to read the oracles to know precisely where he was in order to avoid him. Almost all extant bark books and often inscriptions in bamboo boxes contain a drawing of the naga padoha, with accompanying text on how to divine his current position so that new journeys could be started on auspicious days.[26] A carved lizard, a representation of the naga, often adorned the front entrances of many Batak public halls in Toba and Samosir, where surviving works date back to the early nineteenth century.

The myth of the naga padoha survived primarily in Toba and Samosir, but its symbolism ran deeper across the highlands in the way that founding new settlements conferred leadership. The naga emphasized one key aspect of the highlands' pre-monotheistic sacral ecology: movement gives birth. There was a sacral connection between movement and new life, embodied in the perpetual circular motion of the serpent. To illustrate how moving created new life, let us trace the footsteps of a Batak chief moving out of a village to found a new one with his followers. He would clear a path in searching for a new settlement area, read the signs for a suitable place in which to settle, and clear patches of primary forest so that his people could build dwellings and cultivate land. A high bamboo fence, often encircled by a deep pit, protected the new village (*huta*) from hostile neighbors.[27] Thus, a settlement was born and, with it, often a new patriclan. These migrations appeared motivated by pressures to find suitable land on which to grow food. Every move involved clearing forestland in favor of settled agriculture that could help sustain human life. The migrants did not necessarily stay in the uplands; large communities of Batak formed in lowland Asahan and Habinsaran as autonomous societies under the nominal rule of sultans in the Deli and Langkat sultanates from the fifteenth century on. The economic motive is also captured by the Batak term for migration, *marserak*—likely affiliated with the Malay word *berserak*, which means "to scatter." This term later came to encompass not only migration to a different settlement outside the lands of one's clan but also economic and social mobility.[28]

Islam first entered Sumatra in the twelfth and thirteenth centuries and spread extensively among the coastal Sumatran polities during the fifteenth and sixteenth centuries. The persistently animist Batak in the hills appeared to be insulated from these developments. This appearance was misleading, however, since there was extensive contact between the Batak and their Malay neighbors on the coast, as well as with the Acehnese and Minangkabau to their north and south, respectively, particularly through trade. When Muslim Aceh aggressively expanded during the seventeenth and eighteenth centuries, however, the Batak reacted by closing themselves off from neighboring religious and state interference.[29] It was not uncommon for Batak individuals to convert to Islam, but in doing so they no longer adhered to the adat of the Batak and thereafter often did not identify as being solely Batak. Similarly, coastal peoples who moved to the uplands and embraced the Batak adat sometimes formed a new clan and became Batak. In between, the lowland Batak straddled both identities, but even among them, few converted to Islam prior to the nineteenth century.[30] The two identities—Malay and Batak—were thus neither inherent nor stable but could be adopted, albeit through a new birth.

From both sides, the migration from highland to coast (and vice versa) was crucial in an identity conversion. Two examples illustrate this phenomenon. The Batak clan Nasution was formed, most likely in the fifteenth century, from a pact made by a group of Bugis, Tamil, and Malay traders with a Batak datu, Na Sang Tiong, to adhere to Batak adat and live in the highlands.[31] From the opposite direction, local history also provides examples of the birth of a new person and place through religious conversion. In the sixteenth century, a man named Guru Patimpus, from Sembiring clan in Karo, converted to Islam after he lost a bet with a learned Muslim sage from Java. As a condition of his conversion, he had to follow the sage to the Sumatran east coast. This he did, abandoning his wife and children to move to Hamparan Perak, where he married a new wife, the daughter of the chieftain in his new abode. The couple went on to establish a new settlement, which later developed into the city of Medan.[32] Guru Patimpus's conversion was thus a process of creating both a new character and a new space.

Conversion in these cases was not a moment of enlightenment but a physical move to a different landscape to take on a different identity: movement gave birth. In this way the highlands, without being isolated, managed to maintain and replicate their own distinct cosmology in a dynamic equilibrium with that of coastal Malays.

RICE: PRODUCTION, ALLIANCE, AND SUSTENANCE

To demonstrate how the productive ecology of the North Sumatran highlands historically interacted with Batak concepts of divinity to formulate particular forms of social organization, the next two sections examine the social metabolism of two goods that sustained life in the highlands: rice and camphor. Rice, a staple food, was grown largely for subsistence, while camphor, a key export, was exchanged with traders from the coast for necessities such as salt. While these were not the only produce of the region before the nineteenth century—pepper, tobacco, rattan, and benzoin were also important exports—ritual life was more significant in the production of rice and camphor. In these rituals, a web of relations spanned both the heavens and earth.

A discussion of Batak sociopolitical institutions usually starts with either village or patriclan. But at the center of both these spatial and social structures is a primary food crop: rice. A focal point of life in a new settlement, rice barns were often built facing a row of small houses, usually set in a square patch of cleared land. These buildings usually had black-thatched, saddle-shaped roofs, leaving an attic-like space for storage. A curtain of trees or a tall fence made from bamboo enclosed the whole, leaving open two entrances, one on the east side and the other on the west. The eastern entrance was guarded by a *pangulubalang*, a sculpture of a Batak guardian spirit made of wood or stone that protected the village while the villagers were at work in the rice fields.[33]

These villages were a relatively recent invention. Pollen analysis in the areas around Lake Toba has shown that people began clearing primary forests there on a limited scale about 8,000 years ago to grow root crops. This deforestation intensified from 2500 to 550 BP as external migration into the highlands brought new agricultural techniques.[34] The presence of microfossil charcoal, pollen from secondary regrowth, and fern spores from sample soil suggest that rice was largely grown in swidden, noninundated rice fields by nomadic agriculturalists. Dry rice cultivation could have been a parallel cropping strategy to wet rice, with the latter established at lower altitudes near seasonal swamps before being integrated upland onto preexisting slash-and-burn cultivation systems. Wet rice motivated village settlements: to irrigate wet rice plots, water from nearby streams was piped into each patch of cleared land through bamboo ducts or hollowed-out palm trunks. The presence of temple complexes far in the upland interior of Padang Lawas has shown that wet rice had been planted by the thirteenth century.[35] At an altitude of 1,400 meters above sea level, however, wet rice cultivation was not possible.[36] Other than Padang Lawas, the predominant evidence of swidden implied that mobility and social organization centered on settled agricultural villages was not the norm in the uplands before the fifteenth century.

The question of whether early agriculture was ecologically sustainable is contested, given that swidden farming appeared to predominate for about twenty-five hundred years.[37] Much depends on how long the swidden land was left fallow; if allowed to revert to jungle for twenty to thirty years, the system certainly regenerated itself. On the lower limit, a fallow period below eight years is probably unsustainable, leading to less rich and diverse secondary forest as regrowth.[38] Moreover, scholars must guard against an uncritical acceptance of the paradigm that swidden was a form of forest management and conservation. Data from the uplands of Sulawesi, for example, suggest that it created less diverse regrowth.[39]

On the other hand, some anthropologists have called for a reassessment of the view that grassland formed through swiddening indicated agriculturally unproductive land.[40] The Batak, specifically the subgroups Toba, Karo, Angkola, and Simalungun, had developed a method of grassland farming with a long history that existed concurrently with wet-rice cultivation.[41] Grassland farming involved laboriously opening savannah land with mattocks before using fire to kill the grass in the segments of the broken-up sod. Grasslands were also conducive to raising livestock such as cattle, which could graze on young shoots of grass that sprang up after the field was burned; this grass had a higher protein content and a taste that the cattle apparently preferred. The wide expanse of grassland also supported ponies, which were numerous enough for the Batak to export at least as far back as the eighteenth century.

In North Sumatra, evidence from European sources indicates that the system had become robust enough to support about a million people in the Toba uplands by the early nineteenth century.[42] British traveler John Anderson, who visited the Karo plateau and Lake Toba in the 1820s, observed a similar population density and noted that the swidden rice fields were used to grow crops such as bananas and sugarcane, those fields being interspersed among grassy plains.[43] The German naturalist Franz Wilhelm Junghuhn found that the Angkola Batak preferred farming grassland to cutting down more forest.[44] But subsequent European colonial administrators and scholars tended to view grassland as a sign of ecological exhaustion. The Dutch colonial scholars Meint Joustra and Jan Tideman recorded that the fallow period usually lasted eight to ten years and permitted only two to four harvests before grass regrowth indicated the land was depleted.[45] These colonial assessments of ecological exhaustion through early farming methods should be read against the grain, as they were based on the assumption that grassland could not be agriculturally productive.

Rice was usually eaten with salt and fish as condiments, and the trade in salt brought the upland and coastal peoples into each other's orbits. Technology in rice production was similar: both the Batak uplanders and the Malays harvested the crop with finger knives, eschewing the sickles preferred in China and on the Southeast Asian mainland. Harvesting with a finger knife, usually the job of women, was slow, as only one stalk could be cut at a time. But it allowed each stalk to be cut as it ripened, thus distributing the labor load over a longer period of time and cutting out the labor of weeding the plots.[46] The finger knife also pointed toward a belief, shared among the upland and coastal peoples, in spirits that animated rice crops; a number of nineteenth-century European scholars who inquired about the rationale for this method of harvesting were told that the finger knife was more respectful to the female spirit of the rice.[47] Thus, in this rice-diet zone, there appeared to be a basic level of religious and cultural coherence between the uplands and the coast, fed by rice and seasoned with salt.

Unlike among the coastal peoples, however, agriculture did not facilitate the formation of supravillage ties, and none of the upland Batak subgroups achieved a state-level political organization. Before the nineteenth century, warfare among the Batak was largely internecine, or small in scale but endemic. South Tapanuli was more peaceful than the north, where high bamboo walls and deep ditches around each village were ubiquitous, particularly in the Pakpak and Karo areas. Nonetheless, even in the south, frequent war-like conflict between villages was indicated by periods of poor harvests when villagers supplemented their diets with clay from the earth; geophagy was indicated by the word *bange*, meaning "edible earth."[48] Conflicts were also implicit in the datu's bark books, of which protective magic was a significant part. Endemic war between villages suggests there was no centralized authority to mediate or coerce different Batak clans into keeping the peace.

In place of a supravillage or centralized authority, the rice pot symbolically linked various patriclans in a complex network. To cook rice, each pot was balanced over a fire set inside three hearthstones. In Batak adat, the heart of the relationship between clans is named after these "three hearthstones," or Dalihan Na Tolu, which comprise a man's own clan, the clan of his wife (wife-giving clan, *tulang* or *hula-hula*), and the clans that took the man's sisters as wives (wife-taking clan, *anak boru* or *anak beru*).[49] A man's clan had such an obligation to shelter and protect the wife-giving clan, and he called himself the servant (*parhoba*) of his wife-giving clan. His *anak boru* was likewise obligated to him. Such a network of obligations flattened all hierarchy between villages, since, as most aptly expressed by a Toba Batak man, "all people are kings, and all people are servants, and we must be both to be either."[50] Although members of each village and its attendant founding clan were bound by kinship and marriage to many neighboring villages, no other supravillage institution or person possessed the authority to demand labor or taxes from them. In Batak society before the nineteenth century, Dalihan Na Tolu precluded their formation of a state.

Rice provided more than just an imagery of clan obligations, which were sacralized by rituals involved in its planting. The founder of a new village also founded the dominant clan in the village. When a village opened up a new rice field, members from the wife-giving clan would lead the way in the ritual, symbolizing the obligation that the founding clan in the village owed to them.[51] The wife-giving clan also received a larger share of the meat from the buffalo sacrificed when a patch of forest was cleared for planting rice.[52] Cattle and buffalo were favored for sacrificial meat, but in most of North Tapanuli at least, villagers preferred to eat pork, as pigs were more cost-effective animals to raise. In a large feast in which kin from neighboring villages gathered, pork would be prepared especially for the wife-giving clan, to honor them. Moreover, in Toba and Samosir, a pig given by the wife-giving clan was considered an ideal source of prosperity, and upon receiving such a gift, the wife-receiving clan sometimes made an offering to ensure the animal's productivity.[53]

The importance of balancing the three hearthstones conditioned one of the strongest taboos in Batak adat: marrying within one's own clan. A marriage within one's own clan tipped the pot too heavily toward one's own patriclan, endangering the delicate balance of Dalihan Na Tolu. Such a marriage was considered incest, and the punishment for such conduct was often death, a hefty fine, or exile. One of the most sacred objects in Batak magic, the datu's staff (*tunggal panaluan*) embodied the power of this taboo. Carved on the staff from top to bottom were the figures of a man, a woman, and five figures of indeterminate sex interspersed with animal figures of a chicken, broad-horned buffalo, crocodile, and giant serpent. These carvings were rooted in a folktale describing the origins of this magical object. In this tale, a twin brother and sister committed incest when they were reunited after a long separation. Walking home together after this taboo act, the brother stopped to climb a tree and bring down some fruits for his sister. The tree swallowed him into his trunk, and he turned into wood as punishment for his sin; the same fate befell his sister when she climbed up after him. Subsequently, their parents summoned a series of magician-priests to help their children. Five datu, each bringing a spirit animal, tried in turn to free the pair but ended up being trapped in the tree themselves. Finally, a powerful datu advised the parents that the endeavor was useless, as the tree was too powerful. Instead, he suggested cutting it down, carving a magic staff with the faces of the seven beings inside, and using the staff as a channel to draw powerful energy.[54] This staff became a staple tool of many datu. Among the staff's powers was the ability to end droughts by calling down rains and increasing the fertility of rice fields.[55] The wooden staff was a material manifestation of the belief that humans and nonhumans were intermingled in nature and that nature could channel its power to punish violators of the natural order; alternatively, it could subvert that violation to beneficial ends.

Rice and marriage were crucially intertwined. The staff, ubiquitous in ceremonies over which datu presided, captured in wood the sacrality of Batak adat as a framework for order in society. An indispensable tool during rituals to open new rice fields, supplicate for rain during dry spells, and harvest rice, the datu's staff brought human relationships to bear on the fertility of the natural world. A fertile land was embedded in the production of balanced and good social relations within the village. It was, in turn, the fertility of the land that enabled a clan member to fulfill his obligations to feed his family and offer protection and sustenance to his wife's paternal clan when necessary. Marriage was primarily a relationship of debt in which the balance of who was indebted to whom determined which ties were encouraged. There was some variation among the Batak subgroups about how this debt could be managed through the distribution of food; traces of this belief were apparent until quite recently. As late as the 1950s in Angkola (but not elsewhere), the marriage of a man to his female cousin on his mother's side had been forbidden for generations immemorial, since it doubled the obligation, usually met with rice, to the wife-giving clan.[56] In general, though, two rules seemed to prevail in customary law: marriage within one's clan was taboo, while the marriage of a man's daughter to the son of his wife's brother was considered ideal.

Rice, in its cultivation, distribution, and attendant rituals, therefore conditioned social relationships particular to the North Sumatran highlands. Two features are unique to this culture: a patrilineal clan system in which kinship, descent, and property rights were traced through the male line, and a Dalihan Na Tolu network that enmeshed the patriclan with the matriclan by encouraging cross-cousin unions. The web of obligations in this system confined the political power of a dominant clan to the village level, keeping it from aggregating into a centralized state. This distinguished the adat of the Batak from that of their neighbors: the Acehnese, Minangkabau, and coastal Malays. In those societies, kinship was traced through matriarchal or bilateral lineage, making both the male and female line important for the inheritance of wealth and property. More significantly, the wet-rice cultivation predominant among the Batak's neighbors accompanied a tendency toward centralized state polities, from the Buddhist kingdom of Adityavarman in fourteenth-century Minangkabau to the Muslim sultanate of Aceh, established in the mid-fifteenth century. Where the three hearthstones of Dalihan Na Tolu stood at the center of Batak adat, the king (*raja*) occupied the center of the Malay adat, despite being a charismatic figure who played little part in everyday village life.

Fertility, in the North Sumatran highlands context, was not merely manifested in a bountiful harvest of rice but also in the replication of balanced social relationships between villages, sacralized and regulated by spirits via the natural world. Through the expansion of fertile rice fields over the highlands, the social metabolism of rice aided the expansion of the Batak adat. Trade in aromatics shaped that adat in the face of contact with the states of other civilizations.

CAMPHOR, BENZOIN, AND THE STATE

Monsoon winds brought traders eastward over the Bay of Bengal to Sumatra from November to March. Through the harvesting and trade of aromatics, the North Sumatran highlands became a node in a global network that brought not only humans but also the gods into close contact. The term "benzoin" appears to be a contraction of its Arabic equivalent, *luban-al-Jawi*, first mentioned in a travel account in the thirteenth century.[57] The term "camphor" originates from either the Sanskrit *karpura* or Malay *kapur*; both South and Southeast Asia were regions where camphor trees were native and abundant. The term "camphor" was then adopted into the Arabic-Persian and European families of languages. East Asian languages developed separate terms for the substance independent of the Sanskrit-Malay-Arabic-European zones. These etymologies suggest that although Taiwan and Japan became the largest exporters of camphor by the late nineteenth century, the camphor that penetrated the Arab and European markets in earlier times was of the South or Southeast Asian variety.

Evidence of North Sumatran peoples' participation in a thriving trade in camphor and benzoin can be dated back to at least the fifth century, when there was demand for the two resins in major port cities along the Straits of Malacca. By the sixth century, benzoin had become a common substitute for myrrh in southern China and its use had spread to western Asia and Europe. Srivijaya, the maritime empire based in South Sumatra, was one of the most important conduits for this trade from the seventh to the thirteenth centuries. Barus, a port town on the west coast of Sumatra, became synonymous with the camphor trade, which became crucial to its economy.[58] Used in religious rituals on a global scale, aromatics such as camphor and benzoin came to represent a material connection with the world of the gods. Srivijaya was a Hindu-Buddhist empire, one of the major "Indianized" polities of the maritime Southeast Asian regions, and it sacralized the use of camphor and greatly valued its fragrance, whiteness, coolness, and flammability. Praised in Sanskrit poetry, it became a medium for communing with the gods. In South Asia in the first millennium, waving a camphor flame before a sacred image—a rite known as *arati*—was an extravagant way of supplicating for divine protection. The camphor flame was the "climax of worship" in the Hindu ritual of *puja*, in which "the divine and human participants are most fully identified in their common vision of the flame and hence in their mutual vision of each other—the perfect *darshana*. God has become man and a person, transformed, has become god," as expressed by Christopher Fuller, a historian of religion.[59] Perhaps influenced by this idea of transcendence between a human body and the being of God, Malay rituals—while rooted in animism rather than Hinduism—also heavily utilized benzoin and camphor to perform magic spells, for either protection or aggression. In this blending of the supernatural and healing, Malay and Batak both conceptualized the human body as vulnerable to incursions by spirits, and bad health indicated an offense to the spirits. This idea of a permeable body, vulnerable to a malodorous environment, was common in the early modern world. Aromatics such as camphor and benzoin enabled a fresh fragrance to chase away the vile odors; they were central to the notion that healing the soul's connection with the supernatural was healing the body.

In the premodern world, there was more demand for the resin than for the wood of Southeast Asian camphor, which was of the *Dryobalanops* genus. This was unlike the cases in China, Japan, and India, where the evergreen *Cinnamomum* variety grew, yielding wood used to make moth-proof cupboards as well as ship masts and keel joists. Timber from the camphor tree, infused with the scent of its resin, was valuable in the making of furniture that could repel insects and white ants. The Dominican priest Fernández Navarrete, who traveled to China in the seventeenth century, observed that camphor trees' strong odor appeared to drive away insects, such that "for five leagues around where these trees grow there is not one bug to be seen."[60] These trees were often planted around temples and gardens and prized for both their scent and their appearance. Unlike the *Cinnamomum* variety, however, the wood of the *Dryobalanops* genus common in North Sumatra and Borneo was not particularly effective in construction, as it absorbed water and warped in a relatively short time.[61] When freshly cut, the wood was flexible and easy to work but hardened upon exposure to the sun.[62] Therefore, while timber from the *Dryobalanops* variety of the camphor tree in North Sumatra might also have been exported, there is little evidence of extensive demand for it.

The camphor tree's resin, unlike its wood, brought material gains. The quest for healing the body and spirit, profane and divine, drove demand for this elusive substance, sending Batak men ever deeper into the uplands to seek it out. The search process itself brought new divinities into being, as seen in Batak folklore highlighting both the elusiveness and the value of the camphor tree's resin. In one tale, a beautiful young woman called Nan Tar Tar Nan Tor Tor, who descended from otherworldly spirits (*anak begoe*), married a human under the condition that he was never to ask her to dance. However, a romantic rival tricked her into dancing at a feast, and as a result she was carried away from earth by a powerful and malevolent spirit. Her soul escaped, however, then fled to the shelter of a camphor tree and transformed itself into the magical substance. Her human husband, Si Pagedag Si Pagedog, searched for her in every camphor tree, knocking on each trunk with a stick in search of her spirit. But since he had violated the terms of their marriage, he was doomed never to find her. Even as he came to approach the right tree, her soul would flee to a different one, and all he would hear was a hollow thumping sound of "pagedag pagedog."[63] And so, when a Batak man searched for a camphor tree from which to harvest resin, he would avoid those whose trunks made a hollow sound when hit, as it indicated that the camphor had already fled.[64]

Ideas of the divine permeated the quest for camphor. The Batak did not domesticate and cultivate camphor trees but instead sought the resin through supplication of the divine. A Dutch colonial ethnographer described this process as it was carried out among the Dairi Batak, his account further illuminating the social metabolism of the camphor trade. He wrote that in traditional camphor harvesting expeditions, a village chief first appointed a camphor seeker (*bona hajoe*), who would lead a search party and provide the necessary capital for the venture: daily supplies for the men and a buffalo. The camphor seeker then gathered a team of men, and in an area where camphor trees grew, he built a hut to serve as both shelter and base for the team.[65]

The hut was built in tacit respect for the camphor seeker's ability to commune with the spirits. It had two entrances—one for the camphor seeker and the other for the rest of the men. The spirits provided the camphor seeker with guidance to decide which trees should be cut, and his methods of communication with them took the forms of offerings, direct supplication, and dream seeking. The camphor seeker first set out an offering of salted carrots. When ants came to the offering, he would read the signs through their appearance, as their color indicated the color of the animal to be sacrificed. If red ants came to the carrots, then a white buffalo needed to be slaughtered; if black ants came, then a black buffalo had to be offered to the spirits.

When this buffalo was slaughtered, the direction in which it fell at the moment of death guided the camphor gatherers to their destination. The camphor seeker also occasionally ingested opium when seeking to communicate with the spirits through dreams. If a beautiful young woman appeared in his dreams bearing an offering of rice, the camphor seeker interpreted her appearance and the amount of rice offered as signs for which type of tree should be cut. The skin color of the woman in his dream told him whether to cut down a tree with black, white, or brown bark. If she had long hair, then the tree that should be cut must have long aerial roots. If the woman in the dream wore a clean green bodice, then the group looked for a tree with a nice smooth trunk. The amount of rice offered by the woman indicated the amount of camphor that would be found. Following all these clues, the men then chose which trees to cut down.[66]

Until the camphor was harvested, the group was forbidden to use certain words that could bring bad fortune to the expedition. Instead, they used more esoteric substitutes.[67] If no camphor was found after the identified trees were cut down, this lack was often attributed to an imperfect observance of the rituals to the spirits. The offended spirits might take the lives of the camphor seeker or one of his men as forfeit, resulting in a mysterious disappearance during the night, in which the missing person was said to have been taken by the spirits (*dipangan begoe*). To continue the search, a new sponsor had to be found and the process repeated. William Marsden, an East India Company official, observed such an expedition for camphor in eighteenth-century Sumatra, which led him to disdain the role of the "professional conjurer" and note the local efforts' lack of productivity, reporting that "it is said that not a tenth part of the number felled is productive either of camphor or camphor oil and that parties of men are sometimes engaged two or three months together in the forest with very precarious success."[68]

However, the elaborate practice of camphor hunting was more than mere cultural oddity or superstition. Rather, these practices highlighted how the notion of spirits aided a rudimentary system of managing camphor trees as a natural resource. The cost of the sacrifices—in buffalo and sometimes human life—indirectly acted as a check on the number of camphor trees cut. Implicit in the process of seeking camphor was the recognition that the resource was finite, elusive, and nonreplicable. The magical powers associated with the camphor seeker likely precluded men from outside the Batak highlands from striking out to find camphor on their own, which would have threatened an already precarious monopoly. In this case, the natural world provided a sign of divine power; the tree was not an agent in its own right but a medium for the agentive power of the spirits. Capricious and demanding of sacrifices, spirits in nature were not uniformly benevolent. They deterred seekers without local knowledge from coming into Batak territory, thus allowing the Batak to defend their monopoly despite their decentralized, dispersed political structure.

The importance of Barus as a port for exporting camphor outlasted Srivijaya as a maritime empire and survived until the eve of Dutch colonialism in Sumatra at the end of the eighteenth century. Politics in Barus demonstrated how the camphor trade brokered power sharing between Malay polities and Batak groups, who needed each other. Malay chiefs ruling Barus would be unable to withstand an attack if the Batak ever wanted to destroy the port, but the Batak were unlikely to do so, as internecine war checked each Batak subgroup from launching an assault on their own, and their collective dependence on the port provided an impetus to maintain good relations with the Malay rulers in Barus.[69] Two family histories of Malay chiefs who shared power in Barus—Raja di Hulu, the upstream king, and Raja di Hilir, the downstream king—showed that they each bolstered their authority through alliances with Batak clans. Periodically, these alliances took the form of roping in Batak military strength to settle disputes between them.[70] Barus developed into a protocosmopolitan space, where traders of many different identities coalesced around a Malay king. According to the history detailed from the court of Raja di Hulu, "The people who live here [in Barus] are one: Malays, Acehnese, Rawa, Korincies, Bataks from Mandailing and Angkola, Bugis, Javanese and people from Timur. All of these people have mixed together as have their customs and clothing. There are also Hindus, Keling [Indians] and people from Nias."[71] These diverse groups converged in Barus, attracted by a profit-making purpose.

Raja di Hilir's chronicle provided a contrasting account that highlighted not unity but the distinctiveness of the Malay and the Batak. It claimed that Sultan Ibrahim, the second Raja di Hilir at Barus, traveled to Bakkara and was invited to rule over the Batak there. However, when he requested that they convert to Islam so that they could become "one people" (*satu bangsa*), they regretfully turned him down, as they wished to remain true to the spirits of their ancestors. Sultan Ibrahim consequently left the uplands, but not before fathering a son with a Batak woman; the boy later became the first of the charismatic priest-chiefs known as Si Singamangaradja in the sixteenth century. Taken together, the chronicles of these two Malay kings on Barus show that a distinctive Batak identity had emerged by the late sixteenth century and that nonadherence to Islam was one of its key characteristics.[72] As expressed by the historian Anthony Reid, the Batak might show "a symbolic supremacy of the coastal ruler" but did not allow themselves to be culturally absorbed."[73]

The camphor trade thus produced a symbiotic relationship between the Batak and the Malay, while keeping the two peoples distinct. The Batak, as gatherers of camphor, were politically dispersed, clan-oriented, and non-Muslim peoples. The Malay, as traders of camphor, controlled the route to the coast through a polity unified around their king, possessing co-religionist links with Arab-Persian merchants and long-standing maritime connections with much of the region. Uphill lay the adat of the Batak, downhill the adat of the Malay. Balancing this spectrum of identities was a little settlement called Rambe, a collecting center for resin at the lower end of the hills leading to Barus.[74] Rambe was most likely founded in the fifteenth century by a Batak man, Alang Pardoksi, who was gifted the land by a Malay chief who had cheated him. He marked his control over the settlement with the erection of several *pangulubalang*, but he and his children ruled in a manner akin to Malay kings, abandoning the obligations of Dalihan Na Tolu to levy taxes on his subjects for the camphor passing through his territory.[75] In effect, the people of Rambe straddled the religion of the Batak and the political model of the Malay, just as their settlement geographically straddled mountain and coast.

However, this equilibrium did not imply a continuous or frictionless co-existence. The term "Batak" had become a marker for a non-Muslim identity and independence from Malay coastal states. Malay court chronicles at times reflected unease with that autonomy through derogatory descriptions of the Batak. For example, *Hikayat Aceh*, a sixteenth-century panegyric to the Aceh-nese sultan Iskandar Muda, described the Batak as cheaters and murderers. In the epic, a Batak man cheated the young Iskandar Muda of his sword and kris, and two Batak datu were recruited to the service of a rebel Acehnese prince in order to poison the king.[76] This distrust of the Batak stemmed from a larger Acehnese drive to conquer North Sumatra: Aceh decimated the Karo Batak polity of Aru in the 1530s, with Ottoman assistance, and Iskandar Muda attacked it again in 1622.[77] An estimated twenty-two thousand Batak Karo from Aru were enslaved by the Acehnese, and their descendants resettled in Aceh but acknowledged their Batak roots.[78] The seventeenth-century *Hikayat Hang Tuah*, a classic paean to the maritime empire of Malacca, also mentioned the Batak as untrustworthy and outside their locus of control: the Batak warmly received a princess who had fled to the mountains after rejecting the suit of the king of Malacca, and they made her their ruler.[79] These uncomplimentary mentions attested to how the exercise of Batak autonomy weighed uncomfort-ably on patriarchal Malay king–centered coastal states that nonetheless needed them, and they depict how boundaries between Muslim sultanates and animist peoples sometimes hardened into outright animosity. Notably, however, such moments were sparse during the early modern period.

Following the trail of camphor, we thus uncover three epochs in the history of contact between the Batak and the states with which they traded. Running through them was the development not of territorial states but of alliances needed to sustain this trade. The first, from approximately the tenth to thirteenth centuries, connected highland villages with each other on a north-south route from areas where the aromatics grew best to the port cities in Srivijaya. The thirteenth to fifteenth centuries saw the rudimentary emergence of a Batak identity as the highland peoples negotiated with and absorbed peoples from small, Malay king–centered states that controlled trade on the east and west coasts (while slowly converting those peoples to Islam). A northern neighbor, Aceh, was becoming increasingly expansionist. Beginning in the fifteenth century, a clear Batak identity arose in rites and religious rituals for the camphor harvest, which distinguished them from their largely Muslim neighbors while helping them maintain their autonomy, both politically and economically. This new identity was most evident through migration: Batak movement to the lowlands during this period—most numerically significant among the Karo and Simalungun, who came to the Islamic sultanates of Deli and Langkat in the late eighteenth century to grow pepper—resulted in lowland settlements that symbolically accepted the supremacy of a coastal ruler but held their identities and political structures aloof from absorption by the Malays.[80] Intermarriage, trade, and conversion to Islam continued on a small scale, but the Batak identity had solidified and resisted incorporation into lowland Malay states. From the perspective of the coast during the unstable equilibrium of this period, the Batak had grown to become as elusive and ungovernable as their most valuable export.

DEATH AND AFTERLIFE: TOMBS, THE ENSLAVED, AND THE *TONDI*

Death, in its broadest sense, is Janus-faced: on one side, an end in which the body ceases to function in this world and, on the other, the beginning of a process in which material flesh gives way to a metaphysical afterlife. It bridges the world of humans and the world of the spirits. Examining the sacral ecology surrounding death in the North Sumatran highlands elucidates how the Batak body was embedded in a natural world animated by spirits that were enmeshed in power structures within Batak society at the start of the nineteenth century. I examine two forms of death here. The first is physical death, along with its attendant traditions of burial and inheritance. The second is enslavement, which I categorize as a form of death in the Foucauldian sense of being a process that inhibits life.[81]

Driving up the slopes around Lake Toba today, one often finds three-tiered aboveground tombs dotting the landscape, some plain and some incredibly ornate. When I asked a Toba Batak guide about the structures, he explained that they represented three levels in Batak cosmology: the netherworld, the earthly realm, and the heavens. The netherworld was associated with the underground, and thus the bodies of honored men and women were not interred. Rather, such a body was first placed in the bottom tier of the tomb and then removed after some time; the remains were then reburied at the top level, closer to the heavens.[82] Whether this practice is similarly understood across different subgroups and over time is debatable, but there are clear indications that Batak precolonial rituals avoided returning bodies to the earth. Secondary burial—the practice of interring a body in a tomb until it decayed before reburying the remains in another receptacle, this one aboveground—was a prevalent feature of Batak adat as well as many other animist societies before conversion to monotheism.[83] Preserved sarcophagi of Batak chiefs show that bodies of the chiefs were buried aboveground at least as far back as the eighteenth century and probably earlier.

Extant sources contain very few accounts describing death and burial among the Batak. The earliest seems to be Marsden's, whose account of a funeral of a Batak chief in 1783 is worth reproducing in detail:

[Men brought] a buffalo, hog, goat, dog, fowl, or other article of provision, according to his ability, and the women baskets of rice, which are presented and placed in order. The feasting begins and continues for nine days and nights, or so long as the provisions hold out. On the last of these days the coffin is carried out and set in an open space, where it is surrounded by the female mourners, on their knees, with their heads covered, and howling (*ululantes*) in dismal concert, whilst the younger persons of the family are dancing near it, in solemn movement, to the sound of gongs, *kalintang* [gong chimes], and a kind of flageolet. . . . On the tenth day the body is carried to the grave, preceded by the guru or priest, whose limbs are tattooed in the shape of birds and beasts, and painted of different colors, with a large mask on his face. He takes a piece of buffalo-flesh, swings it about, throwing himself into violent attitudes and strange contortions, and then eats the morsel in a voracious manner. He then kills a fowl over the corpse, letting the blood run down upon the coffin, and just before it is moved both he and the female mourners, having each a broom in their hands, sweep violently about it. . . . Suddenly four men, stationed for the purpose, lift up the coffin, and march quickly off with it, as if escaping from the fiend, the priest continuing to sweep after it for some distance. It is then deposited in the ground, without any peculiar ceremony, at a depth of three or four feet; the earth about the grave is raised, a shed built over it.[84]

Marsden did not attempt to interpret the meaning of the dances and animal sacrifices that he depicted as colorful savagery. Christian missionaries to the area later attempted a deeper understanding of the notion of death and the afterlife among the unconverted Batak in line with their interest in saving souls. In these works, missionaries saw in Batak burial practices a belief in what some called the "cult of the *tondi*."[85]

Tondi, variously translated as "soul stuff" or "soul of a living human," had an existence independent of the human body and the ability to influence past and future happenings.[86] Among the Batak, a person's tondi dwells with the High God, Mula Jadi Nabolon, and takes a leaf from the tree of life before being born into this world; the choice of leaf leads to the events in that person's earthly life, whether good or bad. However, the tondi is more mobile than its corporeal, earthly body, although it dwells in all parts of the flesh. A person's tondi could even choose to leave the body unless it received food and honor through communal feasts where presents are exchanged.[87] Honoring the tondi thus entailed honoring social obligations, and its transferable nature also meant an individual's tondi could strengthen those of others. Possession of a person's belongings or body parts, such as a fragment of fingernail, gave another person magical power over that individual's tondi. Consuming the heart, palms, or soles of the feet of another person gave access to that person's tondi and strengthened one's own.[88] Physical or mental deficiencies were often ascribed to a weak tondi.

The strengthening and protection of society through the tondi of an individual could also be detected in the magic spells of the datu. One of his most potent potions was the *pupuk*, which was produced from the sacrifice of a young boy kidnapped from a neighboring village. To make *pupuk*, the boy was gently reared to the age of about eleven with the understanding that he would be sacrificed. On the day of the sacrifice, he would be killed by filling his mouth with molten lead to prevent his tondi from escaping; from his dead body, the datu made the potion, rich in his tondi. The *pupuk* potion was believed to be especially powerful in animating the inanimate; it was applied to wooden or stone figures such as the *pangulubalang* with the belief that these figures would come to life when there was danger to the village.[89]

After death, the soul took on a different name: *begu*.[90] Begu more specifically refers to the spirits of one's ancestors but could also encompass spirits from the heavenly plane, as in the legend of the camphor tree, and the spirits of the dead more generally. The wide definition of begu suggests a unity between the dead and the spirits of the upper world. The dead have escaped the bounds of earthly authority and could traverse the heavenly world as well as the earthly one of the native villages; they could choose to intervene in the latter. The fortunes of the living depended on the goodwill of the ancestors.[91] Thus, traditional Batak adat venerated the *begu* of one's ancestral lineage with offerings and sacrifices. The longer a man's lineage and the more descendants he had, the more powerful his begu would be.

It is unfortunate that this window into pre-monotheistic Batak beliefs about the dead can be accessed only through missionary sources, which color the interpretation of the beliefs with a sense that they are inferior and macabre. Through this distorted window, however, one may glimpse several important features of Batak adat on death, the human soul, and the natural world. The spirit has relatively more mobility than the physical body, and death sets it free to move across different corporeal planes. Spirits have the power to protect as well as to animate the inanimate while enhancing the power of flora and fauna in the natural world. As we have also seen in the legends of camphor, the landscape was largely made potent through these spirits even though flora and fauna possessed a power of their own.

What happens to the *begu*s of persons far from their homeland? Enslavement is a second form of death in the North Sumatran highlands that merits attention because it demonstrates the sacral connection between the Batak identity, spirit, and homeland. The Batak use the same word for both "slave" and an enslaved class—*hatoban*—and the existence of such a word indicates the visible and permanent presence of such a class in village life. Enslavement was a form of death in this context, as the status of enslavement halted a person's involvement in Batak ritual life and very often severed enslaved people from their homeland. A person could be bonded in precolonial Southeast Asia in the following ways: capture in war; indebtedness; sale into bondage by parents, husband, or oneself; judicial punishment for inability to pay fines; and inheriting the bondage of one's parents.[92] Of these, debt and capture in war appear the most common among the Batak. Many Batak were sold into slavery *outside* the highlands, but non-Batak people were not imported *into* Batak society as slaves, making their system a closed one in which no outsiders entered. This asymmetrical traffic of enslaved people in precolonial Southeast Asia meant that people were forcibly moved from politically fragmented societies to more centralized polities.

An enslaved person, while possibly treated lightly in terms of demands of service, occupied a marginal position in village life. The status of enslavement, for a person and as a lineage, precluded participation in communal rituals. For example, among the Pakpak, enslaved persons were not allowed to receive meat from ritual village celebration feasts. Slave lineage could be inherited, but in the case of a man enslaved through debt, his free family could pay it off on his behalf and liberate him.[93] Most of the enslaved class in a village were bound not only by debt but by isolation. They came into being as outsiders—as captives of war who owed a debt of life to their captor, who had decided not to kill them, or as marginalized free persons whose family had disowned them and their debts. Cut off from the support of lineage and family, excluded from village ritual life, and often physically removed from their place of birth, newly enslaved persons were also newly dead in terms of their societal function.

Yet, if slavery was a form of dying in the Foucauldian sense of limiting life, the complexities of slave trading between coastal states and the politically anarchic uplands demonstrated that dying could lead to a new form of being. There have been few studies of slavery in precolonial Southeast Asia, but the most authoritative show that bondage could lead the enslaved to assimilation into the ethnic group of their masters. Using the looser term "bondsman" rather than "slave" to describe a Southeast Asian conception of slavery, Reid considered the system to be more personal than legalistic when compared to similar systems in contemporary Europe.[94] Malay sultanates regulated the hiring of enslaved persons as labor, and this was captured in the provisions of legal codes such as the Undang-Undang Melaka.[95] Legally, little distinction was made between slavery and other forms of bondage such as wage labor. These bonded groups often intermarried with people of the ethnicities that had enslaved them. While the enslaved persons from the uplands may initially be regarded as a race apart, and an inferior one at that, Reid noted that "the Malay population in the coastal lowlands of Malaya, Sumatra and Borneo gradually absorbed animist hill peoples during the five centuries before 1900, by a mixture of raiding, tribute and purchase, especially of children."[96] By assimilating into the Malay or migrant Chinese population, enslaved Batak, even if they were later freed, found themselves cut off from their clan-centered adat and rituals to propitiate the spirits of their ancestors. At the same time, by embracing the adat of their masters and assimilating, they could find a new life with a different ethnic identity, albeit bound to a different landscape.

The flow of enslaved people into the Malay Peninsula emphasizes the dynamic equilibrium of the highlands with the Sumatran-Malay riverine and coastal states that were its neighbors. Bondage of a lower class of Batak tied together the states and the stateless, siphoning off part of the Batak population while keeping the upland hierarchy stable. This equilibrium was also gendered. Within this territorial unit of trade and exchange, enslaved females—Batak and others forced into concubinage—contributed to the regeneration of the coastal populations. By the nineteenth century, colonial powers had superseded Malay authority in some coastal ports, with the British controlling Penang (from 1786), Singapore (from 1814), and Malacca (from 1824), forming a colony known as the Straits Settlements. Enslaved females became a large proportion of the women in this colony, providing a small counterbalance to the burgeoning number of male migrants, mostly from China. For this reason, they were also priced higher. A certificate of sale from Malacca in 1819 showed that an enslaved female named Manees was sold for a hundred Spanish dollars, almost twice the average price for a male.[97] Nor was Manees, whose name connotes good looks or a sweet disposition, a singularly expensive slave. The price of a thousand Spanish dollars to buy a "Nias maid, when all her points are good," was considered unexceptional.[98]

It would be instructive to look deeper into some trends in the slave markets of Penang and Malacca during the late eighteenth and early nineteenth centuries in order to delineate the Batak's position in those spaces. Malay-language documents in the India Office Records regarding the sale of slaves over a thirty-year period from 1785 to 1815 show the ethnicity of the persons sold in each transaction.[99] The documents followed a standard format: the date; the number of slaves sold; the gender, name, and ethnic group of each person sold; the names of the vendor and the purchaser; and the price and the names and signatures of witnesses. Some, however, did *not* specify the ethnicity of the person sold, simply recording instead that the vendor sold "a slave, male" for a particular price.

While people of many ethnicities were sold in the slave markets, the trade was dominated by the sale of individuals who came from animist highland regions outside the control of coastal states (e.g., Batak) or non-Muslim islands also

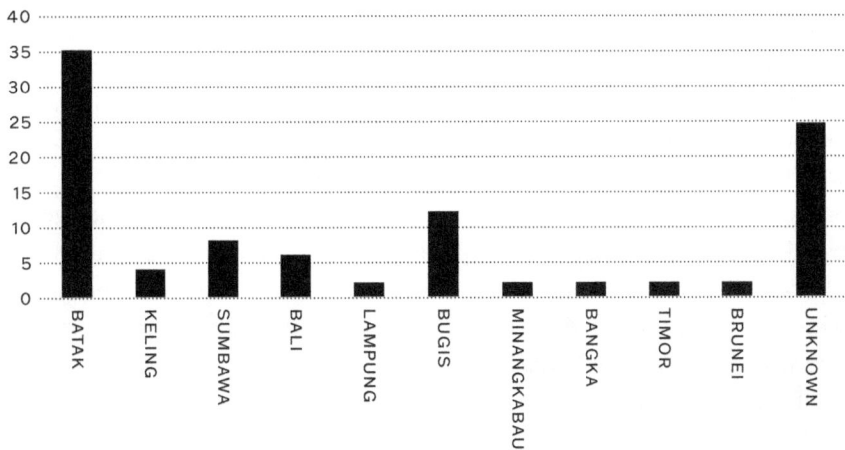

Ethnicity of enslaved persons in Sale of Slaves documents, 1785–1815. Malacca Records, India Office Records, British Library.

outside their influence (e.g., Bali and Sumbawa). The diversity of ethnicities represented in the Malaccan slave market demonstrates how the waterways of the Straits of Malacca, the Sunda Straits, and the Sulu Sea facilitated the churning of bonded peoples from uplands to lowlands. The Batak also participated in selling their own people; one record showed a (lowland) Batak man from Batu Bara selling a Batak person to a Malay woman.[100]

We lack sources on the interiority of enslaved people's lives, but their assimilation and inability to return indicated their estrangement from adat. While the "soul stuff" of illustrious Batak lived on, honored by the sacrifices of their descendants, children of the enslaved Batak likely neither embraced the Batak adat nor had meaningful links to their clan. The option of a different adat was open to them. Enslavement in exile could kill the Batak identity that had been so strongly linked to place and create a new one based on a new adat in a different landscape. Movement once again gave birth. The equilibrium between Batak and Malay identity, also conceivable as the equilibrium between highland and lowland, hinged on this transformative quality of place.

The life cycle of birth, work, and death depicts early upland settlement and how the coalescence of a Batak identity during the fifteenth and sixteenth centuries generated a friction-filled equilibrium between the politically anarchic Batak and the Malay coastal sultanates leading up to the nineteenth century.

Key ideas about power in nature animate this history. We find spirits that could inhabit flora and fauna, creating a potent landscape and a cosmology constructed around a local village and the rice pot; this background of land and belief venerated lineage and sustained spirits in a clan-based system that was closed but not isolated. Adaptation to the local environment of the North Sumatran highlands had led to very particular forms of social order, enforced by axioms in Batak adat that regulated behavior without the weight of state law. The closed nature of the system preserved adat by distancing it from people who moved. Adat was rooted to place, and place was for centuries rooted in a sacred, potent landscape. Yet adat was neither static nor impervious to change. Its adaptive capacity in the face of violence was another facet in its structure.

TWO Rupture and Resilience in Conversion

Two discrete sets of people view the late eighteenth century as the onset of rupture. The first group comprises scholars who promulgate a definition of the Anthropocene that is permanently hitched to its origins in earth system science. This viewpoint is represented by the Anthropocene scholar Clive Hamilton, who warns that failure to recognize the era as rupture dilutes the urgency, range, and scale of human impact on earth: "Geologically speaking, the Anthropocene event, occurring over an extremely short period, has been a very abrupt regime shift, closer to an instance of catastrophism rather than uniformitarianism."[1] Representing the second group, Amitav Ghosh approaches the epoch through literary imagination and suggests that the rupture is characterized by its obscuring in the nineteenth century, when a gradualist strand of geological theorizing superseded interpretations of the data—deemed "unmodern"—as catastrophe.[2] The Anthropocene, from Ghosh's perspective, *is* unrecognized rupture, placing us in a state without analog in historical memory and rendering us unable in many ways to even identify that position.

What constituted religious rupture during the Anthropocene? As I studied histories of the Batak uplands in the early nineteenth century, I was struck by a similar sense of rupture in these narratives. The epicenter was a set of violent clashes engendered by a movement of modernist Muslim reformers from neighboring Minangkabau. Known as the Padri, these reformers, by their presence, revealed stresses in the prevalent equilibrium between animists, adat-inflected Muslims, and an incipient global modernism in Islam. In Batak historiography, the Padri War marked a religious turning point, including abrupt mass conversions to Islam in the southern Bataklands of Angkola and Mandailing.[3] The earliest accounts came from missionaries and Dutch colonial officials soon after the conflict's end; these individuals were eager to draw a contrast between conversions propelled by the Christian Gospels and those that followed the violence perpetrated by key Muslim Padri leaders.[4] The concept of the Padri War as rupture also dogged historical writing on the Bukit Barisan uplands in the postcolonial period. The Batak historian Batara Sangti regards the Padri War as "a door that must be opened" in order to understand the uplands' modern history, suggesting the event formed a threshold between old and new.[5] Likewise, the Batak ethnomusicologist Julia Byl calls the Padri War a "cultural rupture."[6] This conflict brought about ideological dislocation that transitioned into a religious landscape without precedent, producing nominally Muslim southern Bataklands colonized by the Dutch and divorced from a largely animist north.

The Padri were a loose group of Sumatran Muslim reformists who were influenced by the early Wahhabi movement in Mecca and sought to apply a more literal, scripture-based interpretation of the religion at the expense of cultural practices. As antagonists of syncretic, vernacular Muslim practice, the Padri can be viewed as protomodernist Islamists in what is now Indonesia; for these emerging groups, religious life rested on universalist principles gleaned purely from scripture.[7] A case can be made that the onset of the Anthropocene in the Batak uplands was directly related to the religious rupture the Padri caused there. The Industrial Revolution, with its insatiable appetite for coal and markets, reformulated early modern empires into their modern iterations and triggered the relative decline of the Ottoman Empire, enabling the emergence of reformist Muslim ideologies such as that of the early Wahhabis, who briefly took over Mecca in 1803.[8] A world shrinking through trade, colonial, and infrastructural connections during this period facilitated the travel of new ideologies from Mecca to Sumatra, and a changing economic landscape sharpened the motivation to root out what was perceived as syncretism and paganism from its uplands.[9] The long reach of these ideologies and their intimate connections to trade, colonies, and capitalism signposted the cliff's edge of what the environmental historian John Richards terms an "unending frontier," which characterized the centuries between 1500 and 1800.[10] Here, aside from soil deposits and carbon emissions, the end of the religious frontier also signified the Anthropocene.

The Anthropocene serves as both a setting and a metaphor for a new understanding of this first wave of mass conversions from the perspective of the Batak themselves, whose views on the conflict are little explored in the existing literature, which largely focuses on the Minangkabau side.[11] Their perspectives are excavated through family stories told among the Minangkabau, Toba, and

Mandailing, in narratives that tell of catastrophe, of endemic internecine fights giving way to imperialistic state-led violence, of a reconfigured economy, and of dislocated peoples as well as spirits. To argue for a spiritual Anthropocene is to argue for a rupture, and these stories demarcated the limits of resilience and adaptive capacity of the adat-based social ecology unpacked in the previous chapter. Past this door, we can start to address the question of how religion was harnessed so that people could live with the rupture of the Anthropocene.

Stories have been used to redress the lack of documentary sources among the Batak; here I build on the approaches of these scholars. Between story and history lie narratives that draw on both to piece together a personal interpretation of the past.[12] The core of this chapter juxtaposes three distinct perspectives from such narratives: a confessional memoir written by a Padri leader in exile, an oral account of the conflict collected by a Dutch ethnographer, and a sprawling historical epic based on mysterious family papers. These sources are, in effect, one step removed from the immediacy of events. Read together, they provide insights not only into the conflict but also how that conflict is remembered across generations, in a substratum of memory not captured by extant historical analyses, which are largely based on Dutch military reports. Excavated from memory, these stories do not merely portray conversions. More significantly, they show what a new view of human settlement in the uplands should look like: a web of connections that centralized power in specific nodes that were bound by trade rather than kinship and ruled by universalist principles of governance rather than dispersed, suprahuman authority. While the Padri did not win the war, they consolidated religious conversions to Islam that might otherwise have been temporary and nominal.

WARFARE AS A SPIRITUAL EXERCISE

Violent conflict is not unusual in the Sumatran uplands; as mentioned in the previous chapter, most conflicts among the Batak took the form of simmering, internecine violence from which each village (*huta*) fortified itself. A huta founder was also called *sisuan bulu*, which literally means "the planter of bamboo." This referenced the defensive bamboo ramparts that surrounded each village, and many of these ramparts featured sharpened spikes.[13] Defenses, however, were not only physical, as recorded in many writings of Batak datu in their bark books (*pustaha*) concerning war. The linguist Liberty Manik divides her catalog of extant bark book texts into five content categories—

aggressive magic, protective magic, ritual ceremonies, medical prescription, and divination.[14] A bark book that anthropologist Johannes Winkler studied with the help of a datu, for instance, includes magic to harness cosmological spirits to harm one's enemy.[15] *Pangulubalang*, the sculpted ghost guardian of a village, could be commanded by a datu to attack. Defenses included chants while erecting a gate (*pagar*) and rituals such as fighting with a human figure carved on a banana stem (*porsili*), meant as a symbolic substitute offered to the spirits by a warrior to avert his death. Weapons used in these conflicts were also perceived as repositories of spiritual power. Michael Charney, a historian of Southeast Asian warfare, notes that the Batak "made a variety of different kinds of swords, some of which had iron handles and others with ivory handles," not unlike those of the rulers in the neighboring Muslim sultanate of Aceh. They believed that these swords embodied power, evinced by the wielder's spiritual prowess. Among Muslims in maritime Southeast Asia, there was a similar belief that weapons were as much expressions of spirituality as tools that compelled through physical force. In the matter of weapons, Batak adat and adat-inflected Islam largely concurred, even as Muslim communities grew to embrace guns earlier than did upland animists. Charms to increase a gun's potency incorporated and were strengthened by the inclusion of Muslim saints, attesting to the multifaceted role of traders who facilitated access to firepower.[16]

Internecine warfare among the Batak united the living and the dead, reproducing rather than challenging the social order. Batak adat, concisely defined by the Batak scholar L. C. Schreiner, "connects the visible living with the invisible dead. Adat is the social order of the village as a community under law, as a community of producers, and as a religious fellowship. . . . Adat cares for and maintains both the life of law and economics, as well as the vitality of the individual and corporeal life."[17] From this perspective, violence did not seriously undermine adat as long as the bases for law and economic life were maintained; winning or losing, life or death were part of the same social order. Flight was also a popular option in the face of aggression; the populations of small settlements attacked by larger forces fled into surrounding forest until the hostile forces departed, or they might resettle in an area outside the aggressor's reach. In such a geography, the resilience of a village's adat stemmed from its portability.

Initially, the dynamics at the beginning of the Padri War appeared similar to previous clashes. The conflict began with rumblings of discontent from an emerging class of Minangkabau traders in the cash crops of pepper, gambier (used in tanning and dyeing), and, most significantly, coffee. Tuanku nan

Tuo, an initial progenitor of the reform movement that birthed the Padri, was born in 1723 in the Minangkabau region of Ampat Angkat. He studied at the religious school (*surau*) in Ulakan, the coastal settlement where a Sufi mystical association (*tarekat*) had been established in the 1600s. He thus joined a lineage of scholars who traced their teachers back to Syeikh Abdul Qadir al-Jailani, founder of the Qadiriyya *tarekat* in Baghdad six centuries earlier.[18] Concurrently, he was a merchant, actively involved in a burgeoning coffee trade that connected the Minangkabau highlands to the port city of Padang on the West Sumatra coast and to Siak in the southeast. His initial attempts at religious reform appeared to have been motivated by these mercantile interests; he observed that banditry threatened the safety of trade routes to the coast. His religious school included not only Islamic instruction but also lessons in pugilistic skills, and in the 1790s he began to combine his preaching against highway robbery with active policing and rescues of waylaid merchants.[19] According to one of his students, through Tuanku nan Tuo's efforts, "the laws were upheld and people began establishing regular prayers, the roads were made safe even for the meanest traveler."[20] This stricter enforcement of Islamic law served to protect economic interests and sanctioned them with divine righteousness in a way that the royal court in Minangkabau, at this point weakened by loss of revenue from dwindling gold mines, could not.

In 1803, three Minangkabau men returned from Mecca, having conducted pilgrimages supported by coffee profits. The city had been violently occupied by followers of Muhammad Ibn Abd al-Wahhab during that year's pilgrimage season, and their teachings impressed some of the pilgrims. One of Tuanku nan Tuo's students, Tuanku nan Renceh, allied with a returned pilgrim called Haji Miskin, and the pair began a more aggressive campaign that pitted religion against Minangkabau adat in a campaign that was not averse to violence. Tuanku nan Renceh demonstrated his fierce zeal not only by burning cockfighting dens but also by summarily executing his maternal aunt for using tobacco; the killing of the woman was particularly reprehensible under the Minangkabau traditional matriarchy.[21] The pair then formed a group known as the Eight Tigers (Harimau nan Selapan), who styled themselves in the white flowing robes and turbans of Arab dress, earning themselves the local sobriquet "white ones" (*kaum putih*). Women under their rule dressed in white or blue, "concealing their heads under a kind of hood, through which an opening is made sufficient to expose their eyes and nose alone."[22]

The Eight Tigers were more confrontational than Tuanku nan Tuo in provoking or initiating violent clashes with Minangkabau traditionalist Muslim leaders. What ensued was a series of tit-for-tat raids between villages support-ive of the movement and those loyal to traditional leadership, culminating in the torching of the Minangkabau royal house at Pagarruyung in 1815 and the slaughter of many in the royal household.[23] This marked change in conduct and scale of animosity came to the attention of East India Company officials based in Padang, who remarked on it in private correspondence; their messages furnish the earliest documented reference to the "Padri War," which became the accepted term among the European community when referring to the conflict.[24]

The Padri War was thus a civil war that encompassed economics and a new ideology of social order brought by a vanguard of religiously inspired coffee traders. The Eight Tigers' hard-line stance grew to alienate even early reformers such as Tuanku nan Tuo and his student, Syeikh Jalaluddin. The latter acknowledged that the group "established regular prayers, gave alms, fasted during Ramadan and performed the hajj if they could afford to, repaired mosques and bathing places, wore modest clothes and commanded people to pursue knowledge and commerce."[25] But he also denounced them as men who "committed arson, murdered without just cause the brave people who opposed them, killed intellectuals and called them traitors, pillaged and looted, took women without their consent, captured people and sold them to slavery and made concubines from the captives, insulted the elders, nobility and called the faithful infidels."[26] This violent turn in reform efforts represented by the Eight Tigers signified animosity against adat, disdain for unbelievers, and vested interest in commerce on the part of key Padri leaders—all of which were later directed toward the Batak uplands and the adat-governed societies there.

THE BUFFALO AND THE REPENTANCE

The Toba Batak did not call the Padri by that name, instead referring to them as "Bonjol." This term alluded to the name of the Padri base that had launched raids into Batak territories in the 1810s and 1820s and to their leader, known by his honorific, Tuanku Imam Bonjol.[27] After his defeat by the combined forces of the Minangkabau adat leaders and the Dutch, Tuanku wrote a memoir while in exile in Manado to illustrate how Padri thought departed from traditional adat-inflected Islam.[28] Tuanku Imam Bonjol was born Peto Syarif in the arid valley of Alahan Panjang, at the northern reaches of Minangkabau territory. He was somewhat younger than most of Tuanku nan Renceh's Eight Tigers,

Tuanku Imam Bonjol on an Indonesian currency note.

but their reforms deeply influenced his ideas. With a traditional chief titled Datuk Bandaharo as patron, Peto Syarif tried to initiate reform in his home valley, but he met considerable resistance. Datuk Bandaharo was poisoned, and Peto Syarif fled the village to set up a new base with his supporters at the foot of Tajadi Mountain in the village of Bonjol, whereupon he took up the title for which he became known in history.

Bonjol was by no means a thriving market center in 1807 when Tuanku Imam Bonjol arrived, but neither was it completely isolated. A set of footpaths linked it to the Sasak region on Sumatra's west coast; the physical connection was partly born out of kinship, since many peoples in Sasak claimed lineage from the locales of Bonjol, Rao, and Lundar. Due to involvement in the gold trade, Minangkabau had the best footpath and road connections outside Java at the time, despite being in the uplands.[29] Bonjol lay outside the major market circuits, marked by a different set of paths in Tanah Datar and Agam, as well as around Lake Maninjau, where buffalo carts rotated daily between villages, bringing goods and news. Through a series of periodic raids, Tuanku Imam Bonjol expanded his influence over Tanah Datar and Agam.

In the villages he conquered, his leadership was marked by three forms of action: installing an Islamic judge (*qadi*) and imam who promised to "follow the laws of Allah and his Prophet," burning enemy villages, and clearing forest to enable his militants to enforce these laws.[30] He opened a path from Bonjol to Lubuk Sikaping, a Minangkabau village close to the neighboring territory of Rao; the existing route joining these two points could only accommodate two men abreast, but the Tuanku ordered it expanded to a six-man-wide path, which enabled mounted light cavalry to pass through. Elsewhere, his forces

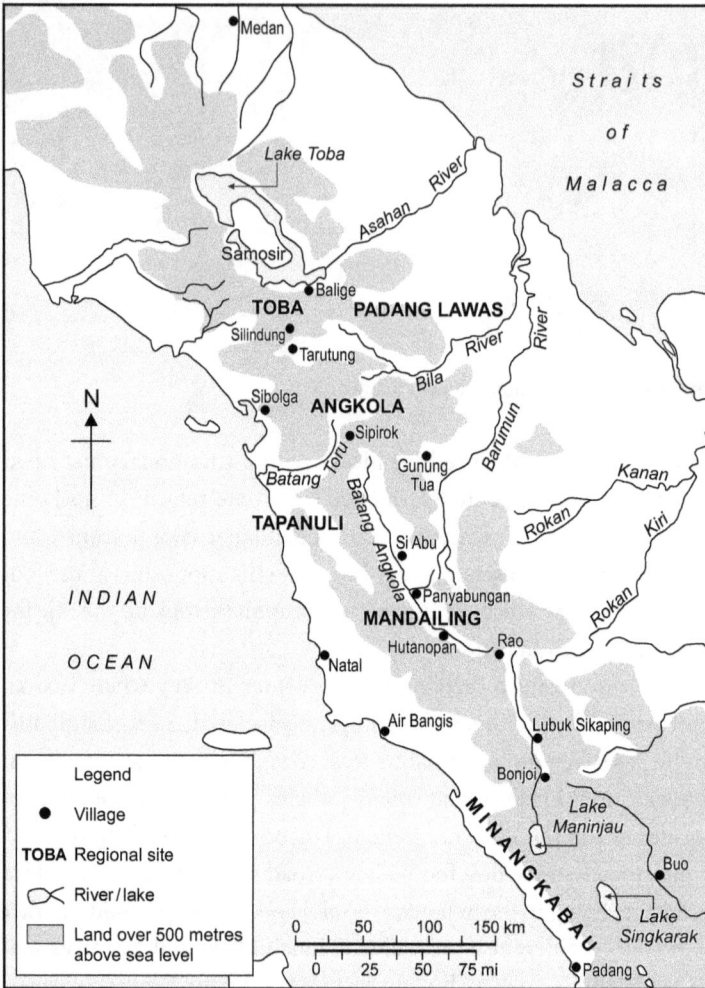

Minangkabau and the adjacent Batak Mandailing territory.
The Padri moved into the Bataklands from their base in Bonjol
and swept northward toward Toba. Map by Lee Li Kheng.

climbed Tajadi Mountain and cleared the trees to gain access to Padang Lawas, where many Batak raised cattle. The effort was so taxing that one of the Tuanku's followers died after a night of forest clearing, but such sacrifices were deemed necessary for the higher cause. After "the religion of Allah and his Prophet was upheld"—a repeated phrase in his memoirs, which skimmed lightly over village burnings—the Tuanku's troops returned to Bonjol. However, adherence to his ideology was shaky; there were repeated episodes of his men having to march forth and again assert their authority.[31] A reformed Islam, in the Tuanku's vision, involved a simultaneous re-creation of leadership and landscape that promoted heightened duality between culture and religion as well as nature and culture.

Such binary views extended to neighboring communities. Instincts in Bonjol grew increasingly expansionist and seemed guided by retaliatory impulses against territories it perceived as populated by the unfaithful. In one such case, the people of Lubuk Sikaping asked Bonjol for aid to defend themselves against an attack from its hostile neighbor Rao. Rao, with its mélange of people who identified as Batak, Minangkabau, or simply as "orang Rawa" (people of Rao), was the back door to Tapanuli, a fulcrum for the lever that would open Batak territory.[32] When Rao surrendered to Bonjol, the Tuanku left the place but put in charge a faithful follower, Fakih Muhammad, who became known as Tuanku Rao.[33] The latter, together with another Bonjol compatriot, Tuanku Tambusai, launched an invasion into Batak territories, with Tuanku Rao sweeping in northward and Tuanku Tambusai coming in from the east up the Rokan River. The pair first conquered Mandailing and then Angkola before burning their way toward Toba.[34]

The Tuanku himself stayed in Bonjol. His memoir noted the conquest of Mandailing but stayed markedly silent on the subject of conversion except in noting gains and losses. One raid by Tuanku Rao, for instance, brought in a hundred cows and ten *tahil* of gold. On another occasion, the aftermath of fighting in Lima Puluh Kota led to the acquisition of cows, buffaloes, and enslaved women. He also gained foot soldiers in the form of convert collaborators; Mandailing men helped him make further gains in Silayang.[35] Over a decade, his tiny settlement had grown into a large and fortified town funded by trade, and it boasted fine herds of horses and cattle as well as enslaved and corvée workers.[36] As reflected in a description of mosque building from his memoir, these herds and gangs of ungulate and human labor powered construction in Bonjol itself:

> And so, the Tuanku called on all his men to build stone fortifications around the village. He sent word to all villages under his dominion and the day came when labor began streaming in from Toba, Mandailing, Nan Tigo Lurah, Kampar Kiri, Kampar Kanan, Mahek, Lubuk Rao[;] they all gathered in Bonjol. He put half of them to work digging ditches, and the remaining half to gather stones and line them four-stones wide. They formed a line, linked arms and passed each stone down the row from one person to another to build a wall that encir-

cled Bonjol and after that, a large mosque. There were about five hundred thousand people working. They managed to build the mosque in one month.[37]

The rerouting of human and bovine power into Bonjol contributed to its quick rise as a node of commercial and sacral authority; in this new landscape, all roads led to Bonjol. The price, though, was many lives, friend and foe each mentioned specifically by name, with their manner of death at times painfully detailed. One of the bloodiest episodes involved death to not only men but also buffaloes. Under three Bonjol leaders—Tuanku Rao, Tuanku Mudo, and Raja Baro—the Tuanku's men attacked a wooden fortress at Kuok and met a fusillade of cannon fire. Battling for many days before finally winning the fortress and its three cannons, the three leaders then rounded up Kuok's buffaloes, with the intention of driving them toward Bonjol. Upon reaching a narrow pass, though, the cattle could not be herded through, and, after several futile attempts, the men trained the cannons on them and killed them all.[38] This willingness to destroy all the animals, rather than let them loose, again emphasized the vision for the landscape—all roads could lead to nowhere but Bonjol. The centralization of ideology was manifested in the centralization of extraction from land and labor.

In a surprising twist, the Tuanku later felt himself assailed with doubt, so he charged three of his followers to return to Mecca and "ascertain the just law of God's Book."[39] While the three were away, violent conflict continued. In 1821, the Dutch entered the fray on the opposing side, and Tuanku Imam Bonjol directed attacks against their bases in Natal and Air Bangis on the west coast, which were blocking trade with Bonjol. The campaign was to be his last success. Soon after, the three pilgrims he had sent to Mecca returned with the news that Ibn Abd al-Wahhab no longer held political power in the city. Convinced that he had misinterpreted Islam, the Tuanku announced after Friday prayers that he no longer wished to fight and would return all his gains. In a public declaration that is today often cited as the quintessence of Indonesian Islam, Tuanku Imam Bonjol proclaimed "*adat basandi syarak*"—that *adat* (customary norms) and *syariah/syarak* (religious law) were mutually constitutive.[40] In effect, at the height of his winning streak, he withdrew and declared the conflict between adat and *syariah* to be over.

The historian Jeff Hadler views the Tuanku's repentance as an "act of moral bravery" that promoted cultural resilience. I would instead argue that his legacy established a tension between Islam and adat, one that resonates in the present.[41]

In effect, Tuanku Imam Bonjol's actions promoted a duality between culture and religion along with the latter's primacy. His penitence and acceptance of adat were followed by a short-lived truce after which his followers attacked Dutch forces who had defiled a mosque. These subsequent military campaigns were pitched as anticolonial, or crimes for which he was eventually exiled, but their galvanizing spirit was a modernist Islam that utilized scripture for military and economic ends. Neither adat leaders nor the Padri who opposed them shied away from self-interested renovations of the landscape and taking forced labor, but the Padri broke new ground in harnessing those changes to a higher purpose. For the Batak, Padri raids and occupation were experienced as a neocolonial enterprise. It was not clear from the Tuanku's memoir whether he returned what he had taken from the Batak, whether converts or dissidents. As seen from the Batak stories discussed below, their losses resulted in a long-lasting disorientation and a different geography.

BUFFALOES AND BAD SPIRITS

The Minangkabau had built their traditional identity around a fabled contest between two buffaloes. The buffalo duel was decisive in a territorial dispute between the people of the West Sumatran highlands and a more powerful, centralized state, usually identified as the Javanese Majapahit. The Minangkabau won when their champion, a baby buffalo with sharpened horns, ran under his huge, aggressive opponent and gored his stomach; the name Minangkabau derived from *menang kerbau*, the "winning water buffalo."[42] The apocryphal baby buffalo, however, had grown to become the aggressor in the Batak uplands, where some remembered the animal with terror. In one account, the sight of an untethered male buffalo sent the people of Silindung, in Toba, fleeing "with only the clothes on the[ir] backs and whatever possessions they could carry.... There was no one capable of fighting[;] even the strongest were frozen with fear."[43]

This account was part of a longer narrative called "Kedatangan Bondjol," found in a collection of the papers of Victor Emanuel Korn, a resident of Tapanuli in the mid-1930s. Along with a narrative collected, translated into German, and published by C. Gabriel in 1922, this was one of the earliest stories from the North Sumatran front of the Padri War that specifically sought a Batak perspective.[44] For almost a century, the written historical record had been silent, with family stories circulating orally in Batak dialects before being committed to paper in Indonesian or German when the territory was solidly incorporated into the Dutch East Indies. In 1920s Tapanuli, a resurgent interest in writing family genealogies formed the impetus for a spurt of written stories.[45] For this reason, oral histories collected by Korn and Gabriel showed some preoccupation with explaining a particular family's present situation. For instance, "Kedatangan Bondjol" included a tragic anecdote about a desperate Batak father from the Aritonang patriclan who killed his child when its cries threatened to give away the family's hiding place as they fled the marauding Padri. His action helped explain why that branch of the family died out, as "for years and years, he could not have more children and he died childless."[46]

How did these sparsely documented family histories reflect changes to everyday Batak religion under pressure from the Padri? These two accounts differ in their details, but both evoke a sense of resilience after the enormity of the damage caused to the spiritual and material landscape of the Toba Batak. Demonstrating the capacity for intertwined political and natural ecologies to recover, the two stories connected the traumatic attack to an adat infraction and a subsequent recovery and reassertion of moral order, made manifest in the landscape. Central to these stories was Tuanku Rao, whom we met earlier as one of the men that Tuanku Imam Bonjol sent to lead the attack in the Batak uplands.

In these Batak memorializations of Padri turmoil, Tuanku Rao is related to an influential lineage of Toba Batak–area priest-kings holding the dynastic title Si Singamangaradja. He is said to have been born to the sister of priest-king Si Singamangaradja IX, who married her own uncle.[47] Marrying within one's clan was considered incestuous, and the couple was banished for their taboo relationship. Si Pongki Ngolngolan (The One Who Yearns for Home), as Tuanku Rao was named at birth, signified that isolation. Si Pongki Ngolngolan's parents eventually separated, and his mother, now unencumbered, returned to her birth family in Toba. Initially accepted by her brother Si Singamangaradja X, now the incumbent ruler, her son wore out his welcome. Pasturing cows sickened and died when the little boy was put to work caring for them, and birds attacked the rice fields while chickens and dogs raided the rice stocks. In light of these calamities, Si Singamangaradja X sealed his nephew in a sarcophagus and threw him into Lake Toba, praying to the gods and his ancestors to spare the boy if he could be made to lead a useful life.[48]

Si Pongki Ngolngolan's incestuous birth was thus paired with an unnatural capacity for upsetting the order of things. However, he managed to use his father's dagger to escape from the sarcophagus. He swam to the shore, where he was brought up by a Minangkabau family, apprenticed to a student of Tuanku Imam Bonjol, and later converted to Islam. Nominated as Bonjol's representative in Rao, he married the daughter of the Rao chief and took upon himself the task of conquering the Batak. Filled with a thirst for vengeance, he returned to the land of his birth as Tuanku Rao and proceeded to kill, enslave, and convert. In a final act of supreme revenge around 1825, he lured his uncle, Si Singamangaradja X, down to a marketplace in Butar under the guise of a peace negotiation and decapitated him.[49]

These details, while impossible to verify, add the human motivation of personal revenge to the invasion. Particularly significant in this tale is how non-human agents interface between gods and humans. As the destructive Tuanku Rao resulted from a taboo marriage within one's own clan, nature itself—in the form of wilting rice fields and recalcitrant animals—rejected him and reinforced the virtue of the traditional means of social organization. Unnatural marriage begets unnatural violence. This version of the tale did not at all suggest that the Batak faith in their notion of divine social structure needed reconsideration. Instead, it fashioned Tuanku Rao into a bloodthirsty figure who justified the adat taboo against incest.

The number of men involved in the attack swelled as the Padri moved north, augmented by converts who found it in their interest to cooperate with rather than resist them. By the time they first reached the territory of the Toba Batak clan Naipospos, their force numbered three thousand. These conversions appeared nominal rather than heartfelt, given that the Bonjol forces worked to prevent converts from reverting to previous habits incompatible with Islam. To enforce a prohibition on eating the flesh of swine, for example, Tuanku Rao "burned all the villages of the Hutabarat and stole all their livestock that were left behind when they fled. [He did this] because many of his men wanted to eat the flesh of swine, particularly the people from Angkola and Sitomtom."[50]

Unlike the relatively well-connected Minangkabau highlands, the Batak uplands had few pathways for market linkages, a paucity that ultimately limited Bonjol's successes. Toba markets were run as mobile trading posts with a four-day cycle, each a short distance from another local spot. This market relay preempted an uneven concentration of power, energy, and resources at particular focal points and complemented the dispersal of political authority that was markedly different from Bonjol's revisioning of the landscape. Tuanku Rao's forces had limited success in broadening roads and creating new infrastructural connections. In the two Toba accounts, the infrastructural constructions of war were rarely mentioned; these consisted of only rough, hastily built bridges, being little more than logs that facilitated the crossing of a swift river before being swept away. When the Padri eventually left, as was customary in their raids, they returned only twice before leaving the northern Batak territory altogether.[51]

The Batak cautiously returning to their villages after their flight up to high-land forests found existing supplies of rice running low due to confiscation by the Bonjol men and had little means to cultivate more. There was considerable looting, and many people died in the chaotic aftermath. Then disease swept in for a period termed *begoe aroem* (referencing bad spirits), when starvation and disease decimated the population.[52] According to the "Kedatangan Bondjol" narrative,

> When the people returned to their villages from the jungle, they saw that their fields were completely wrecked, their storehouses were gone. The people were [starving] like birds in the cold. . . . Ashes bitter like coffee grounds floated in the paddy fields. So it was that women and children had no chores to do and could only beg for rice. Their tools for cultivation were burned, their blankets were gone, and it was difficult to weave more. . . . Those without houses stayed in the shelter of where bamboo grew . . . and the *begoe aroem* attacked them in their sleep. *Begoe aroem* at that time was so potent that many died. In a household of six, if two survived that was already considered fortunate.[53]

This period of debilitation and death was turned into a moral fable, incorporated into a narrative that the disease and ensuing famine claimed a large proportion of the Batak who had collaborated to profit from Padri violence against their communities in North Tapanuli. The "Kedatangan Bondjol" narrative described how "for five years, the people were uneasy because they kept hearing rumors of Bonjol's return, while those who had spied for him awaited him. . . . The thieves and the spies all died of starvation. The spy, still holding his gun, leaned against a green tree, so still that a passerby would have thought him asleep. But he was in reality dead of hunger, and this was the judgment of God for those evil people."[54]

After the cleansing famine, the land appeared renewed. Rice grew back, aided by the domesticated buffalo. The buffalo was valued for its labor and was a symbol of what had to die in order for others to live. The body of a sacrificial buffalo was buried near the rice field after the seeds were planted; it was an offering by which the people sought divine forgiveness for clearing the forest in this endeavor. Before cutting down a tree to construct the pole to which the sacrificial buffalo would be tethered, the datu began his supplications to the spirits by asking forgiveness "from the rulers of the compass, the compasses that serve me as a wall," as well as "from the gods." He ended it with the hope to be blessed with "the yellow gold, with sons and daughters," according to a bark book collected in the 1830s.[55] Among the Angkola Batak, buffalo meat was served with rice that the animals had helped the people grow; it was part of a feasting ritual in which the "mother seed" was kept for the next planting season.[56] The feasts, harvest, and sacrifices were evidence of a land rejuvenated. Rare European visitors in 1824 indirectly corroborated this renewal: during their visit, they saw that the Toba community appeared to be thriving and that women were in their breast-baring traditional garb, not the blue-and-white hooded robes of women in Padri villages.[57] The Padri did return briefly, in 1829, but for all intents and purposes their hold over North Tapanuli was never reestablished after the advent of disease. Tuanku Rao himself apparently died in an assault on the Dutch-held port in Air Bangis in 1833.[58]

By reading the embellishments of these Toba Batak narratives about Tuanku Rao as representations of a social truth rather than mining the tales for facts, we find a narrative construct that emphasized a vindication of the prevailing sacred order. The exiled offspring of a taboo marriage unsurprisingly grew up to become a vengeful and destructive man. Nature, too, rejected the traitors who had collaborated with him, wiping them out in a tide of pernicious disease. The "bad spirits" were at once devastating, cleansing, and *renewing*. In their retreat, in the waters of the rivers sweeping away the Bonjol's temporary bridges that had facilitated the Padri's crossing, and in the collaborators' elimination by disease, the sacral ecology of the Toba Batak in North Tapanuli asserted itself and ultimately triumphed.

In dealing with slippery sources like these circulating Batak Toba stories about the Padri War, we should bear in mind both what the narrative says and the work that it does. The origins and vexed identity of Padri leader Tuanku Rao were part of a historical myth-making picked up by Batak histories written later in the twentieth century.[59] Such stories served as a reminder of resilience, explaining how a disastrous invasion could temporarily disrupt society but also how the ecosystem—human and nonhuman beings alike—would ultimately heal from their wounds. For the southern Batak communities of Angkola and Mandailing, however, there was little healing from the wounds of the Padri conflict.

ERSATZ CONVERSIONS, REAL COLONIALISMS

Written family stories of the Padri War were sparser in the southern Batak-lands of Angkola and Mandailing. A few emerged after 1945, of which a singularly sensational work written by the Mandailing writer Mangaradja Onggang Parlindungan was the most controversial and detailed. A work with enduring influence that generated support as well as refutations, it demonstrated how, unlike Toba Batak accounts, southern Batak territories during this conflict were remembered as enduring rupture rather than resilience.

Parlindungan penned this voluminous local history in the early 1960s. The flamboyance of the work was indicated by its title, *Pongkinangolngolan Sinambela gelar Tuanku Rao: Terror Agama Islam Mazhab Hambali di Tanah Batak 1816–1833*, which can be translated verbatim as "Tuanku Rao: The Hambali Sect Terrorist of the Bataklands, 1816–1833." Crafting his story as a dialogue with his son, affectionately addressed as "Sonny Boy," he fashioned a family history from what he claimed to be papers documenting ninety years of research by three schoolteachers of different generations in his family from 1851 to 1941 (including his own father) and those of "Resident Poortman," said to be the Dutch *controleur* in Sipirok in the early 1900s. Parlindungan's family was one of the founders of Sipirok, a small market town in the Angkola Batak territories.[60] The result of this intergenerational synthesis was a sprawling epic: he brought readers through centuries of patriclan histories, starting with an overview of early migrations from Toba to form new patriclans in Angkola and Mandailing. The conflicts that generated these migrations were a prologue to the main subject of his text: the invasion of the region by Tuanku Rao, whose origins in Parlindungan's history were basically similar to those depicted by the Toba stories. Tuanku Rao, despite being the titular character, was a fairly minor figure. The key character was Parlindungan's own ancestor, Tuanku Lelo, described as a monstrous convert to Islam who gleefully torched unconverted villages and raped and killed villagers with impunity. As rendered by Parlindungan, one of the three hadjis credited with bringing Wahhabi ideas into the conflict was framed as "a grand old Hanbali Fanatic." He writes of epidemics in Toba that turned the Batang Toru River into the "Red River" and calls Padri leader Tuanku Tambusai, the final holdout against the Dutch, the "Last of the Mohicans."[61] The appendixes that follow this story are almost as thick as the main content, covering details of Padri leaders, a biography of his father, his experiences in Indonesia's revolutionary war, and the history of Chinese Hanafi Muslims in the archipelago.[62]

Parlindungan's voice and mixed diction in this saga, as exemplified by his colorful characterizations of key figures, clearly do not carry academic authority, and the work appears like a caricature at times. The literary anthropologist Susan Rodgers regards *Tuanku Rao* as part of a class of "antic histories" that offer an entertaining romp through historical as well as linguistic worlds.[63] Through it, we may glimpse the panorama of the period while being skeptical of its details. Why then is a work like Parlindungan's historically significant despite the impossibility of verifying either its sources or its documentation? One reason for this is its long legacy: the work and its afterlives provoked and influenced local history about the period in subsequent decades. The Minangkabau scholar Hamka's indignant and detailed rebuke was an early historical refutation that rejected the stories of Tuanku Rao and Tuanku Lelo in particular.[64] Ceremonial orators telling Sipirok histories warned external scholars about the book's untrustworthiness. Nonetheless, while it failed to convince certain keepers of Minangkabau and Batak heritage, it managed to engage others. Parlindungan was a significant source in Sangti's 1978 *Sejarah Batak*, for instance. In the 2000s, there was resurgent local interest in his unabashed account of bloody *jihad*, partly due to the geopolitical situation of the so-called "war on terror," and the book was posthumously reprinted in 2007 by his son, the "Sonny Boy" of the original edition. The reprint edition, in turn, provoked yet another round of objections, most notably by a local scholar named Basyral Hamidy Harahap, whose own work highlighted resistance among the Angkola and Mandailing among several families during the period, rather than their violent conversion.[65]

The vicissitudes of this work over five decades connect closely to a history of violence and show that Parlindungan's book endures because of its instrumental memorialization of rupture. Appealing and repelling for its take on the bloodlust that accompanied religious-inspired violence, Parlindungan's epic pointed toward several aspects of the violent conflict that created unprecedented upheaval, from which emerged a state without precedent. First, the movements of peoples in flight or in captivity became embedded in a family's historical sense of connection to a particular place. Internecine war was an explanation for the migration of Parlindungan's Siregar patriclan out of Toba, while the Padri War explained his family's founding of Sipirok and the flight of his father's in-laws from Gunung Tua to Sipirok. Women, absent in almost all documentation of the conflict, were central victims in this account. Many were forcibly captured and enslaved, and their settlement in a new place generated a new branch of the patriclan. Second, landscape transformations inspired by religious conversions promoted specific ways of refashioning settlements. Padang Sidempuan, for example, was converted into a fortified base, webbed by waterways. Large quantities of the hardwood known as meranti were cut down to create the fortifications.[66] Other villages were relocated when the inhabitants converted to Islam, building new settlements that mirrored the Padri's fortifications and followed the requirements of the new religion. For example, upon conversion, Huta Dolok was renamed Huta Godang and shifted to a location near a river about twenty kilometers away so that new converts would have a convenient water source for ablution before prayer.[67] Finally, much of the conflict was the result of changing economic structures and fights for material advantage, a situation in which a cloak of religion concealed profane goals.

Dutch colonialism entrenched a pattern of displacement, conversion of settlements, and changing economic structures when these Europeans defeated the Padri and incorporated Mandailing and Angkola into their West Sumatran colony. Moving away from family memorialization to documented events, Dutch sources demonstrate that a key difference between the experiences of those in Mandailing and those in Toba (which remained autonomous) was the imposition of policies that began to transform the ways in which peoples of the southern areas related to the landscape. The Dutch entered the conflict in 1821, ostensibly in response to a request for help by Minangkabau traditional aristocrats who had escaped the burning of their court in Pagarruyung and fled to Padang. Their intervention intensified after 1830, for two reasons. First, the British had ceded control of all its bases in Sumatra and Java as part of an agreement in 1824 in return for the Dutch withdrawing any claims to Malacca and Singapore, effectively dividing the region into nonoverlapping spheres of influence. Second, the Dutch had successfully defeated an uprising led by the Javanese prince Diponegoro and were thus able to concentrate their military resources on this theater in Sumatra.

The Dutch entry on the scene was marked on the highlands landscape by the building of forts. This act of construction mirrored the fortifications set up by the Padri, who had fortified their villages with fences and ditches and built wooden forts in Muoro Bubus, as well as stone walls in Bonjol and Daludalu, using Batak slave labor.[68] The Dutch escalated the landscape's transformation with stone fortresses lining the ridges from Bukit Tandikek, Batu Sangkar, and Bukittinggi to Koto Tuo, at the heart of Minangkabau territory, finally encroaching on Bonjol territory in Alahan Panjang. In response, the Padri fortified further, building a double layer of defenses where the elderly, women, and children were ringed in by walls that lay behind outposts on which cannons were mounted.[69] The Dutch forts, for their part, housed professional soldiers, a few drawn from the Netherlands but mostly from the Dutch colonies on Java. Behind their fortifications, Padri fighters were subsistence farmers or merchants who participated in raids between the harvest and market seasons. The net effect was to deepen the trend in centralizing power and authority into constructed nodes. In short, Dutch imperialism—far from protecting adat leadership—dug into the Minangkabau landscape more deeply, uprooting traditional power structures in the same way the Padri had attempted but never truly accomplished.

The capitulation of Mandailing was relatively swift; several chiefs were in fact eager to ally with the Dutch to remove the Padri. The best known of these was a Radja Gadombang, chief in the relocated Huta Godang. In 1832, he took the initiative to approach Colonel Elout on the Dutch side, offering his services and his men to help defeat the Padri. Other chiefs in Upper Mandailing joined him. Bonjol, helmed by the Tuanku, and Daludalu, headed by Tuanku Tambusai, were the strongest obstacles to the imposition of Dutch rule. Mandailing, which provided both groups with a geographical gateway, became the base from which the Dutch launched their operations against these stubborn pockets of the Padri movement.[70] Belying any solidarity for their co-religionists, the converts to Islam became a key part of Dutch military operations into Padri territory, often at the front lines.[71] Mandailing, too, became marked by a chain of Dutch forts erected between 1832 and 1833 at Tamiang, Singengu, Kotanopan, and Rao. The forts signified the end of South Tapanuli's independence as it shifted from Padri imperialism to Dutch imperialism. By 1838, all key Padri leaders had been eliminated: Tuanku Rao was killed and Tuanku Imam Bonjol captured and exiled, while Tuanku Tambusai escaped down the Rokan River under a hail of Dutch bullets and disappeared from the historical record.

Like the Padri, Dutch rule from its earliest iteration sought to transform the sacral ecology of the South Tapanuli highlands. Where subsistence cultivation had previously intertwined with animism to organize South Tapanuli society around stateless clans enmeshed in a web of reciprocal relations of kinship, the Dutch now sought to introduce centralized hierarchy. Once South Tapanuli was brought under Dutch rule, an assistant Resident by the name of Bonnet sent a letter to all chiefs in the region, commanding them to attend a meeting every month in Singengu, where he would listen to updates from each chief and adjudicate when necessary. Any chief who failed to attend would be fined a fixed amount of gold.[72] In effect, conforming to this order would mean undermining the Council of Elders (Namora Natoras) that represented the main families in the village, who had traditionally made decisions in concert with the chief. With the Dutch order, the chief was elevated above this sacralized institution. Already diminished by the Padri's installation of an Islamic judge as a parallel religious figure in South Tapanuli, the Padri receded in power while Dutch picked up desacralization where the Padri had left off.

Such changes were put in place partly to facilitate a new economic base through which the Dutch could profit from their colony. This was structured around imposing a salt and coffee monopoly. Sumatran areas under Dutch rule had to buy salt only from Dutch Java and sell their coffee exclusively to the Dutch.[73] In a hierarchical state order, these measures, along with forced labor and requisitions, could be more easily implemented, although they caused significant unhappiness. Chiefs were incentivized to mobilize free labor for the cultivation and transport of coffee, and incentives were also handed out hierarchically. For every *pikul* (forty-two kilograms) of coffee delivered to Dutch ports in Padang and Air Bangis, the province head (*kepala kuria*) received twenty guilder cents, while the village chief (*kepala huta*) and the elder who supervised a neighborhood within a village (*kepala ripe*) were both paid forty cents.[74] This reorganization oriented the region toward a centralized node of power, now located in coastal Padang, and again intensified a process started by the Padri. The Dutch also created an apex of traditional power: in the formerly stateless region, a high chief called the Yang Dipertuan was appointed, nominally holding sway over all the upland chiefs.

Transport was a key preoccupation of the Dutch, who quickly realized that it ate up a large fraction of their profits from coffee. At first they reduced costs by conscripting Minangkabau, Mandailing, and later Nias men as corvée porters, a move that by 1838 had saved the Dutch at least 15,000 guilders.[75] This was not sustainable, however, as resentment and resistance among the population surged. A long-term solution required clearing more land for roads, further transforming the landscape. Insidiously violent, this transformation could be traumatic for Mandailing peoples coerced into chopping down certain trees. When confronted with a tall tree that would have stood respectfully undisturbed before the Dutch imperative, it was not uncommon for a Mandailing man to refuse to ply his ax until he could pay his respects to the spirits lodging in the tree through a ritual apology, not unlike the apology issued by the Toba Batak to trees cut down for poles to tether sacrificial buffaloes, mentioned earlier. However, the spirit of the apology differed, as the Mandailing man assured the spirits that his action was not of his volition but by order of the Dutch controleur.[76] Such a ritual displaced responsibility for the violation from the Mandailing onto the Dutch, who ultimately banalized what was sacred. Yet each tree hacked down without supernatural retribution against the Dutch chipped away at the notion of powerful sacred spirits dwelling within, bringing the peoples of South Tapanuli closer to the notion of a singular God that had been first brought by the Padri.

This turbulent period was capped by the failed uprising of a group of Mandailing chiefs against Dutch rule. Sutan Mangkutur, the brother of Dutch collaborator Raja Gadombang, convened a gathering at a sacred grove near Huta Godang and extracted pledges from those present to fight the Dutch. A family story that circulated down to his descendants suggests this uprising was shaded in religion—not Islam but animist tradition:

> At this gathering, all the chiefs who were present each handed over a bullet.
> The bullet was then mixed with yellow rice using a magical heirloom dagger as
> each man pledged to bury his bullet into the body of the White-Eyes. To swear
> their oath . . . a chicken whose eyes and anus were sewn shut and a bamboo
> shoot was brought to those present. The *datu* leading the ceremony peeled the
> skin of the bamboo, chanting, "Whosoever betrays this pact will face the fate
> of this bamboo, becoming rootless and fruitless [childless] and the fate of this
> chicken, unable to move forward and back."[77]

Reconstituted as family memory, the Mandailing uprising stood against the sweeping away of animist rituals begun by the Padri and pursued by the Dutch. From the Batak perspective at the time, the two imperialisms were remembered as being indistinguishable in their effects. The former convert-collaborators of South Tapanuli asserted their agency one last time by carrying out a pact to attack the Dutch. Their failure was in no small part due to a Mandailing chief, elevated above others as the newly Dutch-appointed Yang Dipertuan, who backed out and warned the Dutch of the impending attack despite participating in the ceremony at the sacred grove. The leaders of the uprising, including Sutan Mangkutur, were captured and exiled to Ambon. The Yang Dipertuan, far from leading a fruitless and rootless life, remained comfortably ensconced in Huta Siantar with his family for several generations to come.[78] On the Dutch end, a different script explaining this episode of violence emerged in the novel *Max Havelaar*, a famous work by the writer Douwes Dekker. In his telling, "the entire people of the Batak had shortly before that time been converted to the true faith by the Padri and new converts usually show a lot of fanaticism."[79] But whether told through conversions or colonialism, for the Mandailing and Angkola, this failed insurrection constituted a rupture without precedent and without healing.

"Change, or impending change, often inspires the creation of myths, for it both threatens and promises. It threatens the security of the established, while providing hope to the disestablished." So writes a historian grappling with the mutating stories that emerged from a distant past with little documentation.[80] The period from the 1780s to the 1840s was noted for its global upheavals during the decades that world historian Eric Hobsbawm called the Age of Revolutions. The Industrial Revolution and related conflicts in Europe and the Americas have been focal theaters of change in this putative age that coincided with the onset of the Anthropocene. But in the Muslim world, too, we can discern a pattern of discontent and reform. The global reverberations of one such reformist uprising radiated from Mecca to our peripheral theater of change in the Sumatran uplands.

The Padri War facilitated rupture and resilience in the North Sumatran uplands. It upended power structures and introduced imperialism to the uplands through a literalist, violent interpretation of Islam and a military-minded Dutch colonialism. The conflict illustrates the differences between adat-inflected everyday religion and modernist monotheism, including centralization of power, a quest for uniformity in scriptural interpretation, and a push for universalist principles for religious governance based on this uniformity in scriptural interpretation. Religion and culture were inseparable in adat-inflected Islam, which came under pressure from the duality introduced through Padri neo-Wahhabism before the philosophy was reformulated as *adat basandi syarak*. The tense reconciliation did not end the tension, however, and conflicts between traditionalists and modernist Muslims flared up sporadically long after the Padri War.[81]

From an environmental perspective, Batak stories are significant in revealing how the Padri War represented the first stage of the transformation of the stateless and inaccessible Batak highlands into a node in global religious and economic networks. Such a transformation was made possible only by the conversion not just of the people but of their environment as well. Rather than seeing violence as a primary instrument for a coerced switch in beliefs—and converts as hapless victims or fanatical automatons—a study of the Batak stories about this period exposes the ultimate futility of violence as a tool of religious imposition. Batak converts to Islam switched sides continually and strategically, eluded attempts at controlling their conduct, and carved out new migratory pathways to find refuge. There was a dynamic interplay between changing landscapes and changing faiths, with early converts becoming power brokers that the Padri needed to maintain their tenuous grip on the parts of Tapanuli they had seized. Conversion was a rational, instrumental decision for those among the Batak who sought to find a new footing in the context of an unstable environment and a shaken inner faith.

As the tales spiraled out from the epicenter of events in the early decades of the nineteenth century, they started to coalesce geographically around resilience in the north and rupture in the south. In stories of resilience, the nonhuman natural world ultimately synergized with adat as the moral social organization of Batak society. In stories of rupture, power was relocated from natural locales patronized by the spirits of ancestors to human-made landscapes of roads, forts, mosques, rerouted waterways, and cannons. Leadership shifted to the converts who could leverage the chaos and thereby reconfigure their bases of power. During the ensuing decades, the uplands continued to be rent by the tension between the two; arguably, rupture eventually won out. The subsequent chapters examine these changes from two aspects: representation and materiality.

REPRESENTATIONS

THREE Secularizing "Literate Cannibals" through Scripture

Dairi Batak folklore tells of a man, Si Mbuyuk Mbuyuk, who was born with no bones. Through intelligence and some measure of luck, he acquired the ability to speak to camphor trees and thus amassed a huge bounty of camphor. Ingesting some of this camphor enabled him to grow bones, and, with his new fortune gained from trade in camphor, he was able to marry a princess.[1] This metaphor speaks to two things: the human body's seamless integration with the physicality of other beings in nature and the fleeting fortune enabled through camphor harvesting. In the 1850s and 1860s, the uplands were politically and economically bifurcated. The camphor economy—capital free and entangled with nature's caprice—still prevailed in the animist, autonomous north. A cash crop economy, evident in the institution of compulsory coffee planting, was taking shape in the colonized, nominally Muslim south.

The tale of Si Mbuyuk Mbuyuk was also committed to writing in the 1850s and circulated to new audiences through the linguist Herman Neubronner van der Tuuk. He had been employed by a Dutch missionary society, Nederlandsch Bijbelgenootschap, to learn the Batak language and render the uplands more legible for future mission work. This work was to change the function of writing in the uplands and position humans as its managers. During this period, literacy in Batak languages—previously a mode of communication with ancestral and spiritual kin, unseen in the natural world—shifted toward deconstructing and managing nature. These shifts intersected with the landscape changes wrought by the new coffee economy that fueled these religious efforts in the south and had subsequent impacts in the north.

Reading missionary sources and colonial schoolbooks against the grain opens a window to how these changes were experienced by three men from different patriclans. Si Singamangaradja XI was a charismatic leader in the autonomous north, while early Christian converts Willem Iskander and Ephraim Sutan Gunung Tua Harahap lived in Dutch-held Batak territories in the south. All three confronted new texts and the people who brought them. With Christian scripture and colonial education positioning nature as an observable object to be deconstructed, writing gained new power as a means of articulating space and planning what it could become. It generated a new spatiality by privileging the seen over the unseen, a step toward secularizing the potent natural world. Capitalism can be seen as a secular faith, investing wonder in objects rather than a sanctified nature. This secular faith can be articulated in Christian terms by followers of all denominations, from Puritans to Calvinists.[2] A related process was the articulation of a secularized landscape through Protestant Christianity, which was brought to the Batak uplands by missionaries in the mid-nineteenth century. Conversion in this case helped dissociate human spirituality from the nonhuman by investing writing with the power to render the latter as objects.

Literacy was not new to the Batak. They have been called a "curious anomaly" as "literate cannibals."[3] The extent of their literacy is unclear, with some scholars viewing it as the purview of an elite-dominated "oligoliteracy" while others argue instead that the egalitarian social organization of the Batak democratized this skill.[4] These studies nonetheless broadly agree on the precolonial function and pedagogy of writing. The Batak used imitation to learn their letters rather than direct instruction. Writing, on a personal level, was mainly used to communicate feelings through love letters and grief-stricken laments written on bark and bamboo. On a more pragmatic level, writing helped to pass down knowledge of magical cosmology, as evidenced by the bark-based *pustaha* written by the datu.[5] While written words recorded such knowledge, the authority of the datu lay in his performative *oral* communication with the spirits. Speech, rather than writing, was power.

The case for widespread literacy in precolonial times has been made in coastal insular Southeast Asian polities, notably by Anthony Reid.[6] This vernacular literacy might be hidden from view, partly due to religious change; conversion to Islam at the coast favored an elite male clergy educated in Arabic script and had relegated local scripts to the domestic sphere, uncaptured by censuses and used by local women. For the uplands specifically, James C. Scott provides a different explanation for the overt absence of writing in the highlands of mainland Southeast Asia and southern China, positing that "postliteracy" could have been both the outcome of seeking refuge from centralized states and a contingent choice that allowed upland society to remain mobile, socially fragmented, and capable of making nimble adjustments to keep centralized lowland valley states at bay.[7]

As rice-growing, semimobile societies in the highlands, Batak groups were neither a centralized coastal polity nor a postliterate landlocked one. However, the Batak test the arguments of both scholars, situated as they were at the cusp of the religious change that Reid finds significant and in the middle of the growing encirclement by a dominant lowland colonial state that Scott views as an intervening factor. Positioning my analysis within these debates on who was literate, in what ways and why, I argue that religious change freighted writing with authoritative power as short-term material blessings began to be tied to literacy. Opportunities for those who harnessed this emerging, powerful skill were unequally distributed. It empowered a tiny class of educated converts but often at the cost of estranging them from their kin and their local landscape. Meanwhile, even the unconverted also began to perceive in literacy a new source of uplifting power. Viewed from up high, the mountains seem flatter.

BLESSINGS OF NATURE: SOUTH TAPANULI

O Mandailing Raya!
Land of my birth, hemmed in by mountains
Under the gaze of volcanoes that puff up smoke
Upriver is Mount Sihite, facing Mount Barerang
Lubu lies on his back, a brow arched toward Sigantang
If I look north and gaze toward the east coast
I see Lubuk Raya standing upright and a glimpse of Mount Malea
Looking down from Bania, I see the river Batang Gadis
Meandering on, earth pressing on both her sides
Although the river is muddied, its waters are beneficial,
Irrigating our fields, flowing into the bay.[8]

This stanza opens one of the first modern poems written in the Batak Mandailing dialect. Composed in 1873 by a Mandailing schoolteacher, Sati of the Nasution patriclan—better known by his Christian name, Willem Iskander—it pays tribute to the land while bringing it into being. Its lines define the physical boundaries of Mandailing in South Tapanuli for the first time through its featuring of volcanoes and rivers from various vantage points: in a valley, looking up at the mountains, horizontally across a river, and scanning the view below from above. From all these perspectives, humans were essentially separated from the land, and the power of the natural world was erased; the author was the outsider looking in. As a commemorative portrait that freezes the reality of its subject in one unmoving pose, the poem bound Iskander's homeland to these lines.

Early European surveyors and naturalists had, in the 1840s and 1850s, begun rendering the topography of the uplands more legible to the Dutch colonial state.[9] Part of this work was carried out to assess the potential profits that could be reaped from South Tapanuli through the export of products, harvested from the woods, that were both high value and easy to carry. These early studies identified Mandailing as a distinct province anchored to the meandering Batang Gadis River and distinguished its more fertile soil from the arid Angkola and Padang Lawas. In the 1870s, Iskander approached his poem similarly, centralizing the river as a landmark while emphasizing its role in irrigating a fecund land. As he wrote these lines, however, he saw in the land not potential but a wasted opportunity not taken up in two decades of Dutch rule:

> O you, owner of vast farmlands, if you scatter a basket of seeds
> You will get sixty in return and you can always sell the rice
> Your land is so fertile; only you are neglectful
> Even though your harvest comes easily, no one comes to trade with you

We glimpse in these lines the logic of intensive resource extraction for trade that presaged a deep transformation of Sumatra. Iskander's poetry did not fade into obscurity but became a classic in Mandailing; his collection *Si Bulus Bulus Si Rumbuk Rumbuk* (which literally translates as "Mr. Quick on the Uptake") was printed and reprinted over the next few decades. This book had several lives. It was the first textbook reader written in Mandailing dialect designed to introduce Mandailing speakers to a Latin script. It was then utilized as a training text for native Mandailing teachers in local teacher training schools. More than fifty years later, his poetry was repurposed as a rallying cry against colonialism in the Tapanuli Residency.[10] *Si Bulus Bulus* was thus the most resilient work of a prolific educator who was one of the first in the province to embrace Dutch-style education and convert to Christianity.

Iskander and one of his students, Sjarif Anwar Harahap (later known by the title Sutan Gunung Tua), were early converts to Christianity and were relatively highly educated. Their entwined histories illustrated how popular unschooled literacy gave way to schooled learning for elites in Dutch-ruled South Tapanuli. Through schools, the two men not only turned toward a new deity but also converted the animistic sacral ecology of the land into an aspirational one of progress that fostered a desacralization of the natural environment.

Willem Iskander and Sjarif Anwar Harahap were both born in 1840, and yet the former was to become a teacher while the other very likely became his student.[11] This circumstance was likely an accident of geography rather than a measure of talent. Willem Iskander, or Sati as he was called then, was born in the district of Panyabungan, the administrative center of the newly established Dutch colonial government in South Tapanuli. In the 1840s, the area included 197 villages and more than 11,000 households under the supervision of an energetic official: Assistant Resident Alexander Godon.[12] Godon opened a school in Panyabungan, and among the few families that took up this early opportunity to become versed in Dutch-directed learning was that of Sati Nasution. His uncle, the chief of Huta Siantar who had helped quell the Mandailing insurgency against the Dutch at the end of the Padri War, was then the designated Yang Dipertuan of Mandailing.[13] His family's decision to collaborate with Dutch rule proved rewarding. In his teens, Sati was hand-picked to become a clerk in Godon's office. When Godon returned to the Netherlands in 1857, he took Sati with him and fought for financial support from the Ministry for the Colonies to educate the seventeen-year-old youth in a teacher training college in the Netherlands. Sati attended elementary school in Vreeswijk and made sufficient progress to move on to a *kweekschool* (teacher training school) in Arnhem a year later. By 1860, he had graduated with a certificate qualifying him to be a teaching assistant and become a Christian, baptized as Willem, a name he apparently chose as a tribute to the Dutch king. Now identifying himself as Willem Iskander—a mix of his baptized name and his Mandailing title Sutan Iskander—his clan affiliation, so crucial in traditional Mandailing society, was submerged under the weight of his new religious identity. The creation of Willem Iskander thus started from his birth to the right family in a location that intersected with an educational path to the Dutch metropole.

Sjarif Anwar Harahap was also born to a family of chiefly lineage, based in Huta Baringin, in the district of Sipirok, where his parents had settled after fleeing their ancestral village in Gunung Tua during the Padri War. Sipirok lay much farther to the north of Panyabungan, at the border with the autonomous Batak territories. Although it was still within the Dutch orbit, as evidenced by its chiefs flying a very visible Dutch flag in a procession to greet a European visitor, it was essentially a frontier settlement.[14] There was no Dutch military presence there, as most troops were stationed in the south. Sipirok's population was a mix of Batak Angkola clans and traders from the independent territories in the north who brought in livestock and salt. Both the Toba and Mandailing dialects were spoken and understood in Sipirok, but Toba men were distinguished from their Angkola Mandailing counterparts by their pierced ears.[15] Dutch authority was loose enough that, in October 1851, Toba Batak men were emboldened to carry out a raid in Sipirok and capture thirty people. Although the Dutch sent a military detachment of seventy-five men into the Toba region, this expedition was later called off without it having achieved success.[16] Another frontier marker was the presence of pig farming in Sipirok, absent in much of South Tapanuli, indicating Sipirok's position straddling animism in the north and Islam in the south.[17]

To get a sense of the relative environment and lived distance between Sipirok and Panyabungan during his childhood years, we can turn to an account by the linguist H. M. van der Tuuk, who traveled between these two points in 1852. Traveling mostly by horse, a traveler took seven days to make one leg of the journey. Van der Tuuk wryly observed that in Sipirok there were "no *datus* (witch-priests) and an abundance of tigers," indicating a flatter social hierarchy in the villages of the province embedded in borderland wilderness.[18] The altitude of the journey can be deduced by the rising price of transporting a load of coffee from point to point. A native porter on foot, carefully balancing his goods on a long bamboo frame laid across his shoulders, was paid thirty duiten for a north-south trip but forty-five duiten to travel a similar east-west distance.[19] The latter trip was clearly steeper and more demanding of energy. With such a prohibitive distance and altitude between Sipirok and Panyabungan, children like Sjarif Anwar Harahap at first found few, if any, opportunities for Dutch-style schooling in 1850s. However, coffee and missionaries would change that. Coffee production became steadily more lucrative; in 1846, the value of coffee exported from West Sumatran ports, mainly destined for Europe, was 1,190,783 Dutch gulden. This figure doubled in five years and had more than tripled by 1856.[20] Sipirok, like much of the new Dutch Tapanuli Residency, was pressed into mandatory coffee cultivation through production quotas imposed on its villages. By 1856, the town had a *koffiepakhuis* (coffee warehouse) and had become a stapling point—a destination for raw coffee beans to be packed for export.[21]

Headed by a Dutch *controleur* and staffed largely by Dutch officials, the coffee warehouse facilitated the import of a new form of education. First, the export coffee crop required locals to staff the new production centers and local chiefs to work within the Dutch colonial administration apparatus. Driven by this need, schooling in West Sumatra and its subsidiary province, the South Tapanuli Residency, developed faster than on Java. By 1861, Sumatra had two teacher training schools to cultivate a cohort literate in Malay, the administrative and trade language, whereas Java still only had one such school.[22] Both schools were in the administrative district of West Sumatra, where coffee production was significant: one at Fort de Kock in the Minangkabau region and the other in Tanobato near Panyabungan.[23]

Like others who lived far from these administrative centers, Sjarif Anwar Harahap was unable to take advantage of the first educational track laid out by the Dutch in South Tapanuli. However, church missions paved a second way, again assisted by coffee. In 1856, a Dutch evangelist named Gustav van Asselt arrived in Sipirok and worked in the new coffee warehouse as manager for a year while proselytizing the Batak. Sipirok was particularly attractive to Christian missions, as it provided a gateway to the independent Batak territories in the north, where their message might be better received than in the now largely Muslim South Tapanuli, subsumed under larger West Sumatra.[24]

The early classes that Van Asselt organized in 1856 and 1857 were informal and, from his own description, as much a learning experience for him as for his students. He described learning the local language by stacking up objects in the open porch of his house and gesturing to curious passersby to let him know the Batak word for each, which he wrote down together with an equivalent Dutch word. By the end of each day, he had accumulated a "considerable vocabulary list of plants, household objects and body parts."[25] From him, some Batak villagers became acquainted with the message of the Gospels and the miracle of modern medicine. A smallpox epidemic broke out soon after Van Asselt arrived, and his assistance rendered to some villagers in Sipirok during this period of sickness gained their trust such that "even girls confided in him and asked for help."[26] He also reached out to the people in and around Sipirok by freeing children from enslavement and housing them. Some months after his arrival, he bought and freed five children at an average price of forty gulden each, housed them near his lodgings, and began teaching them to read and write, as well as the message of the Gospels. This effort attracted the attention of some local chiefs, who requested that he also take their sons into his classes and "teach them the ways of the white man."[27] The class grew to about twenty students, of whom twelve were formerly enslaved children, and this appeared to be about all that he could manage with his resources.

He continued to spread his religious message by inserting himself informally into Batak ritual life. Participating in Batak feasts that venerated the collective spirit, or *begu*, of a village's ancestors, he claimed to sow the seeds of skepticism in the villagers' minds by taking part in a dialogue with the spirit as it entered the body of the medium. One such conversation is recounted here:

> "Why have you come, Grandfather?" I asked the spirit.
> "I have come to bless this group," the spirit intoned.
> "Good, that makes me happy because they are brothers and sisters of mine. And I too seek a favor. Tell me, Grandfather, what do you consider a blessing?" I asked.
> "Richness, respect, honor, and a long life," the spirit answered through the medium.
> I turned to the crowd and asked, "Are you rich?"
> "No," one and all said.
> "Are you respected?"
> "No."
> "Are there many among you who are old?"
> "No."[28]

This conversation, self-congratulatory tone aside, demonstrates how interest in the divine was intimately linked with the everyday gains of the world, where religion invested in ritual for pecuniary rewards from spirits that haunted the world. Van Asselt, representing both Christianity and the coffee trade, offered entry to a different eschatology that eschewed ancestral spirits but could reap similar gains.

How would a Batak youth like Sjarif Anwar Harahap perceive a man like Van Asselt? Perhaps he was one of the youths who curiously contributed a Batak word or two to identify the objects that Van Asselt held up. Perhaps he was one of the sons of a chief's family sent to learn alongside the children whom Van Asselt had freed from enslavement. Perhaps he was a listener to putative conversation with the spirits. Not even his descendants today know. Very likely he witnessed the arrival of more and more missionaries. In October 1861, four of them, including Van Asselt, held a conference in Sipirok and agreed to divide up mission work under a unified Protestant church, with the Dutch concentrating on Angkola and the Germans focused on Toba.[29] A community school was formally set up by this church that same year in Parau Sorat, Sipirok. This 1861 conference is now celebrated as the day that the Batak Protestant Church (Huria Kristian Batak Protestant, or HKBP) was founded.[30] Momentous as the event was retrospectively, to the people living in Sipirok at that time it only vaguely impinged on their consciousness, if at all.

What *was* clear in family memory was that Sjarif Anwar Harahap was enrolled in mission classes—probably with August Schreiber at the new school in Parau Sorat—and converted to Christianity in 1868.[31] He was baptized Ephraim but assumed his birth-given Batak title, Sutan Gunung Tua, as the name by which he was more commonly known. When he was in his late twenties, equipped with some basic literacy in Batak and some Dutch of indeterminate level, Ephraim Sutan Gunung Tua Harahap apparently headed south toward Tanobato and entered the teacher training school set up by his peer and fellow Batak Christian, Willem Iskander.

NATURE OF BLESSINGS: SOUTH TAPANULI

> Over there is a house, with rows of benches and chairs
> There we sit, to seek knowledge
> And those who love the schoolhouse
> They are more honorable than the contemptuous noble
> Those dedicated to school, their knowledge will multiply
> He knows the score, surely he will acquit himself well
> Those who do not come to school, they will remain ignorant
> They would only know this spot of earth, in the big wide world
> Those who say that wisdom lies only in their lands
> We can compare, with a frog in a well
> Because of that, dear children, to school you must go
> And I tell you friend, do not be content to be a beo
> A beo and his kin, this is his habit
> To recite as if singing but without knowing the meaning.[32]

The young Mandailing teacher Willem Iskander composed this paean to school-based education as part of the same collection in which he published his ode to his homeland in 1871. If Ephraim Sutan Gunung Tua had been a student in

Iskander's school during its twilight years in the early 1870s, he would have read this poem as he sat in the schoolhouse trying to master written Batak and Malay in the five years of classes that the school provided. He would have read about the light of a sun that "glimmers like the flutter of a winged insect and in that incessant oscillation, who would not want to praise God in his heart?"[33] He would have read a whimsical short story about the ridiculousness of a man who sold his rice field to hunt imaginary deer and a moral tale about a man who saved himself through his wits after sacrificing for his brother. He would have pondered the legend of Si Baroar, putative historical father of the Mandailing, in a narrative that began defining a Mandailing history.[34] The importance of school-based learning was the core of Iskander's message in his book, and this message was propagated by placing humankind in a special position with respect to the natural world and God above the world itself. A Christian-inspired hierarchy suffused each poem or story in which God, humans, fauna, and flora interacted on a shrinking spectrum of power, denuding the landscape of its animated potency. Moreover, to add to his teaching materials, Iskander translated many books from Dutch and Malay into the Batak Mandailing dialect, including mathematics texts, Dutch reading primers, books on Dutch law, and a contemporary Malay-language book on the wonders of the Western world by an author of Arab-Indian descent in Singapore.[35] Iskander appeared to see translation as part of his mission to open up the worldview of people in his homeland, whom he perceived as trapped in provincialism.

At the same time, his motivation to educate stemmed from a desire to introduce his new religion to his people. The financial support that Iskander had received in the Netherlands from the Dutch Ministry for the Colonies at least partially hinged on his conversion: when a motion to fund Iskander's school was raised in the lower house (Tweede Kamer) of the Dutch parliament, the argument that won the day was that he would be an ideal candidate to encourage the propagation of Christianity in the Dutch East Indies.[36] The funding he subsequently received also distinguished his school from the other two teacher training academies on Sumatra. Starting with an initial cohort of five students in 1862, it grew large enough that Iskander hired some of his senior students to teach, and he was able to pay them a decent stipend of ten gulden per month from the financial support provided by the Dutch. Given that many schools in this period were underfunded and lacked trained teachers, the position of the Tanobato training school was unusual. As one of the few teachers—foreign or local—who was fluent in Dutch, Malay, and his own local Mandailing dialect,

Iskander was a product and a producer of language. Through his translations of agricultural texts, fish farming manuals, and mathematics books, Iskander fashioned the Batak Mandailing script into a means of entry to a different world and was able to communicate his vision to his students in their own vernacular. In this vision, colonialism was depicted in positive terms as a step toward learning useful knowledge from other civilizations in how to be a steward for a landscape in God's broader dominion. South Tapanuli, nudged toward monocropping, found renewed spiritual meaning in parsing the land into its extractable parts—coffee beans, fish, and rice. This adds a new dimension to scholarly analyses of the enchantment of capitalism that have largely focused on its secularizing impact and/or the deification of the means of production or consumed objects.

The extent to which schoolbooks could effectively transform one's beliefs and mode of thinking is an open question, and we must not assume that Iskander's teaching objectives matched his students' learning outcomes. School reports provided by Dutch officials who visited the schools indicated pedagogical effectiveness, but even here the conclusions were mixed. J. A. van der Chijs, general inspector for native education in the Dutch East Indies, visited Iskander's school for three days in 1866 and was apparently astounded by its success.[37] He observed that the students could solve arithmetic problems and write well in both Malay and English. J. J. van Limburg Brouwer, assessing native education in the same capacity a decade later, was more lukewarm about the school while reporting on the dismal and patchy efforts to establish schools in general.[38]

Nonetheless, the students in Dutch-supported schools and, to a lesser extent, missionary schools, obtained much material benefit. Perhaps the impact of schooling is best glimpsed through the life of Iskander's peer-cum-student Sutan Gunung Tua, who became a new convert and was christened Ephraim. At the relatively late age of thirty-five, Ephraim Harahap entered the Dutch colonial administrative service.[39] After some years of service in the colonial administration in Sipirok and Barus, he was appointed as a state prosecutor (*jaksa*) in the newly formed Justice Department in Sumatra. The colonial government's regulations actively prevented office holders like a *jaksa* from serving in the province in which they were born; they were instead rotated across different administrative zones. Sutan Gunung Tua was posted to Sibolga and took up a post in the growing city of Medan on the Sumatran east coast with his growing family, which included two young sons, Djamin and Humala, toward the end of the century. In this way, his education and the career it brought him weakened his connections with Mandailing proper while linking him with a wider cross section of peoples from the Dutch colony. Several other students of Willem Iskander followed suit, becoming teachers, administrators, and writers in Dutch-controlled provinces far from the North Sumatran highlands and raising their children in these distant areas, unmoored from their parents' place of birth. The scattering of this small, educated group across the Dutch East Indies differed from previous migrations of the Batak and the identity shifts that had accompanied them. This new group now held onto the ethnic affiliation of their place of birth and positioned themselves to be part of its governance as a native, but only from a distance. Since ritual communications with a potent land, blessings bestowed by the spirits of one's ancestors, and clan-based social relations were closely intertwined with the place of one's birth, the rotation policy adopted by the Dutch began to hollow out the meaning behind these rituals. It later enabled them to imagine a larger nation-state that supplanted one's local place.

Dutch education thus conferred not only intellectual enrichment but a very material form of power, at the cost of being distanced from one's village of birth and the web of relationships emanating from it. Schools provided a route to honor, respect, and the means for a longer and easier life—all the elements of a good Batak life defined by the spirit who spoke to Van Asselt—but through controlling, not propitiating, the land and the spirits that inhabited it. This schooling cultivated an ability to imagine, grasp, and express new ideas for changes to the land, all of them disconnected from the sacral relations governing it.

The effect of being disconnected from sacred and social relationships had deep personal impacts, of which the emotional aspect has left no documentary trace except through conflicts that surface patchily in family or archival memory. Willem Iskander, despite returning to Mandailing committed to contributing to his homeland, did not seem to be able to revive a closeness to his family. They accepted his conversion but, to keep the family peace, forbade him from proselytizing his relatives.[40] When one of his relatives passed away during his first sojourn in the Netherlands, he was denied his portion of the inheritance.[41] He successfully fought to regain it when he returned and notably freed all the enslaved individuals he had been awarded, signaling yet another break with adat. These threads of conflict suggest not only personal emotional struggles but also a limit to the drift away from traditional kinship-based authority. While schools were transforming *individuals* into a new elite capable of reimagining the land for the future, the traditional patriclan and village chiefs held on to their authority to manage village land and maintain order in their local sacral ecology. While Iskander could structure his homeland within the framework of an aspirational progress in his mind and encouraged his students to do the same, the tenor of Batak village life had yet to be fundamentally changed. In 1874, Iskander decided to accept a position to lead a group of three native candidates, two Javanese and one Mandailing, to the Netherlands for training as teachers. He closed his school and left Mandailing, penning this final stanza:

Nonetheless, despite your drawbacks, I will not abandon you
Because this is where I first opened my eyes
Goodbye my love, for an unknowable number of years to come
When I look upon you again, may you not be as ignorant
When we part, I will ask this of you,
Do not forget to ask your children to seek true knowledge.[42]

Neither Willem Iskander nor his three charges saw the Dutch East Indies again. The students all passed away from various illnesses during their sojourn. These tragedies, perhaps a distressing culmination of his long struggle to reconcile the many facets of his identity, appear to have sent Iskander into a self-destructive spiral of despair. A Dutch friend reported that "the man who bears the name of a king is not a constant Christian . . . his steps lead instead to the gambling house and the dance house."[43] Iskander married a relative of Alexander Godon who was much younger than him. Despite this marriage, Godon worried for him, stating that "his scholarship provides substantial support for his upkeep, but he visits iniquitous places. . . . I have had to speak to him about his conduct."[44] His concern was warranted. In May 1876, at the age of thirty-six, Willem Iskander shot himself. His body was found in a park in Amsterdam, with an enigmatic suicide note to one of his former teachers: "I end my life not because I no longer believe in God, in writing these lines, I acknowledge that God had lifted me above thousands of my fellow men, but this life is to me so heavy, the grief that I carry with me made living longer entirely impossible."[45]

By the time Iskander died, there were forty-five schools supported by the Dutch colonial government on the island of Sumatra and the neighboring island provinces of Riau, Bangka, and Belitung. Most provided basic primary education. Sixty teachers and trainee teachers served 3,000 students drawn from a population of about 1.5 million people.[46] Directed by the head of the Tapanuli Residency, Iskander's teacher training school was reopened in Padang Sidempuan in 1879 under the stewardship of a Dutch-born teacher. Iskander's students and their children formed the ranks of a new professional class of administrators, lawyers, teachers, and journalists, all aspiring to progressive changes in an expanding homeland. Their positions were enabled through coffee, literacy, and in some cases religious conversions—everyday blessings that stood apart from the land and their spirits.

KING AS PRIEST: NORTH TAPANULI

Interest in harnessing the divine for everyday gain cut across religious difference. In 1824, a Batak chief sat down with two English missionaries at the marketplace in Sitahuru and listened to their message on the Gospels. At the end of the conversation, he reportedly said, "I have lived a long time and have always found that our customs are good. Never will it occur to us to change them. If you strangers want to come to do away with our customs, we shall know how to defend them. But if you want to instruct us on how we can become rich and happy, we shall gladly be your pupils."[47] Yet, years later, the grandson of this man, Radja Pontas Lumbantobing, belied his grandfather's words and became one of the earliest and most prominent Toba Batak converts to Christianity. In church-centered histories, the conversion of Lumbantobing was considered a turning point in the Christian mission, as it galvanized a turn toward Christianity in the North Tapanuli highlands starting from the late 1860s, while the territory was still independent of Dutch rule.

The Singamangaradja dynasty was often depicted in early mission and colonial reports as an impediment to these conversions. Current historiography elevates both the church founder, German missionary Ludwig Ingwer Nommensen, and the Singamangaradja dynasty, conferring an outsized emphasis on their joint agency even though their histories developed separately despite intersecting significantly during the nineteenth century.[48] Of equal importance, but somewhat neglected, were the spaces in which they organized, occupied, and represented through writing. In their tussle over reorganizing the autonomous North Sumatran uplands, writing, even for the unconverted, became freighted with authority, conferring the power to rule. Here, unlike in the south, Christian missions and the knowledge they brought were understood through the prism of adat and a precapitalistic economy. A deeper understanding of the latter helps illuminate the changes that early Christian penetration inspired.

The Singamangaradja dynasty was founded in the sixteenth century by a man from Sinambela, a Toba clan. As the family legend goes, the birth of Si Singamangaradja I was marked by powerful supernatural signs: his mother was pregnant for twenty months, thunder and lightning rent the earth at the moment of his birth, and he was born with all his teeth.[49] These were common birth tropes in Malay chronicles of royal lineages; moreover, the Singamangaradja dynasty's authority to rule was recognized through the regalia bestowed to him by a powerful king, Raja Uti, in camphor-exporting Barus: a white elephant, a magic dagger, and a magic staff, which he used as tools to militarily wrest control of Bakkara in Toba and parts of Silindung Valley. In this myth, Raja Uti had the snout of a pig and supported Si Singamangaradja I on the condition that he should never reveal Raja Uti's true form to anyone. However, he broke this promise and accidentally revealed this information, causing friction between upland Bakkara and maritime Barus. Nonetheless, the dynasty continued to play a significant role in mediating between the highland peoples and the lowland kings controlling the coastal trade. Si Singamangaradja XI's influence was thus defined through the acquiescence of the upland spirits inhabiting nonhuman natures and a supernatural king with a pig's snout on the coast.

Ompu Sohahuaon, the eldest son of Si Singamangaradja X, only succeeded to the chieftainship after fending off a challenge from his uncle, Ompu Radja Ihutan, who had married one of his father's widows. It was said that the contest was eventually decided through a ritual known as *upacara gajah dompak*, in which the two claimants had to successfully pull the magic dagger known as *piso gajah dompak* from its sheath in order to ascend to the position of chieftain.[50] The dagger was not the only uncanny instrument. The staff, wielded by the right man, had the legendary power to create new water sources during a journey or a drought.[51] A nineteenth-century bark book in the collection of a datu from the Simbolon clan in Samosir contained a prayer glorifying the Singamangaradja and highlighting these powers:

> O my lord Si Singamangaradja!
>   I call on you, I beseech you, I pray to the soul of our leader, the Singamangaradja. He who crosses boundaries and is never crossed, who organized the realm of the men with black eyes, who is of the lineage of Si Raja Batak from Bakkara Toba, which is walled by mountains, curtained by dew, and contains

waterfalls that will flow everlastingly, feeding the rivers of our villages. . . . He is the light from the most High, the light from the gods, who illuminates straight and crooked words, who provides a place for discussing ideas, who provides freedom . . . repels enemies and defends Toba and her sacred places. . . . He is the pillar of the earth, the horn that could not be turned, the sun that could not be faced, and the trust that could not be betrayed. . . . He is the owner of the *gajah dompak* dagger, the spear that can create water, the cloth that can call on wind. . . . It is he who frees the fish from traps, he who frees the enslaved, the one to whom we supplicate for harmonious prosperity and fertility, for wise sons and daughters and the reproduction of our domestic animals.[52]

The prayer not only highlights his special powers—the ability to control water, wind, and fertility—but also indicated the spaces that he inhabited geographically and politically. This was not a state centered around Bakkara. Rather, his most important political role, as indicated by the paean above, was in mediating conflicts and officiating in supravillage feasts. Bakkara, his geographical base, did not draw followers into its sphere; it was Si Singamangaradja XI and his prestige, which radiated out as he moved from village to village, that attracted them. In this respect, he was not unlike the many mobile datu in the Batak territories who had begun helping to solidify a Batak ethnic identity in the sixteenth century. His rule, such as it was, confined itself to people rather than territory. He did not seek to conquer land, did not set up a systematic rule of law, and did not collect taxes or nominate others to do so.[53] In short, his authority was largely spiritual.

The space of Si Singamangaradja XI's influence was thus not easily defined in terms of territory and thereby mirrored the political authority in the uplands, which featured a loose federation of clan-based villages. A village in the independent Batak territories during this period was essentially an autonomous entity with its own chiefs (Raja Huta) running its day-to-day affairs and top priests (Raja Baringin) leading ritual life in the village. Supravillage connections also existed with some level of formal organization, often to facilitate religious life. Neighboring villages, in groups of two or three, formed a loose unit called a *horja*, while a cluster of two to five *horja*s constituted a *bius*.[54] A bius generally gathered at least once a year to make sacrifices during planting season as well as during times of crisis, such as epidemics or droughts.[55] When a feast or council gathering at the bius level was convened, a temporary leader, along with a leading priest, was selected by the leaders of the villages constituting that bius. The position of authority at bius level could thus technically rotate between different village leaders, preventing the accumulation of power by any one chief.[56]

Within this framework, Si Singamangaradja XI gained his reputation as a man of prowess. He and his representatives were a prominent presence at these feasts. Stories of his miraculous feats, such as creating a freshwater spring in Siulokhsa and Ambarita on the island of Samosir, and his generosity in liberating many of the enslaved people became part of local historical memory.[57] Si Singamangaradja XI appeared to lead with moral and religious authority, legitimized by his charisma and unseen spirits in nature revealing themselves through his supernatural feats. While this hold was mainly affective, it gave him some political leverage over territories run by other Batak chiefs, as well as those ruled by coastal Malays or the colonial state, such as Habinsaran, Asahan, and Sipirok, even though his base was in Bakkara.

This political organization had important implications on the running of the camphor economy. The loose supravillage arrangement that facilitated the Singamangaradja's expansion of influence beyond Bakkara was checked from coalescing into a state-like structure by the physical and spiritual boundaries put up at the huta level. Villages in camphor- and benzoin-harvesting Batak areas maintained a barrier (*bongbong*) that restricted the right to extract from camphor and benzoin trees and to trade the extracts. Barriers took on many forms in times of war: the physical erection of bamboo walls edged with sharpened spikes, magic defensive spells guarding the sacred trees, and the limited granting of the right to trade salt for benzoin to merchants who applied for such permission from the Batak chiefs.[58] Barus was reportedly surrounded by barriers: the barrier of Siambaton, Rambe, and Tukka in the north, of Pasaribu in the east, and of Naipospos in the southeast. Only a privileged handful of traders and some intrepid smugglers managed to gain access to these mountain passes. With these barriers, which invoked unseen spirits, the Batak chiefs were able to enforce sacred protection over the price and production level of benzoin and severely punish those who violated these boundaries.[59]

The British and Dutch imperial presence on the island impinged only lightly on this trade. Traders at Tapanuli Bay before the Padri War were impressed by the camphor trees that dominated its forests. They were the "monarchs of forests," wrote one such trader, "being of a hundred feet perpendicular and straight as masts."[60] But these traders had little access to those forests; Sumatran camphor seldom made its way to Europe. In the 1850s, the Dutch colonial government coveted but ignored the camphor trade and overtly maintained a policy of nonintervention (*onthoudingspolitiek*) in the independent Batak territories. On a practical level, it found the *bongbong* an onerous barrier to trade and tried to remove it. However, even after repeated negotiations, the Dutch failed to persuade the Toba chiefs to abolish it. Suspicion of the Dutch as well as the Malays in Dutch-ruled areas grew when the former tried to bring a vaccination program inland in the early 1850s, further dimming their hopes of penetrating the interior.[61]

The persistent presence of the varied *bongbong* and their dispersed implementation highlight a few important aspects of the territorial organization of the independent Batak uplands before 1860. These barriers demonstrate how environmental management of forest resources was carried out at the huta level, in a manner that was replicated throughout large parts of the independent Batak highlands but without coordination by a central political authority. Moreover, an absence of coordination was also evident in religious life: the religio-magical pillars of these barriers were put up by priests at the huta level, rather than the higher bius or *horja* levels, showing once again that the influence of charismatic transvillage chiefs such as Si Singamangaradja was largely affective rather than material. Although he was respected in these benzoin- and camphor-producing areas, Si Singamangaradja did not interfere with the territorial management of the huta nor was there evidence that exerting power in such a manner would be recognized beyond his own base in Bakkara. And it was precisely this dispersion of authority that made such barriers to trade effective: Dutch access to camphor and benzoin trees was possible only when the region formally came under Dutch rule. Although religion and politics intersected in the enactment of forest resource management, the two forms of authority appeared to run on separate tracks and held off Dutch colonial incursions.

Fragmentation of sacral and political authority in upland Batak society did not appear evident to contemporary Dutch observers such as Van der Tuuk. The latter perceived the *bongbong* instead as a sign of oriental despotism in which Batak chiefs impeded the participation of their own people in trade through brutal imposition of their power over natural resources. Van der Tuuk connected this despotism with moral laxness and lamented that the spiritual barriers impeded the reach of Dutch ethics. Such despotism, he opined, resulted in the peoples of the Batak uplands being vulnerable to the chicanery of the few Chinese traders who were allowed into these territories to trade and who paid a fraction of what the benzoin was worth on the open market while selling salt at higher prices.[62] Moreover, he viewed the extraction of camphor and benzoin in the Dairi areas in particular as highly undeveloped and wasteful at the same time, conjecturing that "in the past, the camphor must have overflowed."[63]

Trade statistics from this era partly contradicted Van der Tuuk's views about how the *bongbong* stymied Batak trade. Trade in forest products at the Dutch ports of Barus, Singkel, and Sibolga dipped in the period between 1846 and 1859 but by 1869 had rebounded to surpass the totals of previous years.[64] Most of these products were bound for China—thus supporting Van der Tuuk's observation that Chinese middlemen had seized control of the forest trade—but in fact the relationship was more symbiotic. Through Chinese middlemen, the Batak evaded direct trade with the Dutch. The restrictions Batak chiefs imposed on the extraction of camphor and other forest products through the *bongbong* allowed them the autonomy to first scale back and bypass the Dutch and later to reorient trade toward China rather than limit it altogether. Moreover, both Si Singamangaradja XI and XII, whose reigns spanned 1840 to 1907, had close relations with Aceh. Trading links with the latter increased during this period, suggesting that independent Aceh was an alternative channel for export. This structure also allowed these chiefs to retain the authority to direct camphor-harvesting expeditions as they traditionally had, instead of opening their forest to unregulated trade with Dutch ports that offered higher prices.

If political power was restricted through this mode of organization, so was the potential to accumulate capital. Even as they took part in the camphor, benzoin, and pepper trade, multiple Batak chiefs limited the flow of currency accepted for these goods, allowing coins to replace rice as a medium of exchange at coastal markets but keeping the coins in the highlands for use as ornaments rather than recirculating them freely. Batak chiefs coordinated the production of pepper by providing their followers with rice and implements for pepper growing in exchange for their produce to sell on the market. The limited flow of currency was such that a British surveyor to the Toba region lamented that, while coins came into the territory, "not a dollar left the country again." He claimed that "the greatest difficulty and discouragement to which the pepper trade had been subject, had arisen from the extreme aversion of the Batta [*sic*] cultivators to receive in payment any other than dollars of Carolus the 3rd and 4th, which have a remarkably large and full bust; the Ferdinand the 7th being all small and spare."[65] Such an emphasis on aesthetics rather than the value of the money indicated that the trade structure was still very much akin to barter within Batak society. Only the chiefs negotiated the boundaries between upland

and lowland, barter and cash economy in a manner that enhanced their social prestige. Within this context, the trade with the Chinese that Van der Tuuk had observed was a continuation of this earlier trading pattern that decentralized production among multiple villages while restricting capital accumulation to a small segment within each village. Therefore, mobility and power-sharing between chiefs who financed the gathering of forest products, which was accomplished by mobile priests mediating with spirits, acted as a brake to profit accumulation as a result of harvesting these resources.

Even for the chiefs' families, accumulation was stymied through religious ritual. Funeral rites for a dead chief necessitated the purchase of large amounts of expensive camphor to preserve his body so that his spirit could guard the village during rice-planting season. German naturalist Junghuhn, one of the few Europeans to visit Toba, described how "bodies are stored in sarcophagi made out of the hollowed-out trunks of durian trees and the corpses were entirely covered with camphor. . . . To purchase so much camphor, the family of the deceased king must make the greatest sacrifice, and often sell all their cattle. Every village has such a rajah."[66] In short, the camphor economy required much propitiation, restricted cash circulation, and promised only chimerical, temporary gains. To an outsider like Van der Tuuk, this conduct of the camphor trade appeared immoral and illegible, symbolic of the society that his employers wished to renovate.

PRIEST AS KING: NORTH TAPANULI

It was missionaries rather than the Dutch colonial government who first penetrated the spiritual and material barriers of North Tapanuli, and they did so through the mission schoolroom. Ludwig Ingwer Nommensen, the iconoclastic figure at the center of this transformation, embarked on spreading the Gospel in the Batak highlands in 1861.[67] His journey, successes, and challenges were well documented in church histories. They and the primary sources from which they are constructed highlight two ways in which Nommensen reorganized space: physically, through the construction of mission stations, and abstractly, through the literacy propagated in his schools. What he brought was not simply a new religion but a new order.

The construction of Nommensen's mission stations took place with much difficulty. Suspicious of changes in South Tapanuli, several hostile Batak chiefs asked him whether he had been sent by the Dutch colonial government to build roads and schools and take away their children.[68] No one was willing to secure wood for him or accompany his helpers to obtain it, possibly due to fear of retribution by ancestral spirits inhabiting the trees.[69] In desperation, Nommensen bought a vacant house in a different village at the western part of Silindung Valley, stripped it down to its wooden components, and had the wood transported back to his building site. However, several Batak residents at the site objected to the presence of the wood from a different village and asked him to remove it, causing much unhappiness and heated verbal exchanges—including a threat to throw Nommensen and the wood into the river—before they finally gave in.[70] Their hostility continued even after the house was built. Constructed roughly in an A-shaped frame, bound by rattan ropes, and roofed with reeds (*arung*) in the style of a traditional Batak gathering place (*sopo*), the building collapsed during a minor earthquake after some of the ropes had been deliberately cut. Nommensen rebuilt the house on a sandy riverbed that no one was likely to claim because of the threat of flooding. He protected it from the overflow of the swollen river by encircling it with high mounds of earth.

The mission school opened in August 1864 with 16 children enrolled. In a year, this number had increased to 22.[71] Nommensen planned for a school with the capacity to house 150 children and gradually expanded his compound as well as its perimeter. He named this compound Huta Dame (meaning "village of peace"). By 1867, 75 people had come to live in Huta Dame, of whom about 50 were baptized. Those who were not baptized included forsaken widows, the sick, men addicted to gambling, and orphaned children.[72] Nommensen had thus founded a village within a village, and despite propagating a different religion, he attracted followers and accumulated prowess similar to that of a Batak chief like Si Singamangaradja.

Nommensen at times wielded his literacy like a weapon. The edge it gave him was not through the systematic application of knowledge but through the way in which accoutrements in the process of becoming literate were perceived and at times mistranslated by his audience. For example, to avoid further conflicts over his settling into the area, Nommensen called a meeting of all the chiefs in the Silindung area after his house was built and first read aloud a letter of permission to reside in Toba that he had received from the governor in Padang. Next to him sat an assistant with a large book and pen and ink. Then, he asked each chief if they opposed his plan to stay there. If they did, he would enter their name in the book. Nommensen noted that the fear of having their names written down in a large book led the chiefs to unanimously agree to let him stay.[73]

The association of a material book like Nommensen's with the magic re-corded in the bark books of the Batak seemed to have given Nommensen the prestige of a datu. Likewise, many Toba Batak were fascinated by his magnifying glass, which appeared to draw fire from the air; his compass, which seemed to unerringly find true north; his watch, with its different conception of time; and the music he drew from his violin. They began to be wary of his rattan staff—another tool associated with the datu—that he used to keep dogs and pigs at a distance. At least once a man who had touched the staff without per-mission came to Nommensen, asking for medicine to ward off the misfortune and calamity caused by his deed.[74] The expansion of the school as a space in which to heal the sick who were housed there also added to the new religion's prestige over the old. It became an even greater focal point when there were epidemic outbreaks of diseases such as cholera and smallpox. Nommensen was not trained as a doctor, but he supplied homeopathic medicines based on German medical tradition. In 1865, an outbreak of cholera among the Batak contributed to a short-lived spike in the number of conversions, as did a chicken pox epidemic the following year.[75] In Nommensen's reports, it appeared that datu—competing for influence and prestige on religio-magical terms—were among those most vehemently hostile to him.

Education at the mission school upended social order in the village. En-slaved persons were accepted in the school and then freed by Nommensen. Their subsequent position within Batak society was uncertain, as they had no place among free persons linked by kinship in the village or among its enslaved underclass. The freeing of the enslaved was not uncommon in Batak society, since most of the enslaved were bound and unbound by debt and repayment, either their own or that of their families. The Singamangaradja dynasty, in many retrospective historical accounts, was apparently also against the practice and often helped the enslaved progress toward freedom.[76] But those who had once been enslaved and their descendants were often excluded from religious life, as when a chief slaughtered a buffalo for a feast and the formerly enslaved and their families were not allowed to partake of the meat.[77]

Equality before a divinity was a departure from this old practice. In Huta Dame, the formerly enslaved were joined by the dislocated—those early Batak Christian converts who had been disowned by their families after refusing to contribute to feasts that venerated their ancestors. Further, the fledgling Chris-tian community sometimes visibly rejected customary rites associated with the old sacral ecology. For example, Christian Batak women went to weed the rice fields on days when it was traditionally taboo to work in the fields; non-Christians gathered on such days to propitiate the spirits of their ancestors. At first, some unconverted Batak chased them out of their rice fields but eventually left them alone.[78] In Huta Dame, which overtly rejected Batak rites of respect to the souls of their ancestors, the rice fields thrived.

Nommensen's accumulation of personal prowess occasionally put him in conflict with Si Singamangaradja XI. Their personal relationship was fraught with a certain degree of mutual distrust. In 1865, Si Singamangaradja reportedly called on his followers not to sell any food to Christians in Huta Dame; he made this announcement at a marketplace. On July 22 in the same year, twenty persons were baptized, and a few days later Si Singamangaradja XI was reported to have threatened to attack the mission. However, the attack did not take place, as a bigger conflict apparently broke out between the clans of Lumbantobing and Sinambela when the brother of Radja Pontas Lumbantobing was shot by the latter, leading to a feud that lasted several years.[79] Si Singamangaradja XI instead made peace with Huta Dame, visiting Nommensen in 1866. Interpretations and memories of this meeting between Nommensen and Si Singamangaradja XI varied widely. One incident in particular showed the potential for misinterpretation of the exchange between the two. During this visit, Nommensen admired his visitor's white horse and jocularly asked for one. The horse, beloved and so personally associated with the Singamangaradja that it had its own special term (*sihapaspili*), was not for sale. Si Singamangaradja XI, however, reportedly offered it to Nommensen in exchange for his white wife. A Batak Christian observer to the encounter, recounting the incident much later to a historian, characterized it as a joke meant to maintain rapport.[80] By contrast, missionary accounts recalled this moment as a crass and immoral demand for a white woman.[81]

Despite this high degree of mistrust, by the mid-1870s the Christian community had grown so large that a new mission station was needed. Radja Pontas Lumbantobing and a few other Christian chiefs allocated a plot of land to Nommensen on a small hill overlooking Silindung Valley.[82] Materials from the old church were used to construct the new one, but the new structure had timber walls designed for greater safety during an earthquake. This new, secure Pearadja mission station, completed in 1872, marked his leadership among the Batak. Over time, additional classes were offered in this new station, including teacher training.[83] Survival spoke for itself. Decades earlier, Radja Pontas Lumbantobing's grandfather had rejected the Gospel but welcomed pragmatic knowledge on how to live well. What he had failed to foresee was that such knowledge could not be separated from sacred customs; maintaining the latter depended on acquisition of the former. Nommensen gained his status through successful management: of hostile woods, of the dislocated people in Huta Dame, of diseased bodies. He exercised authority over a space to propagate literacy that could potentially help others do the same. Material power and sacred power were embedded in an inseparable circle of nature/culture and found expression in each other.

An exceptionally long life was not the lot of Si Singamangaradja XI, who passed away in 1875 when he was in his late fifties. Mindful of the power in the developing world of authoritative literacy, the new Si Singamangaradja XII became the first in his dynasty to use paper and a royal seal, with at least one Simalungun chief following suit.[84] The seal was patterned after those in Aceh, with twelve points denoting royalty. The words at the center of the seal were written in Toba Batak script: "I am the seal of the Singamangaradja in Bakkara." Around it, in Malay-Arabic script, a similar message was repeated: "This is the seal of the king in Toba, his capital in the village of Bakkara in the Islamic calendar year 1290."[85] Through these words, the seal combined two traditions: it spoke for itself as a potent actor through the declaration "*I* am the seal" in the Batak language, and it sublimated itself as a tool in the style of Malay royal seals in Arabic script. Writing, even for the ruler, was no longer light, portable, private, and optional; it had become weighted with state-like authority. In both Bakkara and Huta Dame, the priest was king, and the king was priest.

Writing took on different functions with missionaries' arrival in the Batak uplands. In the poetry and laments scribbled on bamboo, writing had communicated feelings between humans. Through the magic bark books of the datu, writing recorded ways of communicating with these spirits that inhabit the landscape. Early conversions and a burgeoning coffee economy in South Tapanuli changed writing into an entry pass for a world in which men became managers and thus elevated from the rural subsistence of peasants. Such a transformation involved new thinking about the natural world, by viewing it in more transactional terms and atomizing it into parts devoid of potency. The few who attained high levels of competency in this new language found themselves distanced from the nonhuman worlds that had sustained their ancestral villages. Meanwhile, in North Tapanuli, the cashless economy represented by the harvesting of camphor remained relatively intact. But even in this autonomous zone, the message of the Gospel brought by missionaries such as Nommensen tended to graft itself onto the prevailing everyday concerns of the time and succeeded when it could translate into ways of becoming successful. In both regions, these early conversions were responses to production and reproduction as the concerns of everyday religion. Moreover, they hinged on mastering a secularization of nonhuman natures through writing.

Such changes were still limited. In North Tapanuli especially, these early missionary efforts did not displace the charismatic leadership, kinship system, or economic activity that had governed relationships between humans and nonhumans in Batak society. However, they paved the way for Batak peoples to understand and relate to deeper changes within their environment and society when the adat basis of their society was fundamentally shaken. Whether learning to articulate the world in a way that precluded the presence of spirits was a form of disenchantment, as Max Weber argues, or a misenchantment cast by capitalism, as Eugene McCarraher posits, is an issue that will be taken up in chapters 5 and 6. The advent of modern literacy and its dominance over vernacular forms of communication through conversion and colonialism centralized an extractive logic in the Anthropocene.

Conversions were also to affect the genres through which personal experiences were expressed and pondered. The next chapter explores fresh environmental representations that emerged through two of these new modernist genres: autobiography and biographical history. These genres came into being when reflective, rationalized writing was coupled with a new adat landscape that formed through migration.

FOUR Mountains, Waters, Derangement

In the mid-nineteenth century, there was a discernible turn in Malay-language writings that centralized the authorial self and eschewed the fantastic in favor of the realistic.[1] Unlike the sparseness of Batak written documents, there was a relative wealth of literature in Malay, encompassing court chronicles, localizations of stories and religious texts from the Muslim world, and poetry, all of which revealed complex literary engagement with mythology and history.[2] The personal narrative with the authorial self at the center, however, was a new genre. Two rare narrative sources discussed here represented a pioneering departure from a mode of historical storytelling that had emphasized genealogy and featured lineages that often breezily included the nonhuman. The first is a personal memoir of a Batak boy's enslavement, forced migration, freedom when bought by a preacher in Singapore, and subsequent conversion to Christianity. The second is a family history recounted by a second-generation Mandailing Muslim telling the migration story of his great-uncle and father. Both histories spanned the 1850s to early 1870s, although parts of them were written decades later; each writer was a convert making sense of recent experience. Their narratives build on the rationalization of landscapes afforded by school-based learning. How did working with the land, specifically mountains, and the water figure into these stories? And how did conversions shape these interactions? Such writings frame how conversion to Christianity and Islam democratized human power over nature while narrowing converts' ecological vision: these faiths empowered the individual to succeed in personal enterprises regardless of their ability to interface with spirits of the local landscapes.

The "Great Derangement" is a term used by Amitav Ghosh to refer to our present era's failure of the imagination in discussing climate change, a failure that Ghosh identifies as a hallmark of the Anthropocene. This contraction of the literary imagination, he argues, occurred at precisely the moment when the scale of human impact reached epic proportions, operating through a "rhetoric of the everyday" that excluded the uncanny from the written page and privileged theories of gradual change over sudden upheavals.[3] The stories in this chapter, though nonfictional, reflect a change in religious imagination enacted through realistic family histories that erased or banished the fantastic to the margins. Religious imagination is key to them; unlike Ghosh, who makes a distinction between the uncanny in the environment and the supernatural, the authors of these stories tell of a context in which the environment *was* the supernatural. These family narratives arose from this understanding but began to de-link humans from genealogies originating from nonhuman sources while also slowly bifurcating the supernatural from the environmental. Whereas the nonhuman was exiled into the pages of genre fiction in literature, it gradually receded into folklore in the religious life of the converted. This shift did not occur in a vacuum but in a context of migration, capitalization, and urbanization, all of which were to vastly increase human impact on the land.

Centralization of the experience of Batak migrants to the Malay Peninsula is a perspective hitherto unexplored in much of the historical literature.[4] Connections between Sumatra and the Malay Peninsula have long geographic roots. The naturalist Alfred Russell Wallace remarked on the "wonderful similarity on the whole of the animals in Sumatra with those of the Malay peninsula" and observed that this "rendered it perfectly certain that the two countries were at one time joined, and at a not very remote period."[5] Those days of unity were "remote enough for the intervening land to have sunk down and then for the volcanoes to have arisen and poured such a mass of matter into the water as to form the enormous expanse of undulating country, which was largely formed of a red clayey substance such as was seen in almost all regions where volcanoes abound. It had been deposited in the sea, then uplifted and then cut through by rivers."[6]

Even as geological processes sundered Sumatra and Malaya, the two places remained a shared cultural zone connected by layered stories heavily influenced by Hinduism, Buddhism, and Islam. The *naga*, a creature of Hindu mythology recast in many of these stories, was a central motif in myth-making, shaking both mountains and waters.[7] Mount Merapi, a volcano in Sumatra's Bukit Barisan range, was part of a small island that rose suddenly above the water and was inhabited by a naga that spewed earth to enlarge it. It could be subdued with the right supernatural alliances; among the Batak, a fallen goddess stilled him with a sword to stabilize the land, while among the neighboring Minangkabau, Kubu, and Besemah peoples, a group of men from Mecca was said to have killed this guardian serpent, after which the island expanded and flourished.[8] On the other side of the Straits of Malacca, there were similar stories: a persistent Malay belief that the world is encircled by a serpent chasing its own tail and an Islamized version in which God asks the angel Gabriel to kill the naga Saktimuna.[9] In many stories, the naga was associated with creative destruction; landslides in the mountains and floods after heavy rains were sometimes attributed to the serpents slithering their way back to the sea after a retreat in the mountains, after which the land renewed itself.[10] The naga was a creature of mountain and water, uniting the uplands with rivers. Moreover, it was a creature of moral ambiguity, simultaneously a symbol of fertility, creativity, and destruction.

With the naga at the center, we can see the uplands as an amalgamation of two symmetrical realms: mountains of great height and waters of great depth, where supernatural powers were once thought to reside and mingle with the world of humans. Each realm paired the human and the nonhuman. On the mountains, Sumatran upland tradition tells of the first humans emerging from Malin Deman, who married an angel by hiding the coat of feathers that had enabled her to ascend to the heavens.[11] As for the seas, the *Sejarah Melayu*, a Malay genealogy of kings, speaks of Raja Chulan, a descendant of Iskandar Dzulkarnain, exploring the depths of the sea in a glass box, marrying the princess of an underwater realm, and fathering three children before becoming restless and returning to earth.[12] The new genre of family biography, however, questioned and critiqued these origins. To understand why, we must traverse a vertical axis from the mountains of North Sumatra to the Malayan Peninsula and its waterways.

"HIKAYAT HIKAMAT": CONVERTING MOUNTAINS

In 1861, a young Batak boy named Hikamat started a personal journal about his life. A conversation with his teacher, the Reverend Benjamin Keasberry, who was running the sole mission school in Singapore at the time, sparked the journaling effort. He recounts his mentor gently urging his newly literate students to better the world with their acquired skill. "There are many to whom I give fragrant flowers and they are returned to me, mixed with rotten blooms,"

Keasberry reportedly said in reference to the mixed success of his missionary efforts. "My students, remember this: plant every seed with the hope that it will become nourishing fruit. Even if you do not get to eat it, its green leaves will long flourish."[13] Taking these words to heart, the boy wrote in his memoir's preface that "it would be good for me to create a *Hikayat* (narrative), speaking of how I came to be with this master, his conduct and all his works as well as the works of his students. . . . [The writing endeavor] could be like an alloy of iron and old gold, never losing its luster over the years. . . . If it [the narrative] is worthless iron, it will rust away and disappear. If it is valuable gold of much benefit, many will demand it."[14]

For a while it appeared that iron might have won over gold. This reflective piece outlining the youth's motivation to chronicle his life appears as a manuscript appended to a long *syair*, or Malay court poem, initially separate from another manuscript comprising entries that made up the main text. Both manuscripts were likely gifted to the Singapore Training College after 1880 and were at some point bound together and collectively titled "Hikayat Hikamat." It then became part of the library collections in two later iterations of teacher training institutes in British Malaya during the early twentieth century—the Malacca Malay College and the Sultan Idris Training College—before being requisitioned by Malay scholar Za'ba just before World War II. The manuscript sank into the anonymity of Za'ba's voluminous papers after his death and only resurfaced decades later as the subject of a brief study by the Malay literary scholar Raimy Ché-Ross, who had retrieved it from a collection of Za'ba's personal correspondence and ephemera at the National Archives of Malaysia.[15] Ché-Ross's careful analysis is primarily concerned with establishing the origins and chain of ownership of the manuscript to lay the foundation for further study. The following discussion of "Hikayat Hikamat" is the first to focus on the content of the main text, particularly the tropes it employs as a modern conversion narrative. The features in its writing and story arc that marked it as "modern" were also precisely what domesticated the potency of the landscape and provided evidence for a contraction of the eco-religious imagination.

Of particular interest is the motif of mountains. "Hikayat Hikamat" roughly follows a narrative arc in which the protagonist travels from one peak—the Sumatran highlands—to the allegorical city on the hill, Reverend Keasberry's Mount Zion (Bukit Zion). Keasberry was the only Protestant missionary left in British Malaya after the London Missionary Society withdrew from the field in 1844 to concentrate its resources on China. Unable to speak Chinese but proficient in Malay, he felt called to stay in the region despite his meager resources and not being supported by any Christian society. An unnamed patron high in the colonial government subsequently gifted him with fourteen acres of ground on a hill covered in tropical jungle.[16] The description of how Keasberry transformed this hill is a textbook depiction of an idealized ecology of cultivation often associated with and critiqued in Christian eco-theology:

> This hill, Mr. Keasberry accepted in the name of the Lord, and bowing upon
> his knees, consecrated it to his service, and gave it the name of "Mount Zion."
> On this summit, rising two hundred feet above the surrounding plain, he be-
> gan at once to clear away the jungle, and built a small bungalow to be occupied
> by a native who was to aid him in the work of his mission. Afterward the entire
> hill was cleared, and planted with various tropical fruit-trees; and now may be
> seen there, in healthy growth and fruit-bearing, mango, mangosteen, bread-
> fruit, coconut, cinnamon, pepper, nutmeg, cloves, cardamoms, vanilla, papia,
> India-rubber, laichi, rambutans and all varieties of the beautiful and fragrant
> tropical flowers.[17]

That such a description was considered worthy of mention in Keasberry's obituary reflects a sense of the spirituality attached to the work of transforming wilderness into cultivated agro-landscapes, a Protestant Christian ethos that has been debated and explored in many works since publication of the religion scholar Lynn White's classic 1967 essay on the Christian roots of the present environmental crisis.[18] The encounter between Hikamat and Keasberry brings together divergent spiritual attachments to highlands.

The two are in contrast because spiritual power in Southeast Asia tends to reside in the unstructured, in the flux of creativity, rather than in controlled construction. The art historian Stanley J. O'Connor writes of how the ancient art of iron working evokes this notion of power:

> Mountains in Southeast Asia are regarded as the powerful manifestation of
> the boundless creative power that irradiates the cosmos and links all being,
> animate and inanimate, into one field of diffuse, unstable and pulsating en-
> ergy. The same force that buckled the earth's crust and drove the mountains to
> shoulder the clouds is seen at work in the endless flux that marks the visible
> spectacle of the world's processes, *natural and cultural . . . all beings can be read
> as a text rather than an assemblage of matter that is opaque and inert.*[19]

"Hikayat Hikamat" alludes to and then questions this notion of nature as a living text. Opening the narrative with the dramatic circumstances that drove him from his childhood village, the author writes of how his mother was abandoned by his father, who had left to sojourn in Tanjung Padang.[20] Soon after, his mother was gruesomely murdered by a group of robbers who attacked her village during a gathering, burned down the house where she had taken refuge, and chopped off her hands to take her bracelets. Hikamat was adopted by a maternal aunt but nonetheless found little stability. For reasons that appeared confusing to the child, he recalled the family being forced to move when he was "old enough to know right from wrong" but still young enough to be carried when the trek was too strenuous.[21] Memories of moving from peaks to valleys, past waterfalls and lakes as well as arid plains, dominate this part of his story. The magic of the mountains surfaces as he tells of the brief moments of refuge this wandering family found. In one episode, they travel through the forest to avoid unfamiliar strangers and find a cave that he describes as magical (*ajaib*): "the light comes in from the north . . . [through] a natural door and it was protected in the south."[22] In another, he wrote about how altitude became a refuge in "Haru," a settlement that used to be located in a lowland area but was relocated to the mountains when its *raja* found it necessary to evade an unspecified hostile enemy.[23] Higher up, its inhabitants could easily spot the enemy and throw rocks to deter them. The settlement was fortified, protected by deep gorges, and surrounded by cliffs. The family could never stay in isolated protection for long, however, as there was very little food available, and hunger was persistent.[24] The mountains and forests of the author's childhood offered protection but no sustenance, while houses and settlements signified sustenance but little security.

In these wanderings, Hikamat sometimes retrospectively sounds notes of skepticism about the agency and potency of the nonhuman within his natural surroundings, often through fragments of conversations with his aunt and uncle. "Why does the owl [*punggok*] make a mournful sound on the nights when the moon is full?" he asks once, as the drowsy trio are drifting off to sleep in the forest. "The people of old says that it misses the moon," says his aunt. "Then why doesn't it call in the day?" he persists, falling asleep only partly mollified by his aunt's answer that the owl was too busy looking for sustenance. In another conversation, the group had reached a grove of trees and rested briefly under the shade of a Malacca tree. They cannot stay, his uncle explains, because this was a place where "the spirits had warred." The boy questions him: "How could you know that?" These things, his uncle explains, could not be seen but could be heard and felt. The group then moved on, careful to avoid disturbing a solitary ambling elephant.[25] These episodes demonstrate an early skepticism of his elders' personification of nature and an envisioning of the supernatural in what Hikamat later perceived to be inert, after he had come to understand the world in different terms.

Hikamat's uncle and aunt passed away from illness, still on the run, and the young boy was later captured by a slave trader he referred to simply as Nakhoda, or commander. It was Nakhoda who gave him a new name for his changed circumstances, as he narrates, referring to himself in the third person: "Hikamat was asked: 'What is your name?' And so Hikamat told them what it is. Hearing the name, Nakhoda said: 'I want to change this name of yours into a good one.' He opened his divination book and proclaimed: 'From today we will call you Marjan!' From then on, the crew began to address him as Marjan.'"[26]

The boy was then brought to Singapore and sold to a master who, in his account, seemed decent. Slavery had been technically outlawed in Britain's Far East colonies since the passing of the Felony Slave Trade Act in 1811. However, the enforcement of the law was spotty and opaque, especially with regard to women, whose trafficking and prostitution were often disregarded by officials in the East India Company as a necessary evil that catered to the needs of an overwhelmingly male population in the colonial city.[27] By the 1850s, however, tolerance of this practice was wavering and the colonial authorities in Singapore acted on this case. According to "Hikayat Hikamat," Marjan was seized along with a group of other boys, and their masters were charged in court. In 1856, Edmund Blundell, governor of the Straits Settlements, took the boys under his charge and handed them over to Reverend Keasberry to be schooled.[28]

The second half of the narrative spotlights the youth's experiences at a new peak in Keasberry's Hill of Zion. Initially frightened, with several episodes recounting how the boys burst into tears whenever the missionary approached, the group eventually settled into their new home and routine of study. Keasberry had built a number of houses on the hill: a bungalow for his own growing family and another for guests, along with several buildings for a girls' day-school, a boys' boarding school, and a lithographic press.[29] These neat out-cropping of buildings appear to have left the biggest impression on the young Hikamat. When he first arrived, his fear was mixed with astonishment at the "many houses without occupants and with open doors . . . through which came through sweet sounds of singing."[30] He later expands on this idyllic picture:

[Hikamat] observed the panorama of the hill; how beautifully it was ordered and arranged by the master much like a garden. He had built houses on the hill in pairs and with perfect symmetry. The hill itself was nicely situated. The wind blew from the north and the south was sweetly shaded. At the foot of the hill was a stream, winding its way to the sea . . . [and] at the highest point of the hill, the master had built his [own] house. Around it, over the slopes, he planted many fragrant flower bushes and many fruit trees. At the right time, fruits sprouted and the flowers bloomed.[31]

This idealized depiction of Mount Zion was a turning point in Hikamat's life, when he ruminated on the protection offered by a built environment compared to that gifted by the natural one. Where gorges and caves had once lent him some refuge in an unstable childhood, houses and gardens represented security wrought by his own human hands. It was a world with clear, desirable cause and effect—plant a seed and a tree grew; create the right shelter and the winds blew gently around it.

Scholars of precolonial Asia have remarked on a mode of thinking about the climate and environment as barometers for good conduct, memorably phrased by historian Mark Elvin as "moral meteorology."[32] Often, however, the most important agent of precolonial morality is that of the leader, whose lack of integrity might invite disaster. For the majority who lived under the leader's rule, avoiding disaster through morality was still an unpredictable exercise predicated on hitching one's star to the right ruler.[33] Moreover, nature's creative force, perpetually in flux, sided with neither good nor evil. In contrast, Hikamat's nineteenth-century conversion narrative contained a new meteorological morality that hinged on the humble *individual* as an agent of good who could domesticate restless, unstable powers.

The promise of security based on an individual doing right comes across even more strongly at the narrative's ending. Hikamat closes his story with Keasberry preaching to a large flock of congregants at the public baptism of a girl called Mariam, which took place at Keasberry's hill: "You have now accepted and upheld the religion of the Lord Jesus [Isa Al-Masih] and proclaimed it to all who are here. Thus you should take care not to stray from the path of God. Praise him and pray to him that no disaster shall befall our works, and we shall escape the temptation of the devil and his whispers and that if one of our companions should fall, do not neglect to pray day and night for help from God, who had promised Jesus that you shall obtain salvation."[34]

With this ceremony at the top of the hill, the mountain was repositioned as a peak to scale, whose right path led to a summit where one could stand close to God in triumph. Hikamat's story arc reached civilization through wilderness, journeying from Sumatran uplands haunted by ghosts of tragedy to the gently rolling hills of Bukit Zion, with its clear path to salvation. The elements that arguably position this work as "modern" Malay literature—the strong authorial voice, the clear trajectory from disaster to upliftment, the focus on the everyday—are also those that negate causeless catastrophes. To convert, in Hikamat's telling, is to take one good path and eschew all others. Such a view necessarily narrows his imagination of the landscape. On that one good path, the possibilities for human empowerment through God became magnified, while powerful churnings outside receded into a blank otherness.

"TARIKH RAJA ASAL": CONVERTING WATERS

The contraction in religious imaginaries of nature was not restricted to converts forcibly dislocated to a Christian mission. Muslim Batak migrants to Malaya, despite being of a different class and religion from the formerly enslaved youth called Marjan, also faced uncertainty, violence, and risk in their journeys, to which their response was a rethinking of sacrality. The following account reflects on this period that is one step and one generation removed from its tribulations, providing a glimpse into how a family history is disciplined into a narrative that foregrounds human agency and submerges the natural as well as the uncanny. The author, Raja Yacob, was a British-appointed *penghulu* of the settlement of Papan in Kinta Valley, Perak, and a son of the previous headman, Raja Bilah.[35] Upon on retirement in the early 1930s, he wrote an account of how his family came to the peninsula, beginning with the migration of his grandfather, Raja Asal. In a short epilogue at the end of the manuscript, he clarified his intention and his sources: "My intention in writing the story of Raja Asal bin Raja Ter'ala is solely to remind my family of their history so that in the future they may know [not only] that history but also that of their people who had sojourned to peninsular Malaya and finally settled in Perak. These stories have been collected from old letters and recollections from the late Raja Bilah and some of the elderly Mandailing folk here."[36]

The family papers were deposited in the Perak branch of the National Archives of Malaysia in the 2000s. The papers contain a sprawling maze of personal letters, daily work diaries, record books of dispute resolutions, ad-

Migration routes from North Sumatra to the Malay Peninsula.
Map by Lee Li Kheng.

ministrative memorandums, and correspondence that help us appreciate the monumentality of Raja Yacob's task in shaping a narrative. The story arc presented in his family history, in the end, was a trajectory of piety opening with an invocation to God and his prophet along with the statement that this work was to be the history (*tarikh*) of Raja Asal, a ninth-generation descendant of Sutan di Aru. The Arabic word for a time-based history imputes linear time and a Muslim identity to the work; *tarikh* literally means the counting of years. The more commonly used Malay or Indonesian word for history is *sejarah*, a localized derivation from the Arabic word for "tree." *Sejarah*, unlike *tarikh*, centralizes genealogy rather than chronology.[37] Raja Yacob's manuscript was thus a history that transcended traditional genealogies and patriclans.

In 1840, he wrote, his grandfather Raja Asal left his upland village in Maga,

Upper Mandailing. His reasons were unstated; there is persuasive indication that he was against Dutch rule. Crossing the Straits of Malacca to Raub, in the sultanate of Pahang on the Malay Peninsula, Raja Asal began mining for gold, together with Mandailing, Minangkabau, and Rawa companions from Sumatra whom he had accrued along the way. Raub was so named because "people found that for every pan (*dulang*) of sand there was a handful (*raub*) of gold."[38] For more than a decade, the Sumatran men stayed in Pahang. Hearing news of a tin rush in Selangor, however, the group moved on to the neighboring sultanate. It was then that his nephew, Raja Bilah, migrated from the North Sumatran uplands to join him and the group of Mandailing that he led in 1860. Then, their fortunes slipped, and they found themselves in a serious downturn.

"And so, the world ebbs and flows, never still, always changing from one form to the next," Raja Yacob wrote of this tumultuous period. "Through the will of the Mighty One God, there arose a conflict between Raja Mahdi (the patron of sojourning tradesmen) and Tengku Ziauddin of Kedah, the Viceroy of the Realm, which stretched from 1867 to 1873."[39] Those six years of civil war proved difficult for the Mandailing migrants. Raja Asal and Raja Bilah then decided to move to the sultanate of Perak together with an estimated one hundred to two hundred followers. They traveled up the river Bernam and forded their way to Slim River, where they settled down to mine and plant rice. The group was in dire straits as there was no food to be had, "even with cash in hand."[40] Raja Bilah then sought assistance from James Birch, the newly appointed British Resident of Perak, to grant him safe passage to Malacca and allow him to transport food from the port town to Slim without hindrance.[41]

In Raja Yacob's narrative, this was the first mention of Birch. However, in Birch's own diary, he recorded a meeting with Raja Asal in which he proffered financial help in exchange for a commitment that the latter would be "responsible for peace, would allow no *gados* (fights), and would drive out every bad man who came there."[42] As the first Resident exerting colonial authority in Perak, he hoped the Mandailing would temper their restlessness and help him keep the peace in the face of hostile Malay aristocrats. This alliance proved to be pivotal in changing the fortunes of the Mandailing, though not in the way that Birch, who was killed in 1876, had hoped. Following his death, Raja Asal and Raja Bilah helped Deputy Commissioner Frank Swettenham to apprehend Birch's killers and pacify the turmoil in the sultanate. For this service, Raja Asal was awarded the right to open mines in Kinta Valley, a new tin frontier that was opening up at the upper reaches of Perak River. There, the family eventually established a settlement called Papan. Their tin ventures ultimately failed, but by that time they had achieved financial stability through Raja Bilah's work as a colonial headman, for which he received wages and a portion of the tin duties (*chabut*) exacted on the mines in his area of influence. Settling in Kinta Valley marked the end of their economic precarity; as Raja Yacob noted, "[We are] grateful that with respect to food, Allah has sustained us and there are no difficulties."[43]

Raja Yacob's narrative from this point alternated between discussing the vicissitudes of mining life that the Mandailing faced and his father's work as an administrator, laying stress on how the settlement maintained peace and prospered. With prosperity came attendant gratitude and with it a marked expansion of piety, articulated through the building of a mosque and a school to teach the Qur'an, as well as the establishment of the legal office of *qadi* in the village with the support of Raja Bilah.[44] The climax at the end of Raja Yacob's narrative was a short account of the family's trip to Mecca just after the turn of the new century. When the family returned, they changed their names to reflect alignment with a Malay-Muslim identity. Raja Bilah's new name was Haji Abdur-Razzaq, with *haji* being the honorific given to those who completed the pilgrimage to Mecca. His wife and daughter became Hajjah Zabedah and Hajjah Rabiah; these names similarly downplayed their status of *raja*, which had traditionally marked a chief's family. Raja Yacob rounded off the family history with a series of appendixes listing an eclectic collection of world events that occurred during the period he was writing about. These included the eruption of Krakatau, the war between the Philippines and United States, a timeline of various rulers of the Malay Peninsula, and events in the Ottoman Empire since 1909. The inclusion of these appendixes allows us to glimpse the larger world with which the family now identified, along with a sensitivity to scale and chronology that marked their history as modern.

Submerged within this arc from adversity to pious triumph was a parallel story about water, not addressed directly but present in key episodes. Water enabled the movement from upland mountain range to peninsula, separated gold and tin from sand and gravel, determined political control, irrigated rice fields that fed the men, and fueled the tides that swept the family on their pilgrimage across seas that ultimately redefined them. The abundance of water on the peninsula was simultaneously blessing and challenge. Hugh Clifford, a junior colonial administrator in Perak at the time, defined these aspects of water in ways that resonated with the Mandailing story:

The Malay Peninsula suffers from an excess of moisture which causes the soil to be quite inconveniently fertile and presents *a grave difficulty to those who mine for minerals at a depth of more than a couple of fathoms* from the surface. . . . In spite of the quantities of water, however, swamp-land is not a very common feature of the Peninsula. *Almost all the rice swamps are irrigated by artificial means*; there are no lakes from one end of the country to another and even the ponds are by no means numerous. *The waters of the Peninsula are almost always in motion*, for stagnant water is soon licked up by the fierce sun rays and return to earth and finds its way back into one of the thousand streams that water the land. . . . *The rivers are the highways of uncivilized Malaya*[;] . . . in the jungle it is the only real landmark and guide.[45]

The availability of water was never an issue; the challenge was in getting it to flow to where one might need it. Conversely, establishing control over a river or stream defined political authority, for doing so meant one had gained the capacity to set things in motion. Almost all significant developments in the family's history took place near rivers. Raja Asal's control of Ulu Klang, the upper part of the Klang River watershed, and later the tributary Slim at the Perak-Selangor border enabled the Mandailing not only to survive but also to establish local leadership that ultimately resulted in a change in their fortunes. To convert water, then, was to transform it from forceful to useful.

All the available mining techniques during the nineteenth century required copious amounts of water. Malays mined for gold and tin essentially by directing mounds of mineral-rich earth into a stream of water that washed away the lighter dirt.[46] The most rudimentary method was simply to scoop out the pay dirt in pans (*dulang*) and sift out the minerals. The creation of the ground sluice (*lampan*) allowed tin mining to expand to the hillsides: the area to be mined would be cleared of trees and a diversion channel dug from a nearby stream. In the channel, the heavier, mineral-bearing sand sank and accumulated at small dams and would periodically be scooped out and then concentrated in a sluice box. Similar mechanics were also behind the open-pit mines (*lombong*), where miners dug several meters deep into tin-bearing hillsides to dislodge the pay dirt, and the water in a channel below would carry away the lighter soil and leave the minerals behind.[47]

"Tarikh Raja Asal" demonstrates the importance of being able to direct water, as it describes a Mandailing settlement that had "a still pool, packed with water lilies. They [the settlers] used the water to wash tin sand. The water was then spun back into the pool to be used again."[48] The revolving waters of the pool were so central to the settlement that they named the village Pusing, after the Malay world for "turn." Moreover, water not only had to be directed in for washing, but unwanted water also had to be directed *out*. Heavy rainfall and excessive groundwater needed to be kept out of the mine to prevent it from flooding. In Raja Bilah's mine in Papan, water was bailed out with containers called *gua-gua*, while wooden supports buttressed the pit to prevent the earth from crumbling into it.[49] In this precarious working environment, inept management of water could be fatal.

Technology to direct water took a further turn when Chinese migrants began to come in large numbers in the mid-nineteenth century. From 1820 to 1830, Selangor and Negeri Sembilan produced on average only two hundred tons of tin annually, but by 1880 Selangor alone was producing four thousand tons a year.[50] Propelled by a global boom in demand for tin due to the rise of the tin-plating and canning industries, the increase in the tin industry's productive capacity over this fifty-year period correlated with a large increase in the population of Chinese in Selangor, which jumped from a few hundred in 1820 to twelve thousand in 1871 and twenty-eight thousand in 1884.[51] One key Chinese innovation was to yoke a wooden bucket-chain mechanism to a waterwheel, thus enabling up to three thousand gallons of water to be removed per hour and permitting open-cast mines to reach greater depth without flooding.[52] Gravel pumps were also introduced, although a geologist observed as late as 1903 that "it was not uncommon to see the water raised from a shallow pit by a chain of buckets operated by a human treadmill, worked by the feet of two or three men."[53] These technologies enabled deeper penetration but did not reduce the enterprise's uncertainties with regard to water, as droughts and heavy rains could significantly derail mining efforts. Still, the years from the 1860s to the 1890s featured increasing tin profits for those with the wherewithal to move water and earth on the western side of the Malay Peninsula. For a brief time in Kinta Valley, Raja Bilah's family was part of that group.

In effect, Raja Yacob's disciplined narrative tells us about intertwining conversions: his family evolved into pious Muslims as they acquired the technology to direct and harness unpredictable waters. Their tin ventures were increasingly successful: Raja Asal's outright failures and debts in the 1860s and 1870s stood in contrast to Raja Bilah's thoughtful ventures, which later generated enough profit to purchase first a horse-powered and then a steam-powered engine from England.[54] Still, the family eventually left the mining industry, unhitching their fortunes from fickle waters and turning toward an occupation unyoked to natural forces. From this point on, the ebbs and flows of fate appeared gentle, exemplified by the family's pilgrimage to Mecca, where "they sailed forth and *Alhamdulilah* (Praise be to God) safely returned, without any untoward disaster."[55] As in Hikamat's narrative, tribulations gradually narrowed into a climactic journey that connoted spiritual success, represented by the scaling of a peak or by overseas travel. In modernist, pious retellings of family histories, the individual's belief in one God was a secure bulwark against the ceaseless forces of nature. However, such disciplined narratives also discard other stories and other possibilities; their silences are as important as their contents. These gaps are important to consider when thinking about what was lost when writing about self and family took this pietistic turn.

ERASURES, ELLIPSES, AND EVACUATIONS

Returning to Ghosh's characterization of the Anthropocene as a great derangement, we may notice that one striking contention he makes is that the essence of our epoch is our textual expulsion of "forces of unthinkable magnitude that create unbearably intimate connections over vast gaps in time and space."[56] Put another way, modernist writing, with its focus on everyday protagonists, rarely addresses power beyond human agency and often limits discussion only to a single human lifetime that cannot conceive of climate change on a grand scale. In his argument, this narrow focus partly stemmed from a late nineteenth-century moment of greater security and a correspondingly reduced awareness of human precarity in nature. This was a moment when, as Ghosh puts it, "nature lost the power to evoke that form of terror and awe that was associated with the 'sublime,'" and urban colonialists were the vanguard of this change.[57] He contrasted this moment with the intuitive, long-running recognition of nature's powers documented in religious ideas ranging from the apocalypse in the Bible and the Qur'an to the *palaya* in Hindu cosmology, also known as the great dissolution.

But religion is not only ideology; it translated into an understanding of the everyday. Such translations permeated personal or family histories, past and present, in which religion was harnessed to make sense of nature. An awareness of the wider environment pervaded "Hikayat Hikamat" and "Tarikh Raja Asal," but what was left unsaid reflected the ellipses that Ghosh critiqued. What was discarded in those translations of Christian and Islamic ideology into the everyday? One conspicuous absence was that of natural forces articulated in terms of supernatural beings such as the naga. These traditional presences were excised in favor of a monotheistic divinity more distant (yet reachable through individual piety) and more powerful (yet more predictable). Modernist Christian and Muslim converts were emerging but still rare figures. When we juxtapose their narratives with other histories from the second half of the nineteenth century, uncanny beings and multiple pieties jump back into view.

One source comparable to Hikamat's reflection was an account of a Batak man called "Tom." The story of this formerly enslaved person was recounted by a pastor named John Beighton, who characterized him as a childhood "cannibal" friend living in the Straits Settlements city of Penang. Beighton's recollection of Tom's experience made much of the competition that Christianity faced from "two other religions struggling to secure him. . . . On the one side was a Burmese priest frequently visiting him, who plied him with rude pictures, and by appeals to his fears through stories of jungle demons; and on the other a Mohammedan hadji who read with him chapters of the Quran and told tales of the prowess of the prophet and the spread of Islam."[58] Beighton, like many Europeans living in the Straits Settlements, was eager to highlight exoticism in the peoples whom they encountered. Even those like Tom, who embraced the same religion, were regarded as being at risk of realigning with nonbelievers. For a brief period, Tom embraced Islam but later turned to Christianity, part of a religious journey that Beighton described as "a man who was by birth a savage and a cannibal . . . found a place for all that was mortal in him among those who sleep in Jesus."[59] Hikamat's narrative, by contrast, excised old gods to push back against those prevailing perceptions of innate savagery, focusing on a relatively straight path toward enlightenment, a path shielded from the risk of going astray. In his religious journey, he had to disregard all other faith possibilities and other peoples, except to highlight his own skepticism of them.

A similar narrowing of religious possibilities and a closed-in sense of community were evident in "Tarikh." Here, the erasure of other gods involved eliminating the optic that viewed tin as a living being. Colonial administrators, European miners, and missionaries provided a wealth of observations on the local view of the uncanny and on how local communities managed environmental risks through ritual, by propitiating spirits that animated tin; all these were absent from Raja Yacob's narrative. "The Malay miner," wrote Abraham Hale, inspector of the mines in Perak in the mid-1880s, "has peculiar ideas about tin and its properties; in the first instance, he believes that it is under the protection and command of certain spirits whom he considers necessary to propitiate; next he considers that the tin itself is alive and has many of the properties of living matter, that of his own volition it can move from place to place, that it can reproduce itself and that it has special liking for certain people and things and vice versa."[60] The notion of living tin came across in many rituals in Selangor, where Raja Asal first mined. Based on interviews with Selangor pawang (Malay shamans), philologist Walter Skeat translates direct commands to tin ore:

> Peace be with you, O Tin Ore,
> At the first it was dew that turned into water
> And water that turned into foam
> And foam that turned into rock
> And rock that turned into tin-ore
> Do you, O Tin Ore, lying in a matrix of solid rock
> Come forth from this matrix of solid rock
> If you do not come forth
> You shall be a rebel in the sight of God.[61]

In these sources, the Malay shaman was ubiquitous in tin-mining enterprises. Dressed in a black coat that only he could wear, he prospected for tin by communing with the spirits; a good pawang had a "wonderful nose for tin," appreciated and sought by Malay and Chinese miners alike.[62] He also kept order in the mines by adjudicating disputes, enforcing rules, ensuring that taboo conduct was avoided, and deciding on compensation for infractions. Significantly, the magician was a personage of considerable importance in *both* Chinese and Malay enterprises.[63] Historian Teren Sevea, in the most broad-ranging analysis of the pawang to date, depicts the tin-prospecting magician as being embedded in "cosmopolitan networks," where Malay *raja* and Chinese mine owners (*towkay lombong*) acted as patrons to sustain these men and their magic.[64] What united these diverse communities was the environment of precarity that they constantly faced: the risks of financial failure, disease, landslides, and fatal accidents while handling water for extraction and fire for smelting. These anxieties were remarked on in British assessments of the tin miners' world and also evident in their addresses to spirits that inhabited the mountain, river, and tin ore and were capable of transforming good or ill fortune at pivotal instances.

These supplications to spiritual elements of the environment ultimately mixed older beliefs with Islam. For instance, an 1892 manuscript by a Selangor magician told of a snake that produced tin and gold ore; it was expelled from the heavens with Adam and sank underground. The geological distribution of mineral-bearing alluvial deposits thus depended on the snake's writhing.[65] The amalgamation of supernatural beings and the serpent from the Abrahamic religious tradition demonstrated that earlier conversions to Islam in the Malay Peninsula absorbed rather than excised traditional elements of religion embedded in nature. The association also worked the other way around, with venerated Muslim figures brought into the world of traditional spirits. The Muslim prophet Khidir, for instance, became known in the Indian Ocean regions as a protector of travelers, esteemed by both Hindus and Muslims, and in the North Sumatran context he became linked to Puteri Hijau, a legendary underwater spirit, with the pair commonly depicted as being robed entirely in green.[66] The fluidity of these folk religious beings encompassed the migrant's world. For much of the nineteenth century, Chinese migrants lit candles at sacred nature sites of the Malays known as *keramat*, such as earth mounds.[67] One such site in Larut, an active mining community from the 1840s to 1880s, was the grave of a female saint who dispensed supernatural milk from her right breast to the Muslim community, or ummah, and from her left breast to the Chinese miners who employed a caretaker for this *keramat*.[68]

Reading "Tarikh Raja Asal" in this light, we find two key erasures. The first is the downplaying of the Chinese-Mandailing associations in the tin mines in favor of emphasizing a bounded Mandailing Muslim community.[69] Comparing "Tarikh" with the historical record of Raja Asal, one may observe a striking gap in events: his heavy involvement with the civil war in Selangor and deep associations with the Chinese mining community there. Far from being caught up in the middle of a conflict between warring Selangor aristocrats over which they had little control, Raja Asal and his compatriots were linked to the Chinese miners who took sides in the power struggle between Raja Mahdi and the viceroy, Tengku Ziauddin. Violence erupted between these competing Chinese tin-mining outfits, organized along ethnic lines. The two most powerful organizations were the Fei Chew, whose members were of the Hakka ethnic group and based in Kuala Lumpur, and the Kah Yang Chew, a Cantonese group whose base was farther north, in Kanching.[70] According to the biographer of Yap Ah Loy, the Hakka Chinese leader, the Mandailing were initially allies in supporting Raja Mahdi, who was a far friendlier figure to migrants than the viceroy.[71] Kuala

Lumpur, Yap's base, was at the muddy confluence of three rivers, and Raja Asal securely held one of them—the Klang River, which enabled supplies to flow into Kuala Lumpur. However, when the tide turned against Raja Mahdi and he was driven out of Klang Valley, Raja Asal and Yap both discreetly switched sides to obtain assurance from the sultan that their territories of influence were secure.

It is their role in this conflict that provides us with an explanation for the Mandailing people being near starvation, as they fled into Perak after finding themselves unable to buy rice even though they had the means. Theirs was a failure of strategic political kinship, explained summarily and euphemistically in "Tarikh" as one of God's trials. In April 1872, Raja Asal turned against Yap, diverting supplies that the latter had charged him to transport down Klang River.[72] The Mandailing-Rao group he led then banded together in a war against the sultan of Selangor and his viceroy. The gambit failed, as the viceroy ultimately prevailed with help from the rulers of neighboring Pahang. The anger and enmity of both the Selangor and Pahang rulers toward the Mandailing-Rao migrants ran deep. Some of Raja Mahdi's supporters were pardoned, but when the Rao surrendered to a Pahang chief who promised to spare their lives, the viceroy proceeded to orchestrate their massacre. Only two Rao men escaped, while Rao women and children were carried off by the Pahang chiefs and enslaved.[73] The Selangor sultan, Abdul Samad, sent out a royal missive forbidding trade with the Mandailing and ordering the execution of their leaders.

Any number of reasons might explain why this bloody episode of shifting loyalties and kinship was left out of familial collective memory; the truth cannot be ascertained from this distance. Nor can we assume that the silence was deliberate. What is of interest, however, is the net effect of the lacunae. As in "Hikayat Hikamat," this silence lends a bounded insularity to Raja Yacob's narrative, thus excluding all other gods, agentive beings, and spiritual means of managing nature's risks to mining ventures, which both migrant communities had shared. Moreover, like Hikamat's resolute Christian faith, these textual disassociations from communities outside a circle of faith served to reposition personal and family experiences in an empowered textual space when this sort of empowerment was denied to them in reality by a colonial structure that utilized the uncanny to define a backward Other. In these personal writings geared for future generations, Hikamat and Raja Asal claimed agency to effect change as converted individuals.

That limited empowerment nonetheless worked through a myopic focus on human lifespans untethered to other scales of time on earth, particularly geologic time. This brings us to a second silence: the environmental solipsism of "Tarikh Raja Asal." This silence echoed in the disconnects among time, event, and space formerly embodied in figures like the naga, whose continuous movements were linked with crisis and disaster. Such silences were loudest in depictions of tin mining that cut out the magical figure of the pawang, thereby leaving the slow disaster of the enterprise—previously expressed in fear of landslides and erosion—unacknowledged.

Small-scale miners worked by directing streams of water against hills, leaving behind not only waste tailings that washed downhill and silted up rivers but numerous pockmarks in the soil. The siltation of rivers was further exacerbated when trees on the hillsides were chopped down as fuel for smelting tin. By the 1870s, this fuel harvesting had resulted in significant forest cover depletion, denuded hillsides prone to erosion, and clogged rivers in Larut, the area most worked by migrant miners. As mining enterprises expanded with the consolidation of colonial authority, the large holes left behind became "a great eyesore" that gave "a bad impression of the country to the casual traveler," according to mining historian Carey Ross.[74] The holes transformed river ecology, with some becoming lakes as they filled up and overflowed due to the constant flow of water directed at hillsides. In at least one case, crocodiles abandoned the silted river and made the new lakes their home.[75] The worked-out areas were too degraded to convert into agricultural land, let alone return to forest. E. W. Birch, the acting British Resident of Perak, fretted over the number of Malay peasants who chose tin mining over agriculture even as it became clear by the 1890s that tin deposits accessible through use of the ground sluice, or *lampan*, were running out. He opined that the colony's stability depended on an agricultural Malay peasantry.[76] While such views stemmed from a broader colonial suspicion of Asian enterprise writ large—in tin mining, European firms had initially been unable to compete with them—they indicated that the environmental impact of these enterprises was nonetheless real and observable.

"Tarikh Raja Asal" was not oblivious to these landscape transformations, as evidenced by Raja Yacob's note on Mandailing Malay vocabulary for the mining process. He mentioned four terms to describe mining, each evoking damage, force, and lacerations to earth: *meludang* (to scoop out), *melereh* (to use the sluice or *lampan*), *mencabik menajak* (to tear out), and *menebuk* (to make holes). There was a place in Papan, he remarked, called Tebuk Seratus, meaning "a hundred holes."[77] Nonetheless, mining was foremost a means of personal uplift for Raja Asal and Raja Bilah, as seen through their pride in the expansive size of their mining enterprise. It was at one point "the largest Malay mine at the time, staffed by hundreds of who[m] were all Malay."[78] Pride was tempered with humility: they reconciled their position in benefiting from the mines by invoking God's will as a reason for their success. In a religious chronotope in which the human lifespan is temporary, central, and divorced from place, personal progress can be privileged and colonization replicated on multiple scales. It was an extension of everyday religion, long primarily concerned with production and reproduction and now newly combined with a sense of empowerment through atomized temporality and ruptures generated by colonial encounters. For a brief human lifetime, risk from and fear of a potent earth could be buried within the space of a disciplined narrative, especially when articulated from a distance.

And yet, can they be retrospectively blamed for opening a path to degradation and loss? As powerless migrants dislocated in a fast-changing landscape, their efforts in focusing on improving their personal lot, adapting to colonial structures of governance, and finding a god that promised eternity apart from this fragile world were empowering approaches. They developed a moral meteorology along a spectrum: on the one end, the pawang, who saw risk as the protests and agency of a living earth, and on the other, the modernist Christians and Muslims who viewed the earth as an entity to be acted upon with appropriate intelligence and conduct. I would argue that the latter optic was less about mindless obliviousness than a purposeful estranging from the non-human natural world, which divorced human action from an agglomeration of natural forces. It was a coping mechanism whereby an individual in a changing landscape could reclaim power: from the naga simultaneously spinning creation and destruction, from competing migrants with shifty alliances, and from the pawang who mediated between the seen and the unseen. This new power extended to a closed community of similar faith and values.

A newfound faith in the individual as an empowered actor nonetheless blinkered capitalistic entrepreneurs, large and small, from anticipating cumulative environmental loss. From 1892 onward, European mining enterprises gained a competitive edge in the industry by using hydraulic mining to target low-grade ores in hillsides unworked by small-scale Chinese and Malay outfits. Hydraulic mining produced five to six times more waste soil, creating "dead zones" on which nothing could grow. This was followed by the development of capital-intensive dredging of valley floors, perceived as less environmentally damaging and wasteful. Dredges, it was initially argued, did not displace earth from the hills into rivers, caused less siltation, and relieved pressure on overworked areas. However, data analysis of sedimentation from long-running dredging activity decades afterward showed high degrees of contamination, reduced oxygen, and increased turbidity in Perak's rivers.[79] Whether this could be solely attributed to dredges was a matter of debate.[80] Only relatively recently has there been scientific consensus on their harm, which Carey Ross evaluates as "mass destruction."[81] This destruction occasioned little mass protest, despite disastrous consequences to the rural population throughout the twentieth century, including the flooding of agrarian settlements and damage to small-scale fisheries. Faced with loss, like the Mandailing tin miners, many felt empowered only to move on.

These narratives of Hikamat and Raja Asal, written almost a century apart, show how Batak migrants experienced the fast-changing landscape in the Malay Peninsula during the second half of the nineteenth century. Our narrators utilized religion to understand themselves and their new environments. Their stories demonstrate how complex, interfaith communities—seen and unseen, human and nonhuman—were reduced in personal and family memoirs into moments of pious triumph meant to inspire future generations. Such reflexive writings were part of a modernist turn in Malay literature; the texts in this case also imbricated conversion in a broader colonial thrust toward development. Focusing on an individual's successful temporal path into a monotheistic afterlife was a significant way in which one could harness religion to imbue with meaning their personal concerns about production and reproduction. It is worth noting that migrant workers in other mines around the world also had their spirit patrons, which similarly lost their potency around the same period. Take, for instance, the widespread belief in Tommyknockers—spirits of the dead who might lead one to rich veins of ore but whose knocking presaged death—spread among Cornish migrant miners in the American West in the nineteenth century. These beliefs had faded by the 1930s, as technology to see better in the mines superseded the miners' instincts and "feel."[82] In the Malay Peninsula, too, technology played a part, but mechanistic knowledge was folded into a religious schema of superior human agency.

As with all microhistories, what has been presented here is an exceptional record of everyday belief and practice in the form of rare narratives that made it to an archive. While they may not be representative of the broad mass of peoples in Sumatra and Malaya who faced dangers and risks from the nonhuman natural world through the pawang and his prayers, these narratives show that a vanguard of migrants driving the push toward modernity dictated in colonial terms various new articulations of everyday religion to meet their everyday needs. On a practical level, religious action lay on a spectrum between the modernist rejection of submission to any power but one God and the fractured multiplicities of spirits whom one could supplicate. Christianity and Islam reconciled the unprecedented technological power that was part of the Anthropocene with the everyday concerns of production, negating constant worries about risk from a potent earth. In some ways, what Ghosh perceives as derangement in the Anthropocene is a long-running extension of a moral meteorology that reflected spiritual progress in an acquiescent natural world, now enacted on a more democratic scale. Seeing the faithful as favored was a means of individual, common empowerment that erased or muted agency from the earth and resituated humans in a spiritual landscape estranged from the power of the natural world. There was a material impact accompanying these new articulations of everyday religion, and it affected two things that once represented the potent landscape: the camphor tree and the elephant.

MATERIALITIES

FIVE Camphor and Charismatic Retreat

"Did it not concern them that something so uncanny was taking place?" wrote Dutch missionary J. H. Neumann after witnessing a ritual dialogue between Batak Karo villagers and their ancestral spirits in 1916. "Elsewhere it is certainly no ordinary event if one crosses the border between the living and the dead! Or does this border not exist in their thought? Do the dead and the living animate each other?"[1]

Neumann's rhetorical question highlighted a significant aspect of animistic religious life in the uplands: the immanence of the dead within the living and the living within the inanimate. Ancestral spirits of the dead protected and haunted a village. Any material body—human, plant, animal, rock—had the capacity to contain an indwelling spirit. The camphor tree embodied this immanence, as was evident in the dancing spirit Nan Tar Tar Nan Tor Tor, eternally trailing camphor while eluding a hostile *begu* and a lovelorn human husband. These trees, along with the village rituals that Neumann observed, rapidly retreated to the margins of national socioeconomic life over the course of the early twentieth century.

The Sumatran camphor tree (*Dryobalanops aromatica*) can be seen as a fulcrum of the changes to this potent landscape that gradually alienated many Batak communities from their local environments. The tree is an endangered species of hardwood, another apparently generic victim of deforestation that ensued from a well-documented, early twentieth-century plantation expansion toward the uplands of East Sumatra, which became encircled by lands allocated for cash crops such as tobacco and rubber.[2] Indeed, the plantation is so central to the Anthropocene that a growing number of scholars are dubbing it the "Plantationocene."[3] Extractive, enclosed plantations often robbed the landscape of flora and fauna for the benefit of a single cash crop and constricted the diversity enabled by small-scale farms, pastures, and community forests. Literature on the plantation economy in various parts of the world has highlighted how flows of capital and labor into this industry destroyed indigenous cultures, reduced biodiversity, and forced the natural environment into an unnatural standardized symmetry while maintaining pockets of subsistence for its laborers.[4] With the rise of the plantation in Sumatra, camphor trees, not being amenable to cultivation, fell by the wayside.

The tree's experience under this assault of plantation agriculture at the turn of the century was nonetheless unique in narrating a larger conversion in which potent forests were rendered increasingly impotent through religious conversion. This aspect is often overlooked. Imperialism did not simply entail ecological destruction or exchange but also reflected a critical moment when affiliations between humans and nonhumans were reevaluated. These interspecies affiliations weakened with the political demise of local charismatic religious leaders, who can be defined in Weberian terms as personages with "specific gifts of the body and spirit . . . believed to be supernatural, not accessible to everybody."[5] Bereft of this leadership, communication between the material and spirit worlds shrank, occluding immanence. Extending the turn toward textualization examined earlier, charisma in all species was rationalized to deemphasize the miraculous and incorporated into a legal system in which governance did not value the personal. The retreat of the camphor tree thus brings into view how the growth of localized Protestantism and political economy mutually reinforced unequal structures of power established during this epoch.

These changes occurred in two stages. First, in the wake of the Singamangaradja dynasty's military defeat by the Dutch, a period of mass conversions to Christianity and emergent millenarian forms of the old religion unfolded. Dutch conquest of the uplands, where the camphor tree grew most densely, set in motion environmental changes that reshaped the religious landscape. One key religious change that occurred here was a shift of emphasis from the immanence of the dead in this world to transcendental possibilities for the living in an afterlife. Lived religious practice, even in new everyday forms of the old religion, became focused on renovating the human faithful, based on the promise of a better future life rather than a continuation of the older lifeways.

What role did these religious conversions play in transforming a subsistence economy into a cash-cropping one? What forms of nature thrived and what declined? Here, the vicissitudes of the camphor tree illuminate the material impact of such conversions. The camphor economy had limited the circulation of cash and the accumulation of capital by underscoring divinity and chance in the allocation of wealth. In the new colonial economy, the fickle economy of camphor was sidelined as a source for potential profits. Smallholdings of vegetables, rubber, and benzoin took its place, encouraged by Dutch policies that facilitated the adoption of scientific agriculture in the uplands and by missionaries similarly keen to bring development to new believers. In this newly rationalized forest, camphor trees were felled on a large scale, not for their resin but as timber. The felling of forest fed into the rise of cities on Sumatra's east coast, which drew upland migrant settlers, estranging the living from generations of their dead. Colonialism and Christianity thus worked in concert to reduce indigenous dependence on the woods as an intact ecosystem that had been crucial in the quest for camphor. The newly Christian Batak, converted into small-scale agriculturalists, were often uneasy with these plantations' effects. They would later reach back to precolonial customary norms (adat) to articulate a local environmentalism, symbolized no longer by camphor but by benzoin, whose trees provided frankincense.

PLANTATION EFFECTS

The man who was to become the last Singamangaradja was just twenty when he declared war against the Dutch in 1878. One night, five emissaries hung a *pulas*, a tapioca root carved into the shape of a man, at the gate of the Dutch base at Bahal Batu. Three tiny spears of bamboo stabbed the tapioca-root figurine, on which was inscribed in Batak script the words "total enemy, enemy by day, enemy by night."[6] The implacable declaration of enmity toward the Dutch colonial government catapulted this man toward death and immortality. Today a national hero for his anticolonial efforts, his image is honored on thousand-rupiah notes, exchanged daily in the same cash-based capitalist economy that precipitated his death. Contemporary reports by Dutch officials portrayed their military actions in Batak territories as necessary intervention against a brutal native who threatened the safety of Christian missionaries, while nationalist histories cast Si Singamangaradja XII as a humanitarian defending the freedom of his peoples. The diversity of these military accounts, eyewitness testimonies, and oral family stories makes up a history we should read through rather than with.[7] Although most of these narratives placed undue focus on the actions of Si Singamangaradja XII as the prime mover of anticolonial turmoil, documentary evidence suggests that his declaration merely capped a years-long tension with the colonial state, which had already prepared itself for a confrontation with the Batak. Two years *before* Si Singamangaradja's rash public announcement of hostility, the Dutch colonial government had already issued an internal memorandum that outlined plans to annex Silindung and its environs.[8] What were the imperatives for such preparations?

The best place to start is perhaps not with the man Si Singamangaradja XII but with the tobacco plantation. Most accounts of the rise of export-based tobacco plantations in Sumatra begin in 1863, when Jacobus Nienhuys, a representative of the Pieter van den Arend tobacco company, obtained the right to cultivate the crop on a plot of land in the sultanate of Deli on Sumatra's northeast coast.[9] Colonial law later opened the way for his success to be replicated across Sumatra. An agrarian land law passed in 1870 by the Dutch colonial government in Java encouraged foreign investment in the colony by permitting local rulers such as the sultan of Deli to profit from granting long-term land concessions to foreign firms.[10] Such investments aimed to shift the burden of raising state revenues away from forced cultivation (*kultuurstelsel*) onto the private sector, in line with what the Dutch later termed a liberal phase in their rule.

The plantation economy runs in contradistinction with the wild, cashless, elusive camphor economy. Cigars packed into boxes of perfectly standardized rolls were the main consumer product from this plant and an apt representation of how spaces were reorganized through its production. When a person removed the tobacco leaf wrapper from a cigar in 1870, a perfect wrapper would be "light in color, rich in grain, thin in texture, small in vein and stem, very elastic and of good burning quality," and it would ideally be large enough to divide nicely into four pieces.[11] Filler leaves were shorter and had a medium body with a rich brown color, and they burned smoothly, producing a desirable aroma. They were harvested from rectangular seed beds, built about thirty centimeters high and surrounded by ditches dug alongside passageways for laborers. These laborers planted the tobacco at regular intervals in holes ideally measuring about ten centimeters deep and seven centimeters in width. They kept the beds well watered and staggered the transplantation of seedlings so that they would all reach the appropriate sizes.[12] The plants had been transferred to these uniform beds after a formative spell in a similar plot of soil that had been well spaded, watered, and spread with just the right amount of wood ashes before being thoroughly compacted by a heavy roller. The flat beds were made possible by burning the land a week before planting, a common practice that simultaneously enriched the soil with the nutrients from ashes while freeing it of grasses and weeds. The perfect space for intensive tobacco cultivation was a bounded, compact grid in an interior alluvial valley, empty of other inconvenient plants, having soil that was deep, porous, and ideally fertilized by the periodic overflow of rivers.

The Batak were familiar with trade crops, but their fields were rarely designated exclusively for them. Pepper and coffee were grown in the interstices of swidden rice fields and crops rotated through several plots of cleared land. Swidden entailed less clearing of land, and as the same field was used for rice, pepper, and coffee, farmers did not remove as many grasses and weed species as monocropping tobacco did.[13] Another important crop, benzoin trees, was also integrated into this mosaic landscape. These gardens retained a biodiversity comparable to secondary forests through the coppicing—the practice of cutting a tree or shrub to ground level to stimulate growth.[14] Moreover, the Batak's swidden rice fields and pepper gardens encouraged mobility. The Batak farm (*ladang*) was relatively more mobile than that of the lowland Malay, perhaps best seen through the differences in their pepper gardens. Pepper vines in Batak gardens were supported by dry sticks staked to the ground, which were easy to place and remove, unlike the pepper vines in lowland coastal Malay areas, which were wrapped around hardwood trees grown expressly for that purpose.[15]

The two systems were essentially opposites, swidden being a labor-scarce and land-rich system while plantations were labor-rich and land-scarce operations. But they were not irreconcilable. Planters could and sometimes did graft tobacco cultivation onto existing subsistence farming systems, extracting what Michael Dove terms a "subsidy" from the land by allowing the forest to regenerate once the soil was exhausted from tobacco growing.[16] From the other end, some 350 Batak and Malays took the opportunity to work for the plantations in 1873, mainly as porters plying goods up and down the river.[17] With large profits at stake, however, there was a growing clamor for more land. These calls were initially resisted by Pieter Philip van Bosse, the Dutch minister for the colonies, who opined in the early 1870s that they had neither the means nor the military might to annex more territory.[18]

RETREAT OF THE CHARISMATIC PRIEST-KING

Conflict, however, seemed inevitable. From the perspective of European planters, their position was precarious. The Sumatran east coast area of Deli, where most of these plantations were based, was connected by the Deli, Hamparan

Perak, and Percut Rivers to the Karo Batak highlands. They were governed by their own chiefs, who were nominally allegiant to the sultan of Deli but in practice largely autonomous.[19] At the same time, migrant laborers were being brought in to work on the plantations, where they created their own autonomous spaces at the peripheries.[20] This influx of cheap, often indentured labor from China and Java, as well as the independent Batak behind their barrier (*bongbong*), created restless pockets of "peri-capitalist" spaces, to borrow Anna Tsing's term, that were simultaneously both inside and outside capitalism.[21] The bodies and living spaces of these groups interfaced with and at times resisted the production process, puncturing it with periodic violence. In 1871, a group of Chinese laborers murdered two European planters: seven of the culprits were subsequently hanged and another fifteen sentenced to forced labor.[22] In 1872, a Batak Karo chief from Soengal who was displeased with the sultan of Deli for granting a land concession in the area killed another chief in defiance and fled to his brother-in-law in Tingkat Langkat to mobilize an army of a thousand Batak and five hundred Malay men.[23] The Dutch had to aid the sultan in quelling this uprising, resulting in a campaign that dragged on into 1873. The conflicts highlighted two major threats that involved mobilized locals who were numerically superior to Dutch forces, despite the latter's colonial hegemony on the island: the first from undisciplined labor conscripted into the production process and the second from a pan-Batak and Malay unity that could overwhelm the plantations.

Missionaries, surrounded by uncertain converts and the unconverted, felt a parallel tension. For much of the nineteenth century, the independent Batak territories had provided a useful geographical and religious buffer against what the Dutch perceived as the threat of a pan-Islamic alliance between Muslim Minangkabau and Aceh. But with the outbreak of the Aceh War against the Dutch in 1873, close on the heels of the Soengal conflict, there were fears that this neutrality was eroding. Thus, when rumors circulated that Si Singamangaradja XII had announced that an Acehnese force was coming to aid him in eliminating mission stations, this threat was taken seriously. In response, a Dutch force mobilized in Toba to confront the *pulas* challenge thrown down by Si Singamangaradja XII. With reinforcements, the Dutch force numbered slightly under three hundred but was equipped with guns, grenades, and mortars.

Weaponry, unlike in the Padri War decades earlier, proved decisive. About 6,000 Batak men armed with rifles, spears, and various blades clashed with the smaller Dutch force in Toba in 1878. To Batak combatants, Dutch bombardments seemed like "fire from the sky," and only a fifth of the Batak men were left fighting two days later.[24] They still outnumbered the Dutch force of 6 officers and 233 soldiers but were no match for them, whereupon the Batak retreated north, first to Butar and then to Lintong in independent Batak Dairi territory. From the Dutch perspective, the fight was "difficult and bloody"; from the Batak perspective, it was devastating.[25] Some villages were burned in an act of strategic violence. When five villages were torched in anti-Dutch Lobu Siregar, news of this destructive act incentivized the chiefs in Tarutung, Sipoholon, and Bahal Batu to switch allegiance to the Dutch and pay a 1,500 gulden fine rather than face the same fate. Bakkara, the ancestral base of Si Singamangaradja, was not spared after surrender. It was destroyed, claiming dozens of civilian casualties, after he and his followers evacuated to the village of one of his fathers-in-law in Samosir.[26] Not all villages shrank back: another of Si Singamangaradja's fathers-in-law apparently burned down his own village during the fight.[27] Such resistance was ultimately futile. By the end of the 1878 campaign, the Dutch controlled most of the larger villages in Toba that had supported Si Singamangaradja XII.

However, the priest-king was still able to regroup, partly because of his multiple marriage alliances. Between 1878 and 1883, he married at least seven women.[28] Marriages, with their reciprocal sacred obligations, increased the soul power (*sahala*) of both parties and burnished his charisma. With his kin by marriage, he harassed mission stations and colonial officials and regained the prestige lost in earlier defeat. Seeking a decisive victory, he then launched an attack on his former stronghold at Laguboti, where he made some territorial gains but had effectively been beaten back by August 1883. More than thirteen villages were burned a second time in the environs of Balige and Bakkara and eighty-four in Tambunan and Laguboti. A huge volcanic eruption at Krakatau in that same month, visible from North Sumatra and causing ash dispersal across the Indian Ocean, punctuated the end of this 1883 campaign.[29] Aghast at this bad omen, wounded, and his forces spent, Si Singamangaradja XII fled. In the aftermath, one of his strongest commanders turned against him and became a staunch Christian, while another founded a new religion. A final campaign in 1889 attempted to retake Silindung Valley but limped to a final defeat.

The Dutch *controleur* Pieter A. L. E. van Dijk visited Toba in 1889, and his report helped to produce the first extensive map of the area, which showed the extent of Dutch knowledge and control of the highlands at the time.[30] Marking out only dense village centers and how they were fortified either through natu-

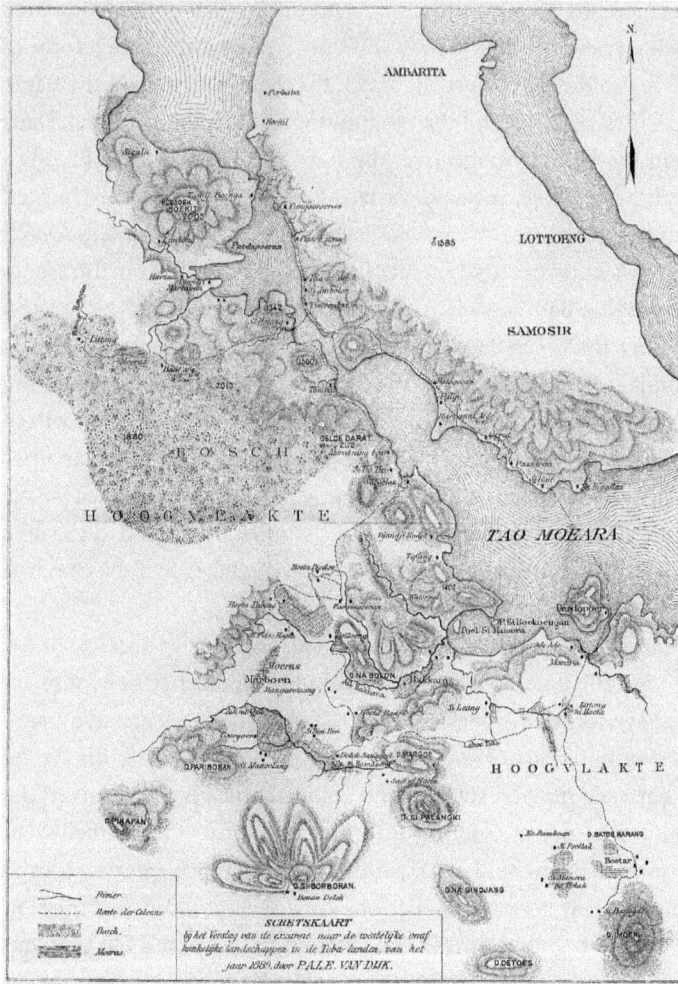

Pieter A. L. E. van Dijk's 1889 map of Toba. Source: P. A. L. E. van Dijk, "De Excursie naar de Westelijke Onafhankelijke Landschappen in de Toba-landen van het jaar 1889," *Tijdschrift van het Koninklijk Nederlandsch Aardrijkskundig Genootschap* 2, no. 7 (1895), map attached as appendix to the issue.

ral elevation or constructed defenses like those at Bakkara and Butar, the map represented the changing landscape of Si Singamangaradja's former territory. The Dutch chose to entrench their position in these villages rather than chase Si Singamangaradja and his followers deeper into the forest for more territory. On the map, the spaces between these nodes of Dutch control reduced the unknown resistance into blank areas on paper.

These blank areas shrank rapidly. Another map drawn from Van Dijk's information about six years later demonstrates how quickly Dutch power was administratively asserted and intertwined with religious conversion. In the aftermath of 1878 and 1883, perceiving the presence of white missionaries as a hedge against the destruction of their villages, many Toba Batak chiefs invited them to set up stations in their villages. Laguboti, devastated in the 1883 campaign, acquired a mission station in 1884, apparently at the behest of surviving chiefs. Others came to Sigumpar (in 1886), Narumonda and Parsambilan (1890), as well as Uluan and Nainggolan (1892).[31] After the 1889 campaign, Christianity reached the island of Samosir in the middle of Lake Toba, which the Rheinische Mission was happy to report as one of the benefits of annexation.[32] Closer to the Deli plantations, Dutch planters began to finance missionary activity in the Karo uplands.[33] Acting on advice from some missionaries, Dutch colonial officials appointed chiefs in service of the new government and motivated their cooperation by exempting them from corvée labor, a privilege also accorded to Batak church elders, teachers, and preachers.[34] This move enhanced an aura of power around schools and churches. "Baptism," according to a Dutch anthropologist's analysis of this period, "became the marker of collective upward socialization."[35]

Batak animist datu were largely excluded from these new colonial chieftainships, although their traditional roles had overlapped considerably with those of the *raja*, or chief. The Dutch defined the datu's role as spiritual rather than political and forcibly separated these two dimensions through their appointments.[36] The new colonial administration then fixed the leadership to territory by restricting movement outside the established villages. Prior to this restriction, a Batak man dissatisfied with his local leadership could gather a band of followers and move out to establish a settlement as a new *raja*, but now this mobility was curtailed by the Dutch. Si Singamangaradja XII continued to fight a lonely guerrilla war at the outskirts of this territory until 1907. But with his charisma spent, the age of the mobile Batak farm on a dense forest's edge was essentially over.

RECONSECRATION IN MILLENARIANISM

Mass conversions to Christianity did not eliminate adat as a social articulation of ecological understanding of the divine. One unexpected consequence of the fall of Si Singamangaradja XII was his almost simultaneous rise as a millenarian deity in a new pantheon that fused Batak animism with monotheism. His death and subsequent consecration through the Parmalim, Na Siak Bagi, and Parhudamdam movements harnessed some aspects of adat to protest landscape transformation effected by colonial rule. These reformed offshoots of animism were nonetheless a break from the past and became invested in everyday resistance, banking hope for a future detached from a dismal present. Si Singamangaradja XII's posthumous potency was less rooted in the spirits inhabiting local natures and partly fed off the landscape's degradation.

The first millenarian movement was founded by a man with the title Guru Somalaing. He was a datu of the Pardede *marga*, whose base was in the northeastern part of Lake Toba. Parting ways with Si Singamangaradja soon after the latter's 1883 defeat, he returned to his ancestral village and claimed he had received a divine prophecy in a dream foretelling how he was to heal the land. "Then the Lord Jesus appeared in my place of retreat and while my body remained on the earth, my soul was raised to heaven by him and brought before God. This gave me to understand that I am the '*anggini Tuhan*', the brother of the Lord, that by Him I am sent in order to preach a new doctrine to the people and that my followers are the *Parmalim*."[37] He found validation for this prophethood when he encountered the Italian anthropologist Elio Modigliani, who was traveling in Toba in December 1890. Modigliani introduced himself as the subject of Raja Roma, a figure whom the Batak peoples associated with Raja Rum, a powerful ancestor in Batak and Malay legends. Modigliani took Somalaing as a guide for his travels through Toba; from this association, Somalaing perceived himself as having imbibed the spiritual prowess of Raja Rum, confirming his qualification to teach a new doctrine.[38]

This validation from a foreign traveler mistaken for the emissary of a long-dead emperor conveys how the movement was looking outward for new sources of divine power rather than tapping into local natures. Those sources were diverse but markedly derived from Abrahamic faiths: the name Parmalim was derived from *muallim*, the Arabic word for teacher, and Somalaing called God "Jahova," from the Judeo-Christian tradition.[39] Parmalim as a faith was not monotheistic, though, and its followers revered a wide pantheon that included

Si Singamangaradja XII and Raja Rum, as well as Batak divinities such as Debata Na Tolu (the spirit ministers of the Batak High God, Mula Jadi Nabolon), the dragon Naga Padoha Ni Aji, and the first human to fall to earth, Si Boru Daeng Parudjar. These were accompanied by the sultan of the Ottoman Empire and the Virgin Mary.[40] Followers sang hymns set to the beat of the Batak drum, praising Lord Jahova, Maria, and Lord Jesus. Spirits of divinities often entered the devotees, giving voice to prophecies that the Dutch would be expelled from the area in seven years. Contemporary analyses of the movement saw this diversity as a desperate search for someone who could save the Batak from Dutch colonialism.[41]

The elevation of Si Singamangaradja XII to this pantheon did not translate into material support of the Parmalim for the man himself, still running a futile resistance in the forests of Dairi. Rather, his title appeared to be a place-holder for a reformulated local charismatic figure not necessarily related to the actual dynasty. Some Parmalim in Habinsaran, for instance, identified the new missionary working in their area as the new Singamangaradja, while another Batak man in Asahan from the Sinambela clan, which was unrelated to the Singamangaradja dynasty, made the same claim.[42] The sacred authority of the Singamangaradja lineage had depended on being able to work miracles in nature and to mediate between upland Batak societies and external powers. With military defeats, the dynasty's prestige declined. Men like Guru Somalaing who broke away from Si Singamangaradja XII perceived divinity when it was manifested through earthly power. In the wake of loss, he sought the source of that power in others while asserting it himself; he claimed, for instance, that acceptance of his teachings would guard his followers from cholera.[43] Ironically, Si Singamangaradja XII's reconsecration reduced his charisma by equating his specific gifts to those of others and disavowing the supernatural cosmology that had previously authenticated the Singamangaradja dynasty.

Moreover, that natural and supernatural world around the Batak was rapidly being converted and meshing with alternate faiths. On one level, there was Christian conversion, which diluted village bonds as differences in religion became awkward wedges in the performance of public duties. Some Batak Christians chose not to take part in rituals to propitiate spirits during rice-planting season, for instance. Others found little use for the magical *pangulubalang* guardian sculptures that had long protected the village.[44] A minister in the Karo uplands approvingly remarked that although converts in the area were few, if the Christians boycott "the feasts of their heathen guru, then the heathens [eventually] do as the Christian does."[45] He further commented, "They [the nonconverts] frequently see that nothing terrible happens to the Christians who lay aside their customs . . . so heathenism dies here because it can give no more that satisfies."[46] This was a decidedly optimistic view of decline; the Karo uplands, distanced from the violence in Toba, were the slowest to convert, and Christians were a minority there until the 1960s.[47] However, it also contained a grain of truth. While official conversion rates were low, a few observers did find that seasonal village feasts held to honor kin by marriage and celebrate the harvest were noticeably fewer after the mid-1910s, attesting to detachment from traditional rituals.[48]

Parmalims, for their part, refused compulsory labor imposed by either the colonial government or the Christian churches. At least one Christian Batak priest complained about Parmalim who refused to help build a community school and church:

> Every day they [the Parmalim] make a circle and play the drum, eating and dancing, for they do not like to go to work. This is because their teacher said, "Let the Christians and the pagans work hard. Someday, Guru Somalaing and Ompu Barnit would come back from their places of exile. Then the earth would be broken, and all of the Christians and the pagans would disappear. But we will be happy. On that day, the kingdom of our raja Si Singamangaradja and our Tuan Raja [Rum] will be declared."[49]

This millenarian heaven, however, seemed more Christian than the adat-based paradise; its hopes gestured toward how everyday religion had grown to encompass a longer-range vision that resisted today and instead hoped for a better, remote tomorrow. Somalaing and several other key Parmalim leaders were arrested in the mid-1890s. Si Singamangaradja XII was shot dead by Dutch forces in 1907. However, millenarian movements in their names continued to pop up with a regularity that alarmed the Dutch over the next three decades. They were religious expressions of ongoing dissatisfaction with the everyday, occurring apace with a landscape that was being rationalized through the intensification of small-scale agriculture, the building of roads, and new circulation of cash.

RATIONALIZING LANDS

A focus on tomorrow became intertwined with an imperial notion of development in which profit became a marker for successful renovation of self and place. An institute for the study of the Batak (Bataksch Instituut) was set up in 1913 to focus on research that could develop the area and its peoples.[50] In report after report by researchers and Dutch officials running the newly unified Tapanuli Residency, large sections were dedicated to analyses on how to push Batak peasants to produce more in the future: experiments on seeds that could give higher yields or were disease resistant, promotion of crops perceived as profitable, scientific studies on soil composition to earmark which area was suited for pepper production, best growing conditions for rice and benzoin, and how to utilize fertilizer.[51] On the surface, the newly annexed Batak areas maintained their sedate agricultural holdings, as plantations on the Sumatran east coast did not lie on uphill slopes. But imperialism left its mark as a model of colonizing land and systematizing agriculture for more predictable yields that deemphasized the miraculous and facilitated the turn away from old gods. The controleur in charge of the Batak Karo uplands in the mid-1910s observed a growing indifference to the spirits of the land, and he attributed this to the rational example of government agronomy programs. "The more the Karo see demonstration experiments of how seed selection, tillage and the use of organic and artificial fertilizers on their scant fields means an increase in yield, the less they worship their old spirits," he reported.[52] We need not accept such perceptions as objective truth. Still, whether or not faith in the old gods wavered mainly due to scientific agriculture, there was a perceptible expansion of agricultural land at the expense of forest in the aftermath of conquest. Although statistics for the conversion of forest to agricultural land during this period are not available, a pattern of acceleration after colonialism and conversion is observable through the proxy measure of tiger-human conflicts. Tigers thrived in the ecotones created between forest and newly cleared land; an increase in these conflicts and an ultimate drop in the numbers of tigers were indicative of the pace at which land was being cleared.

Traditionally, the Batak had managed the tiger threat with a combination of kinship, traps, and magic. Toba Batak women used to carry out rice planting under large baskets made from plaited rattan, which as one European observer noted was "a means to protect themselves against the royal tiger, who was often to be found in this region and who was very dangerous, as it is a well-known fact that the tiger, though usually attacking peoples unawares and from behind, walks away if the first leap fails."[53] Some Batak clans claimed kinship with spirit tigers as patrons and called them "grandfather" (opung).[54] One of Si Singamangaradja's fathers-in-law was a Raja Babiat Situmorang; babiat, the Batak word in his title, refers to the spirit of an ancestral tiger. A Toba Batak bark book (pustaha) speaks of a method of divination that originated from "our grandfather, the striped tiger from across the ocean."[55] Among the lowland Batak in Asahan, the claw of a dead tiger was used as protection against evil spirits, especially those with shape-shifting powers able to take the form of tiger or man at will.[56] Traps were sometimes set for them; such traps consisted of wooden cages made out of young tree trunks driven firmly into the ground with a dog (or a young, bleating goat in Muslim areas) as bait. When a tiger entered, a trapdoor fell, blocking its exit and separating the animal from the bait. It was believed that a tiger would only walk into this trap if it was set with the magic spells of a specialist. Tiger datu specialists might also prepare offerings of rice and fruit to the animal; they laid these gifts at the border between their villages and the forest in hopes that the village would be spared its unwanted aggression.[57]

Tiger numbers swiftly fell as Dutch colonialism redirected agricultural practice. South Tapanuli, infamous for its large tiger population at the inception of Dutch rule in 1840, had seen a precipitous drop in their numbers by the 1880s. Mandailing and Rao, the areas where tigers had been most abundant, saw an average of five hundred to six hundred tigers killed every decade until the 1930s.[58] North Tapanuli had fewer tigers, but after the Dutch conquest in the 1880s, a similar increase in conflicts between humans and tigers ensued, with a corresponding drop in the latter's numbers. Despite claiming kinship with some tigers, the Batak had never been particularly averse to hunting them, and the penetration of firearms during the war with the Dutch gave them increased power to do so. The spring gun (poting), a contraption rigged with a gun to fire when the animal activated a tripping device, emerged during this period. It replaced an earlier weapon called belantek malam, meaning "spear of the night," that used a spear in place of the gun.[59] Such weapons were not only used against tigers. On Modigliani's visit in 1890, he collected a Batak bark book whose colophon praised the datu owner as a man who "kills elephants, wielding his gun."[60] The ability to kill rather than mediate with megafauna became incorporated into a datu's repertoire of spiritual prowess.

Increased conflicts between humans and megafauna sharing the forest were exacerbated by another aspect of the ongoing rationalization of the landscape: a transportation system that rendered the uplands accessible in unprecedented ways. Road building accelerated in the early twentieth century. North and South Tapanuli were united into one administrative unit in 1905, and roads connecting them followed. Without roads, the potential profits from coffee and vegetables grown in the uplands would not have been enough to justify the effort to bring them down.[61] The centerpiece development plan for Tapanuli was a set of roads that looped from the port town of Barus in West Sumatra up to Toba, then south toward Mandailing, downhill to Sibolga, and finally circled back to Barus via a coastal road.[62] Barus was strategically located for the boats sailing up and down the coast from Singkil in Aceh to Sibolga in Tapanuli Bay. Before the roadbuilding commenced, the flooding of the river on which Barus was located had to be stabilized. The Dutch had dug some canals in an attempt to control the annual overflow of Sungai Batu Gerigis, but the effort resulted in such massive erosion that a customs post had to be hastily removed and rebuilt across the river, where the silt had accumulated.[63] As an alternative to these unpredictable waters, the Barus-Sibolga coastal road was to provide a means of transporting goods and facilitating trade overland. A similar transformation was also under way in the Karo and Simalungun areas, which were not incorporated with the rest of the Batak in Tapanuli but administered under the Sumatran East Coast Residency.[64] There, too, roads replaced rivers as a favored mode of transportation between the uplands as plantations mushroomed under Dutch rule.

With roads came cash. Increasing numbers of Batak began to take on temporary jobs at plantations to acquire the necessary currency to discharge new burdens such as buying exemptions from corvée or paying a poll tax, first introduced in 1908. The new cash economy had numerous impacts on the upland forests where the circulation of coins had once faltered. The churches also played a part by stimulating money lending through credit cooperatives, which gave low-interest loans to struggling peasants. This microcredit financing also enabled small-scale cultivation of cash crops such as benzoin, which some missionaries encouraged as a means of helping the parish prosper.[65] From the mid-1910s, the colonial administration spurred the formation of "people's banks" (*volksbankjes*), where small deposits and loans could be made. The first of these banks was set up in Karo in 1915 and in Toba in 1917, with a mix of capital raised by community leaders and a contribution from the colonial state.[66] As banks like the Toba Agricultural Bank (Tobaneesche Landbouw-bank) were established to finance agriculture, they stimulated cash circulation, which in turn promoted land clearing and provided small amounts of capital to migrants and Batak alike. The plantation economy thus pulled the uplands into its orbit through these new circulations of money and credit, which moved from cleared lands in the lowlands to clear lands in the uplands. While on the surface the uplands' small-scale agriculture appeared to be in contradistinction to the expanding lowland plantations, they were essentially two halves of the same system.

Such changes to the land left an imprint on the many iterations of the millenarian movements that followed the Parmalim from the 1890s to the early 1920s. The dynamics appeared standard: a man from rural Toba would claim to have had a dream of prophethood; this self-designated prophet would accrue followers through a message of anticolonial noncooperation based on old Batak values; the movement would simmer down through the arrest and exile of the self-proclaimed prophet, only to flare up again as a new one emerged. However, a closer look showed that with each iteration, Parmalim messaging subtly drifted further and further from reenergizing the kinship between land, humans, and spirits. From the 1890s to the 1920s, the movement instead grew to embrace a renovation of the self not unlike that prescribed by the emergent Protestant ethics that embraced capitalism.

Among the prophets who came out of Toba after Guru Somalaing were Ompu Barnit and Guru Pamosik, whose cases were illustrative of Parmalim movements in the 1890s. Like Somalaing, they located power not only in indigenous values but also in the person of the missionaries. A German missionary named Pohlig appeared to have been particularly subject to Parmalim attention; groups of the latter approached him with offerings from their communal feasts, believing that the soul power of Si Singamangaradja had been transferred to him.[67] It was not only his charisma that drew them but also his knowledge of modern machinery and guns, according to a statement Guru Pamosik made while in detention. Technology, the kind that subdued the tigers of North Sumatra, was being perceived as a source of power, supplanting that drawn from mutually giving forces between the natural world, the living, and the dead. As such, these Parmalim initially submitted to Dutch rule, and they rebelled against taxes only when forced to pay pro-Dutch Batak chiefs rather than remit directly to white Dutch officers. Restricted from moving and taking the mobile *ladang* elsewhere, they were later involved in local quarrels over land (*sawah*) rights with these same chiefs.[68]

At the turn of the century, the Parmalim of the 1890s briefly morphed into a movement called Na Siak Bagi, a term that literally meant "the unfortunate."[69] Its founder, a Toba Batak man named Si Jaga Simatupang, was not a displaced datu but a goldsmith. As gold was currency in the uplands, he doubled as a small-scale banker and partly leveraged this position to gain influence. Although he identified as Parmalim, his preaching and cause differed substantially from that of Guru Somalaing. Eschewing the multifaith pantheon and undue awe of Pohlig, Na Siak Bagi invented instead a communitarian capitalism based on Christian ethics but devoted to the Batak High God, Mula Jadi Nabolon. Drawing on the Christian concept of sin, he preached that the Batak plight was a consequence of personal sin against the High God. He advocated love for all human beings, manifested by, among other practices, the establishment of funds for the unfortunate poor and interest-free loans, which undermined the church's efforts in this direction.[70] This reconceptualization of transgression was markedly different from taboos and offenses against adat. Transgressions against Batak adat were deeply interrelational, as adat was structured to maintain a web of social relations. Sin, on the other hand, was intensely personal. Na Siak Bagi was built on personal accumulation: the development of prowess through virtue, with the ability to be virtuous partly dependent on wealth. Significantly, its progenitor declared that wealth (*hamoraon*) was his staff (*tungkat harajaon*). The foregrounding of wealth downplayed two other traditional pillars of social status—a large number of offspring (*hagabeon*) and esteem (*hasangapon*) through kinship alliances. Predictably, support for his ideas expanded most rapidly in Batak areas closest to the plantations: Uluan, Habinsaran, and Toba Holbung.[71]

Na Siak Bagi retreated when Si Jaga Simatupang was arrested in 1910. In the ensuing decade, the Parmalim caused unrest again through a movement called Parhudamdam, a term derived from an onomatopoeic contraction of their signature chant.[72] Again, taxes were among the bones of contention between the upland peoples and the colonial government. However, new issues arose as the rationalization of the uplands reached a different stage. The flashpoint for conflict was no longer competing visions on how to order the natural, human, and spirit worlds. Rather, having largely ceded control over their territory, the Batak's own bodies were at stake. The Parhudamdam, most active from 1915 to 1918, attracted a new generation of followers too young to have personally experienced Si Singamangaradja XII's struggle. For adherents using traditional charms and magical provision of weapons, a particular pull was the group's promise of invulnerability against bullets; when the time was right, their leaders promised that sugar palm trees would become guns and sticks would become rifles. Convinced of their invulnerability, this group set themselves against several policies instituted by the Dutch colonial government, including a very unpopular compulsory vaccination program.[73] In subsequent clashes between the colonial police and this group, a considerable number of Parhudamdam died, eroding the invulnerability mystique, and the movement eventually evaporated in the 1920s.

The evolution of Parmalim beliefs and organization in this period demonstrated how the connections between humans, spirits, and land progressively weakened even among those who resisted conversion to Christianity. Humans, spirits, and territory were atomized to the point where the human body became the focal unit of faith. Si Singamangaradja XII had fought to keep the territory, with its priests and spirits, autonomous; the 1890s Parmalim withheld their labor from activities such as road building, which wrought deep changes to their land, but began to embrace technology. Na Siak Bagi went further by folding a capitalist Christian ethos into social aims. Finally, the Parhudamdam resisted primarily to protect and limit access to the adherents' own bodies. On the surface, these movements all appeared to be similarly abortive attempts at resistance through religious revitalization, following Anthony Wallace's definition of "a deliberate, organized, conscious effort by members of society to construct a more satisfying culture."[74] All of them used Si Singamangaradja XII as a figurehead and promised his return. At a deeper level, however, each movement successively turned away from what he stood for. With each prophet who promised a reinterpretation of the old faith that could enlighten the dismal present, the focus of resistance and ritual increasingly pivoted on the individual believer rather than more-than-human connections.

The millenarian character of these movements differed substantially from those predicted through existing paradigms, such as Michael Adas's classic argument that violent social protest tends to follow from the displacement of local elites, a sense of relative deprivation, and challenges to the legitimacy of current sociopolitical structures.[75] Unlike this theory's prediction, sporadic violence generally failed to gain wider traction in the Batak uplands. The hallmark of these movements was persistence rather than confrontation. Crafted from successive prophets' capacity to graft the invasive new faith onto the old and navigate defeat in a changed landscape by renovating themselves, Parmalim millenarianism was a religion of persistent resistance rather than conflict. The upland peoples' few confrontations, such as the fight against vaccination, only underscored how much their religion had turned its focus toward the human. Millenarianism essentially rendered the remnants of Batak animism anthropocentric. As mass conversions and prophets stressed a future savior rather than the immediate immanence of their ancestors' spirits in nature, these religious changes would have a material effect on their forest ecology. This is symbolized best by the retreat of the camphor tree.

CAMPHOR DEMYSTIFIED

Amid these changes, what determines which nonhuman natures survive, which thrive, and which die? These questions call for analysis by considering the contrasting fate of the trees that yield two resins that had defined the Batak uplands to the outside world: camphor and benzoin. The camphor tree declined in numbers and density at the same time that benzoin trees became a valuable cash crop and came to symbolize Batak indigeneity. In 1873, an American pharmaceutical periodical predicted the decline of the camphor trees and good prospects for benzoin in the following terms:

> At present the dense forests of Battak [sic] land still contain hundreds of thousands of camphor trees, but the Battak cuts away recklessly without a thought for the future and without planting fresh camphor trees. . . . What is [also] found most abundantly is the valuable benzoin, the fragrant resin that is used for incense and other perfumes. . . . Remarkably enough the Battaks take great care that other benzoin trees rise up to replace those cut down, for in fact, they have nothing else to do than to burn the stumps and scatter the seeds in the ground. The planting of gutta and camphor trees appears to require more trouble and care, more at least, than is compatible with human labor and duty in the opinion of the Battaks.[76]

This view of the reckless Batak, too feckless to engage in the tricky cultivation of camphor, echoed early modern Europeans from Marco Polo to William Marsden to Friedrich Junghuhn and indicated early Dutch interest in regulating the cutting of Sumatran camphor trees.[77] What we see here, however, is that the camphor tree fared no better and in fact much worse under Dutch rule. As the natural world became increasingly more legible to human examination, the camphor tree found itself under the microscope for possible exploitation.

I argue that the central factor in determining the survival of a species of tree was how amenable it was to marketable cultivation. *Dryobalanops aromatica*, with its long history of noncompliance with human commerce, grew acutely vulnerable in this new environment.

The first scientific treatise assessing the properties of the Sumatran camphor tree was published in 1856. Written by Dutch botanist Willem Hendrik de Vriese, it described how *Dryobalanops aromatica*, so named because it belonged to the genus of resin-producing trees, had several unique features that camouflaged its potential bounty.[78] Camphor from the tree came in two forms: natural white crystals or disk-like flakes that collected in the crevices of the tree and an essential oil that flowed through the trunk. The liquid component of the resin did not stream outward but moved inward: "near the pith or heart, are natural fissures in which the juice accumulates, which, gradually coagulating, sticks to the wood in the form of small pieces of camphor."[79] He also drew attention to the rarity of the Sumatran camphor tree's flowers. Very few observers had reported seeing them, as the tree bloomed only every seven years or even less frequently, and when it did, flowering was accompanied by uncannily "unhealthy . . . hot exhalations during that period."[80]

In some ways, these studies were simply offering scientific descriptions of properties that the Batak had mythologized: the difficulty in spotting whether a tree concealed a valuable camphor harvest and the challenge in systematically cultivating a tree that rarely bloomed. De Vriese's analysis went further, however, by comparing the Sumatran camphor tree with its camphor-producing cousins of other genera. The Sumatran camphor tree was unlike its camphor-producing kin in Japan and Taiwan, *Cinnamomum camphora*, an evergreen laurel that was easier to cultivate. This variety of the camphor-producing tree announced its richness through its "shining[,] triple-nerved" leaves and its glistening trunk that yielded the oily resin, which could be gathered in bowls when incisions were made on the trunk.[81] De Vriese's juxtaposition of both trees was echoed in other popular and scholarly articles on camphor in the United States and Europe.[82] It was an indication of the incipient competition between the two species that would soon take off when worldwide demand for camphor intensified to unprecedented levels.

Why were American periodicals interested in the Sumatran camphor tree? In the United States and Europe, camphor had long been a popular folk medicinal drug, a "cure-all for mothers, grandmothers and great-mothers down through many generations."[83] East Asian camphor, however, had cornered the market in this cheap offering for the masses, while Southeast Asian camphor from Sumatra and Borneo fed luxury demand because of its perceived superior quality. Renewed interest ensued from a new use for camphor that upended this market segmentation: the invention of celluloid. First developed in the late 1850s, celluloid required camphor; it was a key input in the production of this lightweight, photosensitive material. Camphor's use in photography was enabled by Alexander Parkes's discovery in 1862 that burning it left behind a solid residue on photographic collodion. Over the next three decades, coated celluloid gradually displaced the heavy glass plates formerly used in cameras, thanks to a process that scientist John Wesley Hyatt refined to make mass production possible. Hyatt's experiments were motivated "by his quest of the perfect billiard ball which would replace the expensive ivory article," as described by a fellow materials scientist.[84] By 1889, his billiard ball project had ended in failure, but scientists in the United States had patented flexible celluloids, a move that revolutionized the film industry by making motion pictures possible. Incorporated into the manufacture of plastics to produce leisure for people halfway across the globe, camphor experienced a boom in demand, which placed increasing strain on both forests and camphor-harvesting communities in Asian uplands.

In this global context, interest in Sumatran camphor was reignited in Europe and the United States, where its high price had previously limited its use to pharmaceuticals. With their expanding authority over the North Sumatran uplands, Dutch colonial administrators were initially enthused about the prospect of profiting from camphor. De Vriese himself saw his botanical work as the cornerstone of a modern colony, declaring that "science and civilization must be the foundation of the prosperity of the lands and peoples of the Indies archipelago."[85] The project to exploit trees was thus simultaneously an effort to modernize peoples, which reversed what Europeans such as the linguist Van der Tuuk had previously perceived as wasteful and corrupt practices in the camphor trade when artificially restricted by Batak chiefs.

With the breakdown of traditional authority, there was an immediate though brief explosion in camphor exports. In the aftermath of the decisive 1883 victory over Si Singamangaradja XII, exports of camphor from the colony jumped more than fourfold, from 26,000 kilograms in 1884 to 106,000 kilograms in 1885.[86] Camphor in the global market would soon become virtually synonymous with the East Asian variety. But throughout the mid-1880s, the amount exported from the Dutch East Indies was comparable to that of that variety's

CAMPHOR EXPORTS FROM THE DUTCH EAST INDIES
AND TAIWAN, 1885–1895

	Dutch East Indies camphor	Colonial Taiwan camphor
	EXPORTS (kg)	EXPORTS (in kg)*
1885	106,000	188
1886	81,000	80,100
1887	101,000	165,400
1888	22,000	230,000
1889	26,000	250,599
1890	2,000	434,510
1891	2,000	1,132,890
1892	3,000	1,052,434
1893	2,000	1,999,196
1894	2,000	2,372,827
1895	2,000	948,280

* Data for colonial Taiwan comes from Tavares, "Crystals from the Savage Forest," 122. I converted Tavares's figures from *pikul* units to kilograms (1 *pikul* equals 60 kilograms).

major exporter, Taiwan. However, Dutch colonial camphor exports began to drop drastically from 1890 onward.

Starting in 1890, however, that initial interest appeared to have petered out. Instead, an arrangement was made to send a fixed amount of camphor to Singapore and Penang for sale, as reflected by the near constant figure of 2,000 kilograms in the colony's annual report of exports in the early 1890s and a note in the 1890 annual report that camphor from Sumatra was now being shipped only to these British trading ports.[87] Despite the rising demand for camphor as a raw material for celluloid in the United States and Germany, the report in 1893 noted that "the decreasing exports can only be caused by reduced demand in the Singapore and Penang market. . . . Camphor trees are still very much sufficient in the forests of Tapanuli [North Sumatra]."[88] In the meantime, prices rose steadily; camphor sold for twenty-four to thirty-six gulden per kilogram in 1893, but the price had reached seventy-five gulden per kilogram by 1911. In the mid-1920s, the price of camphor hit an all-time high in conjunction with the expansion of the film industry. It was precisely at this moment, however, that camphor dropped out of the list of key exports in the Dutch colonial East Indies annual report, having become too economically insignificant to count.

The reasons for this drop in the level of camphor exports are not entirely clear. That it occurred despite booming prices made this drop even more puzzling. "What shall we do for camphor?" wondered a British naturalist, worried about the prospect of British merchants being cut out of the camphor trade in East Asia as a Japanese monopoly appeared likely with the latter's conquest of Taiwan. The answer, however, did not involve looking toward Southeast Asia. Some trading firms in British Singapore did travel to Sumatra in the 1900s to examine camphor samples available in the colony, but they declined to make any deals.[89]

Dutch colonial records suggest that not developing the camphor trade sector despite high worldwide demand was a deliberate policy, which appeared to come from the highest levels. In 1884, the Tweede Kamer (lower house of the Dutch parliamentary body) vetoed a proposal to add research on forest resins to the Dutch universities' science curriculum for future colonial administrators.[90] No money was allocated for transport or research infrastructure to facilitate camphor extraction in this forest frontier. A tentative plan to build a road from upland forests to the port in Singkel was scrapped despite enthusiastic support by camphor traders.[91] The matter-of-fact colonial reports do not explain why these decisions were made, but one possible reason was the political unrest that still pervaded much of the uplands region. Between Si Singamangaradja XII and the millenarian movements, large parts of the uplands remained noncompliant with Dutch rule.

Moreover, the reluctance to leverage camphor as a source of economic development could also be due to the properties of *Dryobalanops aromatica* itself, which deterred both potential sellers and buyers. Camphor remained, as it always had been, tricky to identify and elusive when chased. Moreover, the tree appeared resistant to efforts at systematic cultivation; the Dutch were no more successful in trying to create a camphor garden than the Batak had been. Several American attempts to domesticate *Dryobalanops* camphor trees on their own soil had failed as well. "Neither of these plants [*Dryobalanops aromatica* and *Blumea balsamifera*] can be grown in the United States, except possibly in southern Florida, without protection against cold," reported an American botanist for the US government.[92] The tree was "too tender for the climate of the United States," was the conclusion of another assessment.[93]

Older Batak perceived failure to profit from the camphor trade as a sign those who sought to exploit the trees had neglected to perform the requisite rituals. The younger generation and new economic migrants ended up cutting down empty tree after empty tree. This indiscriminate cutting drew the scorn of old camphor seekers (*bona hajoe*), one of whom was interviewed in 1917 by a Dutch anthropologist called de Ligny. "In the past, the princes forbade the cutting of trees except in certain tree complexes [de Ligny's note: very heavy—thickly forested or very old]. Whereas now, no matter how small or young, if men suspect there is camphor, the tree is cut and the beauty of the forest is lost. You will see," said the aged camphor seeker, "that among the Dairi, those who did not follow adat will cut down more and more empty camphor trees." Referencing the Batak legend, he added, "She (the tree) exhibits the spirit of the ancestors (*sombaon*) but the fools, they are accompanied by [her endlessly searching husband] Si Pagedag Si Pagedog."[94]

There had been a certain symmetry between the legend of Nan Tar Tar Nan Tor Tor and the camphor seekers of the old economy, with the camphor tree acting as mirror. In the world of spirits, a betrayed wife tries to elude the unwanted attentions of a powerful spirit (*begu*) and is doomed always to run and never reunite with the human husband who seeks her. In the human world, the camphor seeker desires to elude unwanted forest dangers, articulated as hostile spirits, and is doomed to chase a valuable harvest that always quickly evaporates. These shared risks and sufferings intersected in the camphor tree, where they "made kin" between human and spirit, to borrow anthropologist Donna Haraway's term.[95] With the evacuation of spirits from the landscape on the heels of religious change, desacralization of the natural beings they had inhabited followed suit. Controleur Middendorp in the Karo uplands observed with some satisfaction that "just as in newly-organized Karo society the sovereignty of the village states was undermined, so also was the sovereignty of the countless spirits undercut."[96] It was an observation with which the Dairi camphor seekers might have agreed. In the asymmetric new economy, risk and grief between human and nonhuman were no longer shared in production.

The magic of the Sumatran camphor flame was also demystified scientifically. One of the first extensive doctoral dissertations on the history and properties of camphor was authored in 1919 by the American botanist William Richtmann, who compared camphor obtained from Sumatran hardwood with the East Asian laurel in terms of their relative melting points. He also established their molecular composition.[97] Viewing *Dryobalanops* camphor merely as $C_{10}H_{18}O$ relative to laurel camphor's $C_{10}H_{16}O$ dismissed notions of its inherent superiority. Skepticism toward the famed quality of Sumatran camphor, once worth twenty times more than East Asian camphor on the market, followed from this clinical unpacking of its attributes. Richtmann's research indicated that Sumatran camphor could be artificially prepared from laurel camphor, further undermining its exceptionalism. Moreover, where camphor was merely viewed as raw material for celluloid, its quality did not matter much. British forester Isaac Burkill, in his definitive analysis of Malayan forest products, reached the same conclusion as the Dutch: the best way to market *Dryobalanops* camphor was in small quantities. He wrote, "The price is partly maintained by the very small output. There is no chance of a larger trade in it, and a greater output would destroy the partly fictitious value that it has."[98] Consequently, the British colonial government in Malaya also declined to expand *Dryobalanops* camphor exports from the trees in its colony.

Imperial disinterest in *Dryobalanops* camphor was accompanied by a corresponding interest in the seemingly more easily grown East Asian laurel camphor tree. In the early 1900s, deterred by *Dryobalanops* but mindful of potential high profits, Dutch botanists experimented with the possibility of cultivating the laurel camphor tree instead, running experiments in the Cibodas Botanical Garden on Java to see whether a fast-growing variant of it could be cultivated there.[99] The initial signs were promising, reported an 1896 article in *Nature*, since the laurel camphor tree "colonizes freely and is now naturalized in several countries."[100] Unfortunately, the promise of laurel camphor trees' colonization and naturalization in the Dutch East Indies dimmed when the fledgling seedlings in Cibodas were decimated by a "red spider" pest outbreak in 1909.[101] The project appeared to have been aborted soon after, leaving the market for camphor to be dominated by the Japanese.

These deliberate decisions not to pursue a larger market share for Sumatran camphor should have been good news for the camphor tree. However, as enthusiasm for camphor resin profits dimmed, attention for profits from another, more potentially destructive use of the tree emerged: timber. Burkill, in the same paragraph in which he decried the fictitious value of *Dryobalanops* camphor, noted that "at the present time, the camphor which the tree gives is far less important than the timber but in former times, the reverse was the case."[102] British foresters in Malaya found the tree "gregarious," as its resin was elusive, and they solved the mystery of its irregular flowering with the discovery that the soil composition of the watershed in which it grew was the main factor for such variance.[103] The foresters concluded that camphor tree stocks could be maintained at sustainable levels through regenerative felling, so trees were harvested at regularly spaced intervals.

It was uncertain whether this technique, spottily practiced in British Malaya in the 1930s, was ever adopted in the Dutch East Indies. In the early 1900s, camphor wood, deemed valuable for its easiness to work with and for its capacity to repel insects, found its way into houses as beams and was used to make boxes and travel trunks, resulting in a spree of apparently unregulated cutting. Thus, even as camphor exports languished in North Sumatra, the tree itself remained in danger. It was felled at such an alarming rate that Tapanuli Resident L. C. Welsink issued a moratorium on its cutting in 1907.[104] But this policy was only temporary, and moreover, it targeted only indigenous timber-felling enterprises. In 1912, the Resident gave a Dutch company called Nijverheid Houthandel Singkel sole license to exploit wood in a land concession of thirty thousand hectares in North Sumatra, half of which had a heavy cover of camphor trees. The company noted that the camphor tree yielded timber of outstanding quality but that there was not much promise in bringing the wood to Europe because of the high transportation costs.[105] The growing demand, in the company's initial assessment, meant that the outer islands of the East Indies should provide affordable wood for cities rising within the colony. From then on, it was for this purpose that the hardwood tree was exploited. Lumbered with other woods, the monarch of the forest's final indignity, it seemed, was in being devalued and regarded as just another type of timber.

GARDEN-VARIETY ACQUIESCENCE

The striking devaluation of the camphor tree was accompanied by an expansion of Batak enterprise in another resin: benzoin, also known as frankincense. Benzoin related the uplands to the plantation and the colony's rising cities. The Toba poet Sitor Situmorang reflects on this connection from the vantage point of his childhood in late 1920s Sibolga, then an important town in Tapanuli: "This was a time that the city [Sibolga] was the center of the world for the mountain people. There they sold benzoin and let their children go to school or had to appear before the court, because Sibolga was the capital of the region. In former times, the trade in incense was one of the main inland activities. Trade in benzoin had seen ups and downs and we could all see this from Sibolga."[106]

Cash crop trading, schools, and administrative power were connected here in a manner reminiscent of Willem Iskander and Ephraim Sutan Gunung Tua

Harahap's experiences, discussed in chapter 3. In this sense, the Toba Batak were playing catch-up through benzoin rather than coffee. The coffee-profiting educated elite had already ensconced their children in the upper echelons of colonial power: Ephraim Harahap's son Djamin, for example, was appointed head district prosecutor (*hoofdjaksa*) in Sibolga in 1915.[107] The Toba and Karo Batak, however, were considered less civilized. To travel down Bukit Barisan on a north-south axis was to journey along a path of what was perceived as increasing levels of civilization among the Batak. For the Toba, Dairi, and Pakpak, benzoin provided access to mobility.

The upland peoples of North Sumatra had traded benzoin for centuries. What distinguished this fresh rise of benzoin trading? One phrase that repeatedly surfaced in colonial reports captured the difference: the Dutch benzoin garden (*benzoëtuin*).[108] What did this garden look like and how did the Batak work it? On a strip of land allocated by a village chief, cultivators planted the seeds of benzoin trees amid crops of sweet potatoes, corn, and sometimes rice. For the first five years, the harvest came from the food crops; the land usually could no longer sustain rice production after two cycles, but the growing benzoin trees shared nutrients well with the root crops as long as other shrubs were kept away. When the trees attained a height of ten meters and a trunk of about twenty centimeters in diameter, tapping for the resin could begin. During the tapping process, a man climbed up the tree with the aid of a fiber rope lashed around the trunk and made a series of incisions about one centimeter long, drawing the resin in the trunk to the wound. After six to eight weeks, the resin would have solidified along the loosened bark, enabling it to be scraped and collected in rattan baskets. The process was repeated after six weeks to obtain a second harvest and possibly a third, collecting about 250 grams of benzoin per cycle, while the tree itself could continue yielding resin for almost a decade.[109]

"Garden" was not the word used by the Batak who cultivated benzoin themselves. They spoke instead of going into the benzoin woods (*tombak haminjon*) to tap trees for resin, making no distinction between cultivated benzoin trees and those that reproduced naturally. But the benzoin woods of 1870 and of 1930 were likely very different. P. H. Brans, author of the first scientific doctoral dissertation on Sumatran benzoin, noted that by 1930 "there is no longer 'rimboe' [jungle] which benzoin tappers had not penetrated[,] and where the specimens had grown in the wild originally, it had been expanded or planted into benzoin gardens."[110] Nonetheless, unlike a monocrop plantation, the benzoin garden still maintained a simulacrum of primary forest ecology. Where peasants were unable to continue pure swidden strategies of the past, the *ladang* plot was transformed gradually into a garden with a "closed canopy structure" that resembled the forest, having a base of tubers and shade-tolerant plants, a middle level of small, fast-growing trees such as banana, and the top level of tall benzoin trees. With the dense canopy, crop diversity, and intercropping of annuals with perennials, yields did not seriously deplete the soil.[111]

The benzoin produced was sold to Chinese traders, mainly in Sibolga, and to a lesser extent in Barus and Medan. With increased access to ports, scientific attention to pest control, and rotated cropping, the garden system intensified benzoin cultivation and enabled it to be sold at an unprecedented scale. Some elements of traditional management remained: when the supply of trees was exhausted, planting and harvesting moved elsewhere, allowing the depleted area to return to forest. Through this hybrid forest-garden system, export levels grew steadily, increasing almost twentyfold, from around 0.1 million kilograms in the early 1900s to around 1.93 million kilograms in 1919.[112]

The amenability of benzoin trees to sustainable garden-making demonstrates why this particular resin-bearing tree thrived. Benzoin harvests were predictable, suited to systematic planting, and appropriate for small plots that could also support subsistence crops. Moreover, it provided a means of maintaining kinship through adat in a disrupted landscape. Benzoin enterprise allowed land rights to upland tracts not particularly suited for tobacco and rubber plantations to remain in the hands of the Batak. These plots were allocated through adat while being divorced from the ritual that had marked animist belief in the collecting of camphor. Both Batak Christians and Batak animists participated in the planting of benzoin trees, and benzoin gardens also became inheritable property in a way that wild camphor trees could not. The benzoin garden, unlike camphor tree culture, did not depend on propitiating wilderness. Instead, it rested on anthropocentric management, and descriptions of rituals linked to its maintenance appeared limited to rice offerings made when the trees were first planted. Benzoin was cultivated largely by Toba, Dairi, and Pakpak peasants, but each Batak subregion had its own "benzoin," namely, a crop that combined small-scale enterprise and new beliefs. The Mandailing had coffee, imposed by force decades earlier but later locally embraced, while the Karo had potatoes, which came in tandem with missionaries.[113]

The prevalence of small-scale agriculture geared toward export showcased how the logic of the botanical garden permeated indigenous enterprise. Dutch botanical experiments, a crucial aspect of this period of European colonialism, were particularly successful when the outcome was a product that had global demand, was relatively easy to cultivate in the colony, and whose raw material supply could be integrated with the manufacturing chain. Chincona bark, used in the pharmaceutical production of antimalarial quinine, is the best exemplar of such a product from the Dutch East Indies.[114] Across empires, the botanical garden became a site for the exchange of easily grown trees. The Japanese in Taiwan tried to learn from the Dutch in cultivating cinchona at the same time the Dutch were trying to adapt Taiwan's *Cinnamomum camphora* trees for their own purposes.

Benzoin gardens were part of this botanic colonial mosaic, even as the enterprise stayed largely in indigenous hands. Cultivating benzoin trees seamlessly placed the hybrid forest-garden into a supply chain, where the resin could be transformed into local aromatic and pharmaceutical products. Demand was global as well as local. Globally, benzoin was an aromatic ingredient in items as diverse as pastilles and toilet cleaning liquids. Locally, it featured in the ritual life of the Batak, especially among the Parmalim, who burned benzoin in rituals to commune with the spirits. This demand was steady, smaller than that of quinine, and paid much lower prices than for camphor, but nonetheless it was sufficient to motivate the growth and regrowth of such trees. Camphor trees, on the other hand, defied the garden. With the greatest demand for it coming from the celluloid industry, *Dryobalanops aromatica*'s chances for survival hinged on its being cultivable in large enough quantities to capture the global market. Given the nature of the tree, this did not happen. Instead, it joined a long list of tree varieties considered superfluous in the new economy and at risk of being cleared for the cultivation of more valued trees. Although once important in the social imaginaries of the upland peoples, enabling miracle harvests and the dead to stay among the living, the camphor tree lost ground to the benzoin tree as a botanical symbol and protector in Toba, Dairi, and Pakpak. Its prestige dropped still further as synthetic camphor came to dominate the production of celluloid in the 1950s, when even laurel camphor was deemed too flammable and expensive.

The legacy of these conversions can still be seen today. The long emotional affinity for the camphor tree and trade that created poetry and myths and spurred patriclan-based formation of Batak identities from the fifteenth century onward retreated into memory. Camphor's kinship affect was supplanted by benzoin as the latter grew more intertwined with Toba Batak indigenous identity over the course of the twentieth century. This botanical affiliation is most visible in moments of environmental protest. Destructive logging in the early twentieth century was superseded by massive deforestation in the second half of the twentieth century. Beginning in the 1980s, Batak benzoin cultivators frequently came into conflict with the Indonesian pulp and paper corporation PT Indorayon, which elicited local protest by seeking to set aside more land for the planting of fast-growing pine and eucalyptus. The benzoin tree became a potent symbol of this struggle. When a coalition of local and international environmental groups produced a short film to draw public awareness to this issue, it opened with a scene of a Batak man wrapped in traditional textile (*ulos*) slowly climbing up a benzoin tree to harvest its sap.[115] The camphor tree, even on celluloid, was gone.

It is said that when Si Singamangaradja XII fled his ancestral village in Bakkara following the Dutch military onslaught, he took the time to dig up the bones of his ancestors and bring them with him.[116] Perhaps he was motivated by a need for protection, or perhaps it was out of a well-founded fear that he would not be able to return. This compulsion to bring the dead with him reminds us of Neumann's puzzlement when he encountered the Batak's fuzzy boundaries between the living and the dead. That blurring maps into more-than-human affinities with beings capable of serving as vessels for the spirits, with the camphor tree being our primary example. The dimming of this immanent supernatural element in nonhuman natural worlds was one significant consequence of the religious conversion that occurred on multiple levels in the uplands. For the camphor tree, as well as the spirits of the dead that camphor had once preserved, these changes estranged them from the living.

The Batak experience at this historical moment is comparable to several others worldwide. At different points in the twentieth century, animistic societies experienced mass conversions that alienated them from their ancestral dead, with these separations also renovating the ways that some beings in nature were regarded. Some of these conversions are ongoing. Many among the Sora peoples in the uplands of South India, for example, converted to Christianity or Hinduism and left for new jobs, leaving a shrinking class of elderly shamans to converse with the dead. The anthropologist Piers Vitebsky found that among the present generation of Sora, who lacked remembrance of the departed and the memories of those interlife connections, "humanity is all there is, and the humans are the people we know."[117] In Taiwan, many aboriginal groups converted to Christianity in the second half of the twentieth century, and roughly

Tomb of Si Singamangaradja XII, Balige, North Sumatra. Photo by author.

50 percent moved out of the forests. These groups simultaneously underwent a cultural renaissance that emphasized human-made artifacts such as textiles and woodcarvings rather than their traditional affiliation with the forest.[118] Closer to Sumatra, the upland Lauje of Sulawesi found that increased forest clearing to plant cacao as a cash crop from the 1990s onward frayed dense intrapersonal networks previously maintained through the reciprocal gifting of rice and further exacerbated inequalities between Christians, Muslims, and animists.[119] The point here is to highlight not chronological causality but a broader pattern in which converting forests into plantations and monocrop gardens also tended to evacuate spirits from the landscape and weaken notions of more-than-human kinship.

The retreat of the camphor tree, accompanied by the rise of the benzoin, created such a space devoid of spirits. Occurring in conjunction with this change was the rise of millenarian animism, which relocated the locus of supernatural power to new pantheons less connected to local natures. This phenomenon highlights the historicity in the notion of what constituted a forest in North Sumatra as well as what constituted animism among those who still identified with a traditional faith rather than Christianity or Islam. Change occurred not just through imposition from external powers but also internal conversion. It is important to note, however, that recognizing the Parmalim as a late nineteenth-century resistance movement against the upheaval of colonialism does not undermine the genuine affect and depth of faith among its present adherents. Nor does acknowledging that Toba benzoin forests have their roots in the early twentieth-century "Plantationocene" undermine current claims for the return of community forests to indigenous Batak communities. Batak benzoin cultivators remain more invested in the idea of the forest and what it represents relative to plantation companies and the state, which recently sought to restrict the land for food production.[120] The rise of the benzoin garden, however, underscores that it is imperative to recognize that linking indigenous claims to pristine forests and timeless ecological wisdom is flawed. Conversion had been, was, and still is an ongoing process for both peoples and landscapes. Even where the religious faith of a population is stabilized, conversions to modernist everyday religion proceed. This not only reduces nature's charisma but also creates disenchanted landscapes.

SIX Disenchanting Elephants

In 1876, the British colonial government in Malaya, whose authority was pressing inward from the Straits Settlements to the peninsula's riverine sultanates, gave the Mandailing migrant Raja Asal four elephants. Three of the elephants, the exception being a female, all had endearing names: Kulub Pilih (Chosen Sweetheart), Kulub Bidor (Sweetheart of Bidor), and Itam Pehangat (Passionate Black One).[1] Their new owner did not share the affection signaled by these names. Raja Asal promptly sent them all back once he had used them to transport goods to his new base in Kinta Valley in Upper Perak, and he included a note expressing his thanks to the British and regrets that the upkeep of the elephants far exceeded their benefits. What can we make of this implicit affective change toward elephants? We first met Raja Asal in chapter 4, as he struggled to make his way from the North Sumatran uplands to a new landscape riven by strife over tin-mining activity. In the period during which colonial rule was established, his family left mining to establish themselves within the local colonial bureaucracy. These structural changes were part of a broader disenchantment of the landscape that rendered both traditional leadership and megafauna vulnerable to demise.

The endangered status of the elephant in the twentieth century is well established, although in maritime Southeast Asia it fared better than similarly sized mammals, such as the rhinoceros. Elephants number in the low thousands in Malaya, while the Javan rhinoceros and Malayan gaur (*seladang*) are already extinct, and the Sumatran rhinoceros population is down to a few dozen, living in fragmented habitats.[2] Such sudden, dramatic declines are part of what some scholars have termed an extinction event, this time modern and caused by human activity. In this context, we can read the juxtaposition of a human family's economic success with the economic rejection of a large mammal once employed in human service as emblematic of an Anthropocene in which the *anthropos* comes out on top. As several studies have shown, spaces for human-elephant cohabitation remained in relative equilibrium while humans viewed the beasts as divine and depended on them for technology and labor.[3] They demonstrate not only that the interposing of human activity into the intimate, deep, and often symbiotic links between elephant and forest co-created a habitable space for both elephants and humans but also that these connections deteriorated once the power to produce and reproduce tipped in favor of the latter.

Behind the panoramic, declensionist view of long-term trends in the population of large mammals is a more complex narrative in which the decline of such megafauna happened in tandem with the disempowerment of particular human groups. The retreat of spirits from human-dominated forests occurred together with the gradual demise of charismatic authority, often enacted through shamanic-inflected religious practices. British Malaya, like Dutch Sumatra, experienced multiple similar disempowerments of traditional charismatic leadership. Further examining this disempowerment through human-elephant relationships allows us to investigate how colonialism promoted disenchantment and relocated spiritual authority in rational, legal, and bureaucratic infrastructure. Remnants of religious reflections and mantras involving elephants recorded during this colonial transition reveal how Islamic monotheism was employed to rationalize the position of humans at the apex of the natural world and to justify the absence of other beings that had only recently shared the same living space.

By disenchanting, I refer to the loss of wonder, a reduction in intrinsic value, and a dis-recognition of agency in the material body of a living being, all of which create a world described by Max Weber as one without "mysterious, incalculable forces," where "one can, in principle, master all things by calculation."[4] Weber thus pointed us toward the role of quantification in disenchantment; mastering the landscape by calculation proceeded apace with a bureaucratic interaction with the forest that decimated the habitats of both free-ranging and captive elephants. This accounting is evident in records of passes given out by Raja Asal's nephew, Raja Bilah, who in his capacity as village headman distributed them to his constituents who requested permission to collect wood from the forest. They contribute to a microhistorical picture of a forest frontier retreating in tandem with mobile swiddeners who were relocated into settled agricultural plots by a purportedly rational, bureaucratic authority. Settled agriculture and bureaucratic management thus created hostile conditions for the previously valued elephants.

The corollary to Weber's disenchanted world is loss, which might not be seen materially, but the reduced capacity of this disenchanted landscape could be sensed and felt. That loss was compounded by the way in which modernist monotheism—in this case, Islam—opened a way toward secularization of the landscape. As the philosopher Marcel Gauchet has argued, the centralization of power in a single, omnipotent God had a dual impact on religious consciousness. When divine power became accessible only through personal contemplation and prayer, spiritual growth became increasingly distanced from everyday human activity.[5] In the uplands, we can sense that lacuna through its reflexive result: the anthropologist Geoffrey Benjamin, for instance, identifies "a dynamic pendulum swing in formalized religion where disenchantment regularly generates a reactive re-enchantment, in which people seek to re-establish a more emotionally satisfying set of practices."[6] Elephants did not disappear completely. In the many markers to elephants that dot the Malayan landscape, including place-names and memorials, we see the resilience of their enchantment. Yet by the end of this chapter, as Gauchet would have predicted, we will see that, after this moment of rupture, affectionate awe no longer depended on emotional intimacy but on, ironically, distance.

ELEPHANTS, ENCHANTED

Who were the owners of Kulub Pilih, Kulub Bidor, Itam Pehangat, and the unnamed female elephant before they were given to Raja Asal? To understand the system of ownership and distribution of captive elephants in the Malayan sultanate of Perak, it is necessary to orient ourselves along its waterways. Like the sultanate of Selangor, the sultan's authority was vested in his ability to tax trade up and down the Perak River. Unlike Selangor, however, which comprises five major watersheds, the Perak River was the only one central to the sultanate. Most of the population lived in small villages lying along this river and its tributaries. A cluster of villages formed a subdistrict known as a *mukim*, headed by a local district chief empowered by the sultan through formal letters of authority (*surat kuasa*) to control principal sources of revenue and tax the produce of his district. These taxes were raised from goods, such as tin, gold, and resins, brought down the river (*hilir*) to be traded for salt, cloth, and other items on behalf of upriver (*hulu*) inhabitants. A district chief's power rested on his ability to leverage this trade to provide for his followers and maintain his position. Traditionally, district chiefs were divided into a four-tiered hierarchy in which the first tier consisted of four chiefs, the second had eight, the third had sixteen, and the fourth, thirty-two.[7] In practice, these configurations were looser, but the Perak sultan's status depended on his ability to gain and maintain the support of this constellation of district chiefs.

The river and its tributaries were the veins of the sultan's realm, but elephants were needed when traveling inland to muster support from the body politic. The forests of Malaya were evergreen, tropical rainforests, characterized by dense, thick undergrowth that was challenging to traverse. As vividly described by British official W. G. Maxwell, "the forest hems in the cultivated area [and] . . . on all sides this area is shut in by a dark heavy line that uprears [sic] itself, around and above it, like the walls of a prison."[8] Elephants, eating their way through the dense vegetation, could easily navigate their way and move a human party or large loads from point to point. They were not necessarily faster than the human walking, but they helped the latter expend less energy while making inroads into untrammeled forest. The transportation system in precolonial Perak can thus be envisioned as a relay from boat to elephant and back again, a relay illustrated by a name given to an elephant of a nineteenth-century Perak district chief—Lancang Patani (Boat of Patani).[9]

Riding the huge mammals was a marker of both class and authority, since the capture, training, and maintenance of captive elephants was an expensive endeavor that few could afford. Unlike South Asian royal courts, however, Malay kings did not have expansive territory or sufficient human resources to maintain large state forests where the animals could be centrally herded. Rather, the herd of captive elephants was dispersed among the various district chiefs and became part of property to be inherited.[10] Their usage as tribute for the king, access to the forest, and mounts for people of the ruling class defined the geographical limits of the king's authority. His charisma, which helped him to maintain support among the district chiefs, was partly enacted through this animal that he rode during his appearances in villages distant from his court. The elephant also helped to define ownership of trees. According to a precolonial legal digest from Perak, trees not planted by a human hand that showed signs of being eaten by elephants were deemed God's property and could not be claimed by anyone.[11]

In this context, shamans (*pawang*) were an important political and social force. We earlier saw them as influential figures in tin mines; the highest among them were also part of the ruling class. In Perak, the court pawang held the title of Sultan Muda (Young Sultan), and his skill set encompassed the use of magical arts to commune with spirits, perform divination rituals, and heal the unwell.[12] An annual court ritual to "rejuvenate" (*memulih*) the royal regalia set the stage for the performance of his power. In this ritual, the Sultan Muda and his assistant, Raja Kechil Muda, summoned the guardian spirits of the Perak realm to a feast lasting three days and three nights. The Sultan Muda and Raja Kechil Muda would pay obeisance to the Perak regalia, whose centerpiece was a set of musical instruments: drums, clarinets, and trumpets. To musical accompaniment, the Sultan Muda offered food and drink to an invisible procession of Perak's guardian spirits, a large pantheon that was inclusive of almost all religious influences in the peninsula—the Hindu gods Brahma and Vishnu, the prophet Solomon in the tradition of Abrahamic faiths, and the son-in-law of Prophet Muhammad, Ali, who was revered in Shi'ite Islam, as well as the spirits of the natural world, such as Sultan Alam Maya Udara (Sultan of the Unsubstantial Air) and the water spirit Anak Raja Gelombang Laut (Prince of the Waves).[13] In this grand public ceremony and other quotidian ones, they were assisted by a group of lesser spirit mediums (*bomoh*), the latter group also including village magicians not directly connected to a royal court.

As with the tin-prospector shaman, or *pawang*, our present knowledge of the role of the court pawang is mediated through contemporary observations of British colonial scholars and officials who appeared bemused and fascinated by them but saw little except long-running superstitions. The pawang's own writings were altogether sparser but reveal a more complex relationship between humans, spirits, and the nonhuman in nature than that captured by a supplicating obeisance ritual. The shaman positioned himself in everyday life as the person with the power to rein in the darker elements of the spirit world in order to ensure success in the material, earthly realm. The "Kitab perentah pawang" is a nineteenth-century manuscript containing a trove of knowledge that stemmed from the lineage of Raja Haji Yahya, whose family members had held the state pawang title; it gives us a glimpse of their position and how it was justified.[14] The manuscript begins with a lengthy exposition on the role of the pawang, describing him as the one who knows the primordial essence (*asal usul*) of all things. Similar to the mediatory role of Si Singamangaradja in the North Sumatran uplands, the pawang "made peace among the seven children of Batara Guru," who went on to populate the world.[15] This history is followed with a set of mantras or ritual invocations to be recited when engaging in specific tasks that might disturb the equilibrium of the natural world, such as clearing forests, planting rice, and trapping and managing elephants.

This last task merited a section on its own, subtitled "Teyib mantra gajah." *Teyib* is derived from the Arabic word for healer (طبيب), while *gajah* is a Sanskrit loan word for elephant. As this name suggests, many of the mantras relate to the maintenance of the captive elephant's well-being. No records of the numbers of captive elephants were kept; anecdotal evidence suggests that each chief might hold about 40 to 50 elephants each, which means at least 640 such elephants might have been kept for riding.[16] Perak also maintained a lively elephant trade with South Asia. This trade had petered out by the early nineteenth century, and the population of elephants on the peninsula increased around this time, in response to greater nutrition available in the ecotones created by parallel increases in forest clearings for swidden.[17] Many of Perak's wild elephants were also found farther away from human settlement in mountainous uplands and tin-rich valley plains in a sparsely populated northern region on the border with Siam (Thailand), sustained by the abundance of salt licks, which provided them with both water and minerals.[18] Wild and tamed elephants encountered each other often in the forest, as captive elephants were turned out to forage for food on their own once they had been trained to obey the goads of their handlers. The latter would then round them up when they were needed; in Malay, the word for elephant handler was *gembala*, the same word for "shepherd." Therefore, at the beginning of the nineteenth century, Perak had two populations of elephants, one wild and one captive. The two groups intersected and mated; tamed elephants were used to lure wild elephants into the fold, and captive female elephants sometimes ran off with wild males, reproducing both wildness and tameness.[19]

Pawang at all levels were involved in the capture and management of the captive elephants. In seeking to assert authority over an elephant, a pawang had to simultaneously assert leadership over humans. Borrowing the sultan's authority, the *pawang gajah* in charge of elephants were allowed to recruit human corvée labor to perform the massive task of trapping them. This labor was employed in the clearing of the forest to erect enclosures (*kubu*) within which to drive elephants; approximately a hundred men were needed in each elephant hunt. The taming process was laborious, with many men involved in corralling the group of wild elephants into small pens (*chelong*) where they were trained to obey the goad. These encounters were potentially fatal to both sides: humans could be trampled by the stronger elephants, while elephants often sickened in captivity as they were left starved for days to rob them of their strength. The risk in these interactions was reflected in the large numbers of mantras, recited in each stage of the operation, which often attributed the source of danger to hostile spirits inhabiting the untamed elephant. The following is an example from "Teyib mantra gajah," with English translation below the Malay text:

Bab ini membuang hantu anak gajah ini mantranya: Om panirong panirak melajut engkau pindah ke hutan penapoh kurab turun engkau ke padang maha luas ke rimba yang maha besar.

This part is about casting away evil spirits from baby elephants. This is the mantra: *Om panirong panirak*, begone to the woods, descend to the wide fields and to the large forests.[20]

When training the elephant, handlers found it important to stamp out idiosyncratic behaviors that might cause it to shake off its load, such as swinging its tail from side to side. Three different remedies were offered to break an elephant from such habits, each involving the application of a paste that contained some mixture of betel leaf, betel nuts, and the roots of *trong asam* (commonly known as "hairy fruited eggplant" due to the needle-like hairs covering the fruit) to the elephant's thighs or testicles.[21] In these endeavors, we can sense the trainers' frustrations with some of the elephants' habits that they could never quite break. Elephants were imperfect domesticates, and these human quests for modifying their behavior never truly reached their goals.

When perceived as enchanted, the elephant was not simply exempt from the processes Weber refers to as intellectualization and "the unmagicking of the world" (*die Entzauberung der Welt*).[22] The enchanted elephant was also a construct that induced anxiety and awe because of the recognition that their interactions rendered humans vulnerable. *Pawang gajah* directly interacting with the animals were said to be susceptible to a disease known in the elephant mantra manuscripts as *chemahang*, in which the human handler became cross-infected by the spirits affecting the elephant.[23] In rural Malaya, there emerged a folk belief about a city deep in the woods where the inhabitants were human by day but turned into elephants capable of rampaging through cultivated swidden plots by night; this interchangeability of human and elephant forms suggests a recognition of elephant agency in these depredations.[24] These anxieties illustrate a local understanding of the elephant's nonhuman personhood that was, as expressed by the anthropologist Piers Locke, "based on a logic of permeability between animals, persons and gods."[25] Permeability complicated the nature-culture binaries inherent in Weber and conferred on the enchanted elephant not only anthropomorphic qualities but the possibility of an alternative human form.

Who then *were* the previous owners of Kulub Pilih, Kulub Bidor, Itam Pe-hangat, and the unnamed female elephant before they were offered to Raja Asal? They were likely district chiefs of the Perak sultanate that preceded British colonialism. They would have inherited and employed a long tradition of trapping and maintaining a captive elephant labor force that was scattered along the Perak River and helped to define the limits of the polity's authority. In their close interactions with elephants, they would have developed an appreciation of the elephant as a being not so distinct from humans. The mantras they would have used to train these elephants illustrated what elephants, enchanted but shackled as labor, looked like: a nonhuman capable of exerting power, not amenable to human domination, and possessing charisma as well as personality that conferred an aura of authority to the humans seen as capable of handling them. The authority of these pawang was to wane along with that of the elephants under their control.

ELEPHANTINE IMPERIAL INCURSIONS

An elephant was said to be the first living being to find a rich vein of tin in Malaya, a discovery that sparked a mid-nineteenth-century expansion of mining enterprises just prior to British rule. Running amok into the jungle one day, this elephant, when recaptured, was streaked with a silvery substance that his handlers discovered was tin. That accidental prospector elephant was said to belong to Ngah Long Ja'far, who later held the title of *mantri* in the Perak court.[26] The mantri leveraged Chinese labor and capital from the 1840s onward and used both to open new tin mines in Larut.[27] From the coast to the mines, elephants proved immensely useful in carrying loads of tin to be exported, as well as in bringing supplies to the miners. They also became useful for impeding unwanted colonialists. As discussed earlier, the chaos of the tin rush gave the British colonial government in the Straits Settlements an opportunity to cement its influence and bring the peninsula under its rule. Through the Treaty of Pangkor in 1874, the British installed their favored candidate, Raja Abdullah, on the Perak throne and compelled him to accept a British Resident. This intervention did not win the support of many chiefs, most notably the mantri of tin-rich Larut. The latter preferred Raja Ismail, a much older man who had been *bendahara* (chief minister) to the previous sultan, a position that traditionally allowed him to hold the Perak royal regalia after a sultan's death and bestow it on the new sultan. Refusing to give the regalia up to a man he perceived as an interloper, Raja Ismail, with the support of the mantri, mounted a passive resistance. On the back of his elephant, he simply disappeared when British officials came calling to secure the regalia for their anointed Sultan Abdullah.[28]

The first British-appointed Resident of Perak, James Birch, was obliged to make several calls during 1874 and 1875 to persuade Raja Ismail to give the regalia up. He found his trips impeded through claims of elephant recalcitrance, writing, "Getting the elephants in the morning was a fearful labor, and in the system which they now adopt as regards their elephants you must always have this delay—a delay which however is unnecessary and would never occur if the elephants were herded, and grass and leaves cut for them. They now turn out as soon as we arrive and go look for them as soon as they get up in the morning, which is very often tolerably late."[29]

Birch viewed this—with a colonialist sense of complacency—as evidence of Malay indolence and inefficiency. The frequency with which he got a late start or indeed never even managed to get beyond a particular point inland, however, suggested active obstruction. Certainly, Frank Swettenham, a British official who accompanied Birch on one of these trips, was more skeptical of the elephant excuse. Swettenham's journal notes that he "had seen three elephants across the river in the evening," and yet, somehow in the morning the mantri, a supporter of Raja Ismail, told him that none "could be got."[30]

Their repeated failures to secure the regalia meant two de facto rulers for Perak: the British-backed Raja Abdullah downriver and Raja Ismail, supported by most of the *hulu* chiefs. This status quo remained as long as travel was dependent on elephants and the jungle consequently difficult to navigate. Clear footpaths inland were scarce; only two could be found on a hand-drawn map from Swettenham's journal.[31] When the British procured elephants, they attempted to turn them from a tool for resistance into labor for the empire. Initial success was mixed. Using hired elephants, Swettenham and Birch led efforts to bring down stockades constructed during the Larut Wars, freed Chinese women sold into prostitution, and sometimes redistributed captive elephants from hostile peninsular Malays to friendly Malays across the broader region. Raja Asal, for example, obtained two elephants as a reward for helping to pressure a Perak chief called Raja Ngah to stop collecting taxes, since the British and their favored sultan claimed sole monopoly over taxes under the terms of the Pangkor Treaty.[32] British officials' use of elephants during these early days of uncertain imperial imposition foreshadowed how they would eventually dismantle the traditional mode of governance: by eliminating the power to tax and enslave, elevating newcomers, and rebuilding conflict-scarred landscapes for economic purposes.

These efforts provoked backlash. Birch eventually lost Raja Abdullah's support due to his efforts to eliminate debt slavery and wrest the right to collect taxes from the latter. These dissatisfactions culminated in his murder. Birch's killing was overtly orchestrated by a conspiracy of *hulu* chiefs, with Abdullah's tacit approval. The latter had hinted at knowledge of the killing through a séance held a few days before Birch's death, an event that he proclaimed the spirits had foreseen.[33] The killing of the first British Resident in Perak invited forceful retaliation that fully upended traditional leadership in the sultanate. The colonial government in the Straits Settlements launched a police expedition to apprehend those involved in the killing. This hunt for the British Resident's murderers was another quest involving the management of elephants. The police at first found it useful to have "native auxiliaries," in many cases Sumatran Malays, precede them on lumbering elephants in breaking a path through the jungle.[34] These men were dispatched to take up stations in the interior and arrange for supplies brought by elephants, and the main party followed on foot. The elephants, however, left huge potholes that exposed the party on foot to the unpleasant experience of floundering in jungle mud, which slowed the chase considerably.[35] Moreover, the use of elephants meant that the policing party was once again susceptible to foot-dragging by unsupportive inland chiefs. Assistant Resident W. E. Maxwell, who was part of an expedition from Perak to Patani in pursuit of a key Malay conspirator, the Maharaja Lela, wryly described one such incident: "Two *Sayyids* of Chigar Gala to whom I had written asking for the loan of two elephants, appeared today. They related with much *empressement* how they had hastened from their village at my call, only too honoured at being asked to lend their beasts. But where were the elephants? Alas! Did not the Tuan [Master] know that this was the *ninring* season and that all the male elephants are *gila* [crazy]? Allah! Such a misfortune."[36]

The recalcitrance of such local leaders was balanced with support from sojourning populations of traders and miners. Their reasons were likely pragmatic rather than ideological, as the British blockade of Perak waterways in

1876 prevented supplies from reaching the mining settlements.[37] Raja Asal and Raja Bilah were not the only supportive Sumatran migrants; chiefs in Mandailing villages dotting the route also provided reinforcements to accompany the police along certain legs of Maxwell's march northward.[38] This assistance was substantial enough to merit monetary benefit; following the successful capture of the Maharaja Lela and his followers, Raja Bilah received $700 and mining concessions in Kinta Valley for his aid, as well as for keeping the peace in his area of influence near the Slim River.[39] Most of the Malay chiefs who were involved in the killing were hanged or exiled, including Sultan Abdullah. Some of their property was confiscated and redistributed to those who had helped the British. The royal regalia was recovered and bestowed on Raja Yusuf, who ruled until 1887 on friendly terms with the British. The settlement of the "foreign Malays" met British approval, geared as it was toward surplus-making profit, technological penetration, and bounded territory. Once the upheaval over Resident Birch's murder was pacified, Raja Bilah accompanied police magistrate H. W. C. Leech as part of a British party to inspect southeastern Perak in 1879 and assess its suitability for agricultural cultivation. Of the Mandailing, Leech commented that "these men, like most other foreign Malays in the peninsula, come from the Dutch colonies[,] and whatever else may be said of the Dutch rule in Malay countries, it appears to make traders and colonists of the people under its influence."[40]

Examining British annexation through elephant movements highlights two major changes to structures of power. First, the move toward British colonial rule provided an avenue for the uplifting of Malay migrants from outside the peninsula whose interests intersected with the British. Second, amid sporadic resistance, it demonstrates a growing colonial reach inland that made previously impenetrable forest "legible," to use James Scott's classic terminology, thereby pushing the forests a step toward disenchantment.[41] The legibility of the forests initially created a new impression of bad magic. Maxwell recounted how he "puzzled an old man not a little by exhibiting a map of Ulu Perak" from which he read the names of kampongs, hills, and rivers not yet visited by any Europeans, a knowledge that the old man called "devilish magic."[42] Some twenty years after these events, Swettenham reflected on the Perak chiefs' vain hopes of having the forests protect them from British intervention: "The Malays of Perak laughed at the idea of a British soldier or sailor making his way through their roadless forests, and there is no doubt they believed that if they could get rid of J.W.W. Birch and me . . . no others would come to seek satisfaction of them."[43]

Colonial success punctured this arboreal mystique. With the forest increasingly legible to the new colonial authority and a trading class displacing traditional chiefs, life for elephants and forests had to reckon with a new accounting.

UNSEEING TREES FOR WOOD

Raja Asal died in 1877. His nephew, Raja Bilah, then became the new *penghulu* of Papan in Kinta Valley but also inherited the former's considerable debts. These he gradually paid off, largely through a stream of steady income from his work as a low-level colonial administrator. Raja Bilah's work as penghulu, a village headman under colonial power, left a trail of paper that was striking in its very banality. He made records of permits given to people in his village who wanted to gather wood for their own use, and he subsequently submitted these records to the Forestry Department, newly formed under the British colonial government in 1898. A typical permit was sparse and brief, such as one from 1903 that simply stated, "Hazara Singh is permitted to take wood for personal use. This free pass can be used for three days only."[44]

The information recorded in these permits appeared singularly useless for monitoring the level of forest resources being used, as it lacked pertinent information such as the type of wood used and the amount taken. What then was the purpose and impact of such copious recordkeeping? These records indicated that colonial management of forest resources in Perak at the local level was frequently more effective in monitoring people than resources. Such managerial work had a disenchanting effect on flora and fauna, as it reduced their overall potency, which was redistributed to their disembodied parts. The forest's retreat would materially impact the populations of elephants in Malaya, both captive and wild, as a manager's success in effectively administering the new system became read as a sign of God's favor on his family.

Kinta Valley, where Raja Bilah and his family settled, became a productive tin-mining area in the state of Perak in the 1890s. The valley produced on average more than 115,000 tons of tin a year during the colonial period, making Malaya the provider of as much as 30 to 55 percent of the world output.[45] The area itself was only about thirty miles long and fifteen miles wide at the southern end, and it tapered into a mountain range in the north. Bedrock in the valley was primarily composed of crystalline limestone, circumscribed by biotite granite in the hills. Besides tin ore, the soil also contained valuable minerals such as cobalt. The surrounding uplands were forested with hardwood trees such as meranti and *tualang* as well as softwood trees such as pine and *kauri*. Forests were brought into the ecology of tin production through the smelting process; charcoal obtained from firewood served to heat tin ore. In the late 1870s, the Mandailing adopted technology, learned from Chinese miners during their tumultuous sojourn in Selangor, to smelt the ore in Papan, their settlement in Kinta, where the miners used hardwood timber rather than ordinary firewood.[46] The furnace, "a compacted earth cylinder of 1 meter by 1.2 meters in height, where the base was wider than the top," was fed at rate of one *pikul* of charcoal to one *pikul* of tin ore.[47]

The use of hardwood in this enterprise was a matter of concern to the colonial government, which through accounting and regulation was keen to prevent the overcutting and overuse of trees as fuel.[48] From the 1880s to the late 1890s, a tax system was instituted to regulate charcoal supply. In it, village headmen like Raja Bilah collected charcoal export taxes at a rate of five cents per *pikul* or forty cents per cartload.[49] Concomitantly, they also enforced British prohibitions in the cutting of trees by issuing permits that confined the collection of timber and wild rubber to specified areas and types. This system thus kept the daily management of forest resources in the hands of local chiefs, although the British colonial government shaped the general policy. This two-pronged regulatory system, however, failed to stem the rapid decline in the numbers of trees.[50] This failure appeared to be used as a justification for further British regulation of Chinese-type tin smelting. In 1888, the British tried to ban the use of Chinese furnaces. Attempts to put the ban in practice, however, incited Chinese-led riots and attacks on the police. The Straits Trading Agency, a British tin-smelting company, was set up in Kinta in 1889 to fill the production gap left by the ban.[51] It did so by introducing blast furnaces, which used coal for fuel and gradually supplanted the Chinese operations.[52]

While Chinese miners managed to maintain their ever more tenuous grip on the business for a few more decades, Raja Bilah found the venture increasingly unprofitable. In 1890, he sold off his mines in Papan and focused his energies on administration.[53] Without the mines as a common enterprise, the ethnic homogeneity of Raja Bilah's constituents gradually disintegrated and his Mandailing followers dispersed. Some of them continued mining, while others focused on agriculture. The dispersal weakened the social organization based on the charismatic system brought from South Tapanuli. The British government assigned Raja Bilah to govern a territory rather than a people, and this territory was becoming increasingly diverse through the presence of immigrant Chinese and Indians. The mystique of Mandailing leadership thus did not long survive the displacement of the Malay pawang when Mandailing leaders were brought into the service of the new political hierarchy.

The British extended their reach into these villages by continuing to be critical of the forestry practices of "the natives," who "cut every available tree down and repeat the process as fast as they spring up."[54] There were murmurs of dissatisfaction in the colonial administration that "we give to the miner what is often fine land covered with magnificent forest, and when he has destroyed the timber, he turns the soil upside down and after a few years abandons it."[55] These complaints culminated in the abolishment of the revenue farm system in favor of direct supervision from a newly established forestry department in 1898. Supervised by A. B. Stephens, who had studied forestry in India, the department was formed with the aim of enabling "a far more effective check to be exercised over the illicit destruction of timber and exportation of jungle produce than is possible at present."[56] Initially, it focused on improving the tree stock through girdling, which removed what were perceived to be inferior species, and targeted a commercial regeneration of trees that had high value in the market. This policy later became a strategy of permitting a five-year regeneration period coupled with several fellings.[57]

For village headmen like Raja Bilah, creating a forestry department meant another layer of reports and bureaucracy that did little to address the actual denuding of the forests. The Forestry Department continued to require those who wanted to collect wood to have a pass or permit, thus providing a record of permits issued by Raja Bilah and his son, Raja Yacob, for the gathering of wood in their village, from 1903 through 1909. Each permit, written in Malay, contained at minimum the name of its holder, the purpose for the wood collected, and the duration for which the pass was valid. An examination of these records reveals several interesting trends.

Analysis of the records shows that the number of permits issued plummeted in 1904 but remained fairly steady thereafter, suggesting a cap on the number of permits from 1905 onward. The average length of the pass's validity increased steadily throughout the six years. Moreover, the allotted times to collect the *same type* of wood from 1903 to 1909 had grown markedly longer by 1909. For example, a permit to collect firewood for personal use in 1903 was generally valid for two days, but a pass for the same purpose in 1909 was valid for fourteen days. This implies that a longer period of time was needed to collect the same amount of wood, an increase that very likely correlated with the distance from

PERMITS TO GATHER WOOD, ISSUED BY RAJA BILAH
AND RAJA YACOB, 1903–1909

	1903	1904	1905	1906	1907	1908	1909
Number of permits	107	27	35	54	69	54	40
Mean duration of permit validity in days	5.11	6.21	8.06	10.39	11.32	13.54	13.43

collection site to village. In other words, the forests were retreating from the village despite their regulation by the Forestry Department.

Turning to trends in how the gathered wood would be used, we may observe that the headmen issued permits only for wood destined for personal or communal use. Unlike during the revenue farm era, individuals were released from farm duty to manage the allocation of wood for commercial uses. This was consistent with the general trend toward shifting autonomous management of profit-making resources from the local elite to the colonial government.

Another interesting facet of the wood-use trends was increased demand for fencing for communal property and private houses, particularly in 1905 and 1906. In this case, communal property referred mainly to mosques that were constructed on land obtained through local *waqf*s (charitable bequests) for the use of the village. The rising level of construction implied more settlement and a visible presence of sacred sites that marked the Mandailing area as Muslim. With the dispersal of Raja Bilah's followers from South Tapanuli, the landscape appeared less inscribed with ethnic affiliations, while a co-religionist bond with Perak Malays was taking shape. Raja Bilah himself established a *waqf* on part of his allotted land in Papan to build a mosque in 1888. As noted in his family memoir, his jurisdiction included four mosques, and he had the power to appoint a judge (*qadi*) to provide Islamic guidance in the increasingly populated district.[58]

As the construction of houses and mosques increased, the presence of a hidden world of spirits retreated with the forest. The banal act of recording the use of wood repeatedly reduced a living tree to the sum of its disembodied parts. The village headmen did not interact with trees but rather with timber, which was cut and sized for specific purposes. Whereas Mandailing and Perak leaders had previously appeased the spirits of the trees through rituals when

PLANNED USES FOR WOOD ACCORDING TO COLLECTION
PERMITS ISSUED, 1903–1909

	Number of permits per year						
	1903	1904	1905	1906	1907	1908	1909
Total number of permits issued*	54	29	35	41	69	54	40
Poles	2	1	1	2	9	4	7
Houses	24	13	13	16	32	26	20
Firewood	18	2	3	4	6	7	3
House fence	0	1	0	4	6	8	3
Communal fencing	0	0	3	5	0	0	2
Roofing	2	7	11	5	7	7	4
Shed	1	2	1	0	0	2	0
Unspecified	9	4	3	7	9	4	2

* A few permits specify two functions for the wood, so the totals in the rows of planned uses sometimes
slightly exceed the total number of permits.

they cleared forests for settlement use, village headmen now appeared one step
removed from the trees that were to be harvested. Spiritually, they could not
see the trees for the wood. Wood, which used to be perceived as a growing tree
infused with spirits, was disenchanted—stripped of its animating, living force.
As part of construction material for a mosque, the no-longer-living wood had
its sacrality located in the building rather than its component parts. And as
these new buildings rose, the concept of a three-tiered cosmology in which
humans existed between two realms of spirits was gradually flattened into a
human-dominated, one-dimensional landscape.

Most important, changes in the contents of the wood-collection permit
indicated a burgeoning effort to fix *people*, rather than wood, in place. In 1903,
as stated earlier, the information provided in the pass was merely a sparse note
recording the name of the holder and the category and intended use for the
wood collected. In 1909, the permit was markedly longer and routinely recorded
information such as the details featured in this permit language:

This permit is issued to Dauri bin Penghulu, Abdullah Hassan and Zawiah.
They are permitted to cut wood in the following dimensions: six logs measur-

ing 12" by 137.6" for the poles of the house; 4 logs measuring 12" by 137.6" for the front cross section (*bendul*), 4 logs measuring 6" by 15.7" for diagonal reinforcements, 4 logs measuring 6" by 137.6" to support the pillars, 18 pieces of wood measuring 6" by 137.6", and another three of the same dimensions as cross beams. [They are also allotted] 1200 bunches of attap for roofing, 40 pieces of rattan for sundry household items. All this is to build a house of their own in their village on the plot of land A.L 552, Plan 2800, Lot 175 in the district of Blanja. The wood should be cut from Pandang. This free pass can only be used for fourteen days from the date of issue.[59]

The extra information included in this permit—an address for the building site and specifications for the logs that could be taken—was of scant use in managing the sustainable regeneration of the forest. However, the new information was markedly useful in identifying where and how the end product, usually a house, was to be built. This facilitated fixing villagers to specified lots in their villages, while the limitations in wood size controlled the spatial dimensions of their own homes. In 1909, the same year the permit above was issued, the autonomously ruled Malay state of Johor was formally designated a colony, putting the entire peninsula under British authority. Wood use permits highlighted the pervasive reach of the colonial state, which extended its grasp over the entire people of Malaya through a department that ostensibly specialized in forest resource management.

Therefore, what we see through the world of Raja Bilah's wood collection passes is a micropicture of a disenchanted, retreating forest that resulted from the sedentarization of not only the Malay peasantry but also the Sumatran migrants who had previously been mobile up and down the region's waterways. This broad colonialist trend toward defining the Malay as a group of settled agriculturalists rooted to village soil has been aptly critiqued in other scholarly works.[60] These studies, however, have largely sidelined how these subaltern subjects themselves took part in the rationalization and accounting of the woods; arboreal disembodying was part of disenchantment. Turning the forest periphery into a productive rural landscape required a spatial articulation of Islam that was built *from* wood but not *of* the woods. Raja Bilah's wood-collection permits performed aspects of calculative logic that reinforced a shift to capitalist-led bureaucracy. What emerges from them is a picture in which the detachment necessary to administer wood use in the colonial system became intertwined with a visibly increasing piety defined through the mosque, *waqf*, and *qadi*. In short, the disenchantment of forests occurred together with the emerging leadership of Muslim-identifying bureaucrats in place of pawang and elephants. This entangled disenchantment of forest and local leadership impacted personal ecological imaginary.

ONEIRIC ELEPHANTS

Raja Bilah was not merely a Sumatran Malay bureaucrat in the British administration system. Inhabiting a world in conversion, he retained a measure of vernacular charismatic authority. A book-length document in his possession suggested that his position as chief still involved spiritual leadership: "Raja Bilah punya ini takwil mimpi" (Raja Bilah's divination of dreams). This sixty-seven-page manuscript written in Jawi script documents how to interpret various kinds of oneiric imagery. While undated, it appears to have been written in the 1890s, before Raja Bilah went to Mecca on the *hajj*.[61] This genre of text is comparable to "Kitab perentah pawang," the manuscript of the Perak court pawang mentioned earlier. Both texts involve an ecological conversation with the divine, including portents that could be read in the natural world and the positioning of humankind in a hierarchy of living, spiritual beings. However, the theological basis of the texts differed substantially. Where "Kitab perentah pawang" drew on a mix of animist-inflected Hindu-Buddhism and Islam to emphasize the special position of the pawang on this earth, "Raja Bilah punya ini takwil mimpi" tapped almost exclusively Islamic imagery to stress the special transcendence of the human soul.

Let us first compare Raja Bilah's dream book with "Kitab perentah pawang" to obtain a sense of the differences between North Sumatran and Malayan perspectives on elephants before relating these religious perspectives to the situation for the elephants on the ground. The contents of Raja Bilah's manuscript can be roughly divided into three parts. The first uses Arabic letters for an interpretation of dreams. Structured repetitively, the text lists what each letter portends in a series of similar-sounding sentences. Interpreting an unknown future through these letters indexes the power of the Arabic script and by extension literacy itself as a vehicle for divine power over humankind. The second part of the text divines meaning for dreams by employing symbolism in the natural world. Readings of nature as portents of the future were consistent with everyday religious practice as depicted in the previous chapters, where the nonhuman natural world anointed leaders, signposted mishaps, and exhibited agency when occupied by spirits. In this text, however, some of the imagery is also Islamicate, including dreams of holy men and mention of Lawh Mahfuz (Preserved Tablet), where it was believed, in Islamic tradition, the destinies of all men were written.[62]

Dreaming of an elephant provides an illustrative example of these melded allusions. In general, dreaming of an elephant was a positive sign: "If one dreams of seeing an elephant or a horse or a water buffalo, this is a good dream, a perfect sign. Should one dream of riding that elephant or horse or buffalo or of climbing up a tree, [the dream] portends future wealth and status."[63]

The grouping of the elephant with the horse and water buffalo as animals that foreshadow future wealth and status is particularly suggestive of the important role of captive beasts of burden in accruing material gains; the labor of these three animals was exploited for transportation, trade facilitation, and the bestowing of status. The inclusion of the horse indexes the Persianate origin of this interpretation, as that animal was not often utilized in Malaya. This grouping recalls and complicates historian William Clarence-Smith's argument that prior to the nineteenth century, the horse displaced the elephant as a preferred mount in the broader Malay world partly because it absorbed interpretations of Islamic theology from the Middle East, which revered the horse more than the elephant.[64] The equalization of horse and elephant in this dream portent indicates that the elephant did not quite lose its status. Rather, it lost its monopoly within the pantheon of revered animals, at least in the realm of dreams.

Nonetheless, a desire for distance between human and elephant creeps into the third part of Raja Bilah's manuscript, which narrates the miraculous journey of Prophet Muhammad to the seven heavens, known as Israq Mikraj in Islamic tradition. This journey identifies a realm of existence beyond the earthly plane, the afterlife of heaven and hell, and the transcendence of the human soul as it moves from one realm to the next. But where in Muslim canonical sources Muhammad simply brings down the gift of five prayers from God to the faithful, Raja Bilah's dream book attenuates this narrative by adding a few mantras derived from local tradition after telling of the Prophet's return to earth, including a *perabun* charm for elephants. Two perabun charms were part of "Kitab perentah pawang," and as this charm for elephants is the only significant similarity between Raja Bilah's dream divination book and the Perak pawang's charm book, it is worth examining them side by side.

The purpose of a perabun charm is implied by its name, which literally means the obscuring of vision. Each supplication in the charm aims to impede the el-

COMPARISON OF ELEPHANT *PERABUN* CHARMS IN TWO
MALAY MANUSCRIPTS FROM PERAK

A *perabun* charm from "Raja Bila punya ini takwil mimpi" (written by a Sumatran migrant)	Two *perabun* charms from "Kitab perentah pawang" (Perak sultanate)
This is a prayer to blind elephants and other animals.	(1) This part speaks of the *perabun* of the elephant.
[In Arabic] In the name of God, the most gracious, the most merciful. O elephant, bend down rattan plant, cringe down among the house of leaves. Among the swallows, I sit [and] you pass, and you think I am a child of the shadows. I sit still as a stump, blind him to my presence like the vanishing of ghosts. Some distance to my left and right, the Singamaraja hills fall silent. Do not follow me across or chase after me. I seek protection. I will be able to obtain [my objective], using this *pelimunan* [magical art], if God covers his eyes and prevents his steps. O my protector, we raise our eyes to the clouds; receive me as I use this elephant *perabun* charm. Please intercept the *siamang* [monkey] from the faraway jungle with the gods of your blessed supplication. In the white west, the child of the proud ones lost and could not overcome me. Fulfilled by God, fulfilled by Muhammad, fulfilled by the honored Prophet.	Twist on one heel on our foot to dislodge some earth and pick it up. This is the mantra [to be recited] three times, [and after] fifty breaths, rub the earth on the elephant's forehead. [In garbled Thai] Om pu pang maha pang pit om tu saham stiakan tanahmu. Tamat. (2) This part speaks of the mantra *perabun*. It is to be recited when entering the jungle or forest so that nothing would impede our work. [In garbled Thai] Om genaling getali pechna tu pechna raha sohot bangkom yang ka betaka yang tupat pechak pi bangkaom isti pada sengkum bong kamuia. [In Malay] Descend to the woods, move to the wide plains and the large jungles. End.
[In Arabic] There is no God but God.	

ephant's sight so that a human endeavor in the forest will succeed. Nonetheless, differences emerge in the comparison of the two charm texts. The use of Arabic in Raja Bilah's mantra and of Thai in "Kitab perentah pawang" points toward changes in the theological underpinnings of everyday dealings with elephants. Moreover, the level of contact with an elephant was also significantly different. Raja Bilah's charm operated at a distance, requiring little direct interaction with the elephant itself. The beginning and end of his prayer appeal to God and his prophet in Islam, with indirect references to magical art that indicate other divinities might have once been worshipped. An element of fear pervades this appeal to dim the elephant's senses and protect the supplicant from it. The elephant in Raja Bilah's "Takwil mimpi" was an adversary to the man, who had God as an ally in the quest to subdue it. On the other hand, the charm in "Kitab perentah pawang" was designed for use in the context of close inter-action with captive elephants. Here the desire for distance is directed toward bad spirits inhabiting the elephant, but not the elephant itself. "Takwil mimpi" views the elephant as a danger coming from the wilderness, while "Kitab pe-rentah pawang" sees in it a dual capacity for tamed goodness when guided by the human, as well as unpredictable conduct when induced by hostile spirits.

Perabun mantras from other documentary sources also show similar mixed feelings toward the elephant. These mantras can also be found in three texts of the same knowledge lineage—through the oral instruction of generations of men who had held the position of Orang Kaya Sri Adika Raja at the upper reaches of the Perak River. The last holder of this title before colonial rule arrived was shot dead by police scouts for supporting the conspiracy behind the killing of Resident James Birch in 1875.[65] Two of the manuscripts were collected by W. E. Maxwell, who was the British assistant Resident in Perak, and his son, W. G. Maxwell. W. E. Maxwell notes that these texts were copied from the mantras of former Perak noble Mantri Ngah Ibrahim, who was ex-iled to the Seychelles in the late 1870s and who learned elephant lore from Sri Raja Adika.[66] Ngah Ibrahim's area of influence was in Larut, one of the richest tin-mining areas, and like generations of pawang before him, he learned these mantras through oral transmission. His exile likely motivated the process of writing them down. Despite their common ancestry, the perabun charms in the two texts show marked differences. One, called "Surat mantra gajah," provided detailed information on mantras that aided in the hunting, snaring, feeding, and training of elephants to carry humans. The other, called "Mantra gajah," omitted most mentions of capture and training, focusing largely on using the perabun to deter the elephant from causing harm, much like the mantra in Raja Bilah's "Takwil mimpi." The differences in these texts pointed toward the growing redundancy of elephant labor in some parts of Perak.

The sense of redundancy and desire for distance from the elephant was articulated during a historical juncture when the animal was being rapidly displaced from its role in the transport system. By 1885, the rivers in Larut were too silted up to serve as waterways, and a rail link was built to replace them. Similar displacement from water to rail occurred in Kinta Valley a decade later, as tailings from tin mining clogged the river and made some parts too shallow for boats. The Kinta Valley Railway was then built to connect Ipoh and Telok Anson, thereby superseding the river as a mode of transport.[67] By all accounts, the numbers of elephants and other large mammals in Malaya plummeted at the turn of the twentieth century.[68] As early as the 1870s, Swettenham wrote about his baffled expectations in encountering big game, seeing "only their tracks on the borders of the bubbling pool" where he had expected them to congregate.[69] Exact numbers before the 1930s are unavailable, but scattered reports attested to their decrease.[70]

Hunters were in a special position to notice the falling numbers of big game, as hunting and policing large mammals were activities often intertwined. Commissioner Harry Syers, the primary organizer of the police force in Selangor, Perak, and Pahang in the mid-1870s, hunted elephants and other large mammals before his death on the horns of an enraged *seladang*, a species of Malayan wild cattle, which he had wounded.[71] The conversion of land from swidden to territorially bound settled agriculture reduced the secondary forest regrowth that had fed these animals, which then began to encroach on cultivated fields and were increasingly seen as pests. Syers wrote that men "engaged in agricultural pursuits complained bitterly of their crops being invariably destroyed by elephants."[72] He encountered such sentiments again as he hunted in the interior of Selangor, where the Sakai, an indigenous forest people, were reportedly frightened of wild elephants and cheered his pursuit of them.[73] William Jervois, governor of the Straits Settlements in the 1870s, reported similar sentiments in his conversations with villagers in Kuala Kangsar, whose first questions to him included what to do about elephants and seladang rampaging through their gardens.[74] When roads, railways, and migrant labor began to supplant captive elephants in the transportation system and tin mines of Malaya, redundant elephants let loose also became a problem for the police. Jervois reported that "they [the villagers] complained very much of the depredation of the elephants who are brought over from Laroot [an exhausted tin-mining area] and then turned loose."[75]

Syers and Jervois were part of a broader group who portrayed themselves as heroes helping hapless agriculturalists. White big game hunters also joined in; William Hornaday, an American who hunted big game in South and Southeast Asia during this period, stated that when he was on a hunt for elephants in Selangor, "our Malay friends . . . hailed our warlike appearance with delight, and gathered in an excited group around the ruins of their pole platform, which the rascally elephants had torn down just the day before. . . . No wonder they begged us to shoot all the beasts, one by one, which we solemnly promised to do."[76] The conquest of elephants became part of a colonial performance of power over peoples whom the colonizers considered racially inferior. European imperialism's *mission civilisatrice* was as keen to show off dead elephants as the elephant shaman had once been to display their authority (*kuasa*) over live, tamed ones.

Their slanted positionality notwithstanding, Syers and Jervois did identify a common fear of elephants among agriculturalists and, later, planters. Human-elephant conflicts were exacerbated with the coming of the rubber tree to Perak and its adoption as a cash crop that eventually provided one of the most substantial sources of revenue in the colony. Planters worried for their rubber crop, as the elephant appeared to be inordinately fond of the rubber tree bark. The conflicts drove the elephant population, increasingly untethered from their work, deeper into the forest and farther uphill, where they ran up against swiddeners who had moved there. From the 1890s onward, many reported complaints about the elephant conflicts came from rural peoples in areas unconnected by roads and railways. This pattern is consistent with Charles Wharton's classic study of wild cattle habits in Southeast Asia, where he observed that wild cattle such as seladang thrived in swiddening upland but not in virgin forests or with settler-agriculturalists.[77] These stories of rampaging in swidden plots, agriculturalist land, and fledgling plantations indexed the retreat of elephants, the reach of the colonial state that was corralling them, and the increasing separation of human and elephant spheres.

Raja Bilah himself could mark megafaunal retreat physically. He accompanied H. W. C. Leech, the British magistrate in the Federated Malay States, on a trip inland in the early 1890s, during which the latter noted the imprint of the wild elephant withdrawing farther and farther from human settlement. At an elevation of 2,500 feet, the party found "the footprints of wild elephants, where

I should have thought few animals, but a goat could have gone, most certainly no tame elephant."[78] The high mountain pass where these footprints were seen led to the neighboring state of Pahang, not under British rule at the time. The locals called the area Batu Gajah (Stone of the Elephant), a name that Leech stated was "derived from [a large boulder on] the right-hand side of the path, which bears a fanciful resemblance to an elephant kneeling down as they do to receive their loads" and was also a testament to the wild elephants that had once roamed there.[79] Batu Gajah testified to the persistence of animist-inflected religious practice in the 1890s—practice that stood in respectful awe of trees, rocks, and nonhuman animals. Everyone passing the stone, which the locals called Toh Gajah, was supposed to pluck a handful of grass or leaves and strike it seven times on the breast to ask for fine weather, leaving the plants as a food offering to the spirit of the elephant. In his journey with Raja Bilah, Leech commented that "having some people in the party familiar with elephants, we were enabled to choose food such as these animals like and were rewarded by not getting any rain till we returned to Kampong Changkat."[80] This nod toward old beliefs was not an allusion to their prevalence; instead, it came with the sense that the Malay Peninsula's era of interceding with elephants' spirits to control the weather was fading. The end of the nineteenth century was an inflection point in accelerating elephants' decline to the few thousand that remain alive today.

The shaman of elephants (*pawang gajah*) correspondingly declined. Captive elephants and their drivers lived on in some rural parts of the peninsula even in the second half of the twentieth century, but their numbers dwindled rapidly. By the 1970s, the Malaysian government had to employ elephant catchers from India to trap and transport wild elephants from a tract of land marked for redevelopment to a national park. Local elephant expertise had vanished.[81] The turn of the century was also a turning point in this family's history. Raja Bilah was likely the last generation to have such a dream book. What survived in the archive of his son, Raja Yacob, was strictly bureaucratic in the mode of an administrator, consisting of details on wood collection permits issued, records of village disputes, and daily work diaries.

In the various elephant mantras highlighted here we see a reflection of landscape change in everyday religious behavior. The downward trend in the population of elephants, Raja Bilah's dream book, and the written record of Malayan elephant charms were subaltern perspectives on broader, rapid, more-than-human changes to the peninsula. Raja Bilah's oneiric elephants pointed toward the centralization of divine power in a single source that accompanied a turn toward less localized forms of relating to nature. Whereas early Perak elephant mantras had incorporated new and old gods for the pragmatic purpose of reproducing an elephant labor force, Raja Bilah's oneiric elephants denoted a more orthodox monotheism of no god but God, with humans as special agents who sought protection from nonhuman harm and a transcendent spirituality beyond this life that did not necessarily include animals. It drew on a rationalized version of Islam, leveraging a single source of power for a single pursuit of a single aim, in this case the welfare of humans. Elephants, disenchanted, were becoming estranged from that aim and superfluous to both the labor force in Malaya's forest landscape as well as the cosmological landscape of many of the peoples inhabiting it.

HAUNTED BY ELEPHANTS

Reenchantment of elephants emerged almost simultaneously with disenchantment, as predicted by Geoffrey Benjamin's thesis of the pendulum-like swing mentioned earlier. Here, reenchantment simulates enchantment by accruing wonder, a heightened intrinsic value, and re-recognition of agency in the material body of a living being—but only in the context of absence. The documenting of elephant mantras attested to incipient nostalgia after loss, evinced in the impulse to record practices that would become wondrous anomalies not even fifty years later. This intuitive reflex to observe, record, and marvel at close interactions between the humans and elephants occurred contemporaneously among North Sumatran visitors to Malaya, who were unaccustomed to riding captive elephants because the animals were no longer used widely on the Sumatran side of the Straits of Malacca. A relative of Raja Bilah, who had a short sojourn in Malaya in 1884, dedicated several pages of his travel diary to elephants. Like Maxwell, he was fascinated by the language the herders (*gembalas*) used to communicate with elephants, listed key phrases, worried over the behavior of the bull elephant he was riding, and illustrated his experience with hand-drawn figures of the animal.[82] He recorded his reactions to the pachyderms during a period in which encounters with elephants were becoming rarer, as the landscape was becoming increasingly secularized in yet another transition in the history of conversions.

Before the 1920s, elephants remained part of Malay sultans' projection of traditional power, despite the decline in elephant numbers. The sultan of Perak, for instance, came to the inaugural meeting of the Federated Malay States

Perak elephants, ca. 1908. Courtesy of Leiden University Library, KITLV 1403887.

Council of Rulers with a procession of fifty elephants that "ranged in front of the house side by side," and in awesome acquiescence, "at a signal from their drivers [they] knelt down and his Highness descended."[83] Such displays were part of what the historian Donna Amoroso calls "traditionalism"—a conscious appropriation of the something from the past as a seemingly timeless tradition for contemporary advantage.[84] The British colonial project used animals and humans to encourage such displays. Elephants were on display at the king and queen's coronation in 1911 in London, for example, while Sultan Abdul Hamid of Kedah was also high-handedly informed that he could participate in the procession only if he wore traditional Malay attire.[85] Tradition with regard to elephants, however, was simultaneously fraying on the ground. As early as 1879, the Perak regent and his council of advisers began refusing applications by their district chiefs to capture wild elephants. The minutes of one council meeting noted that "permission to erect a *kubu* to catch wild elephants is refused by the Regent and Council, the loss of life of these animals being too great owing to the inexperience of the persons employed."[86] This refusal could be an isolated case, since elephants were no longer mentioned in later council minutes, and without further evidence no precise conclusion can be drawn about when the practice was halted. Nonetheless, it indicated that Malayan royals had lost interest in replenishing their captive elephant herd by the late nineteenth century even though the pachyderms were royal mounts well into the 1920s. Where traditionalism replaced authentic tradition, elephants were detached from real links to royal power, although their occasional appearances remained awe-inspiring scenes.

Fascination with live elephants was only one way in which affect for the pachyderm was retained in a disenchanted landscape. More suggestive is the growth of heroic tales around dead elephants, which attested to affective wonder emerging from the human communities most closely associated with their decline: tin miners, men working on the new railway lines, and hunters. The mining town of Sitiawan, for instance, is said to be a contraction of the Malay phrase *setia kawan* (loyal friend) in honor of an elephant who drowned together with an elephant friend he had faithfully refused to leave stuck in mud amid a rising tide. The place used to be called Kampung Gajah Mati (Dead Elephant Village), but after a bad outbreak of smallpox among the Chinese mining community in 1887, a name change was considered necessary to propitiate the spirits that had brought the disease.[87] Changing names essentially transformed a neutral place-name referencing the dead elephants into a memorial to elephantine loyalty and friendship at a time when their labor was growing redundant in tin-mining enterprises. The heroic slant of elephant memorials was also taken up by more secular stories that were not geared toward propitiating spirits. In Teluk Intan, where a new railway line from Ipoh to Tapah bisected the forest, a signboard was erected for a bull elephant that had apparently died while charging a train to defend his family. "There is buried here a wild elephant, who in defence of his herd, charged and derailed a train on the 17th day of Sept[ember] 1894," reads the plaque raised in its honor.[88]

This 1894 clash between elephant and train was remarkable for the way in which the elephant's personality morphed over the ensuing decades. Initial reporting of the incident in the *Singapore Free Press* merely noted that a train in Tapah had collided with the elephant and that traffic on the train line stopped for two days as a result. A memoir by an Australian mining engineer and land surveyor for Malayan roads, published a few years after the accident, acknowledged the elephant's anthropomorphic agency. "One large tusker went so far in his dislike to the innovations of civilization as to dispute the passage of the train. In this encounter, however, he [the elephant] came off badly for he was instantly struck down and killed."[89] When a similar collision occurred in 1926, this 1894 incident was revisited with admiration for the elephant's futile bravery. Citing an unnamed "old resident of Perak" as eyewitness, the *Singapore Free*

Press reported, "The 'gajah' was an inquisitive animal. It stalked up to the engine and, seemingly imagining that the funnel was the trunk of another elephant, it curled its trunk round the funnel . . . the elephant burned his trunk pretty badly . . . he charged the engine repeatedly and tried to capsize it by levering at it with its trunk."[90] There was no mention of a desire to protect on the part of the bull elephant here, but his defiance in the face of certain defeat took on a mildly heroic cast.

Some were skeptical of the bull elephant's protective instincts. Malayan planter Jim Hislop, interviewed in 1965, reportedly scoffed that "the bull scarcely cares two cents about the herd . . . was probably short-sighted and simply got in the way of the train." But even he admitted possible heroism in elephants, especially the females, as "every herd has an 'auntie', a sage and experienced cow with a man's courage and a woman's wits."[91] Unquestioning valorization of the dead elephant reemerged again from the 1980s onward, in the occasional press report, various websites, and contemporary blogs of people who stumbled upon that old plaque of uncertain provenance and lauded elephantine protectiveness in a landscape notable for their absence.[92]

This persistent admiration for dead elephants must be juxtaposed against reports of brutish elephants issued by annoyed and worried agriculturalists and planters, whom the colony's English-language press often mentioned during the 1920s to 1950s. It must also be placed in the context of broad-based participation in the killing of rogue elephants in this period; Malays as well as some interior peoples, most notably the Sakai, appeared to have killed elephants themselves or substantially assisted in their hunting.[93] Besides elephant-human conflict over land, part of the motivation for elephant killings was pecuniary. By the early twentieth century, the price for the ivory taken from a dead elephant's body had apparently reached that of a live elephant on the market.[94] From the 1880s to early 1900s, the colonial government awarded one tusk to any person who could prove having shot an elephant. This practice once led to a dispute between the white revenue collector at Ulu Sengat and his Malay tracker over who had a right to the tusk, the latter alleging that he had fired the fatal shots and that the former only came to shoot the elephant at point-blank range when it was already struggling on the ground.[95] This macabre dispute highlighted the collaboration between imperial authorities and their subaltern subjects, both being invested in the elimination of elephants living in proximity to human settlements.

However, those prevailing hostilities toward the elephant only served to highlight the occasional heroic elephant that *did* become revered. The development, denial, and reemergence of the 1894 elephant's bravery against a steel foe, contemporaneous with voluminous complaints about normal elephant infractions against human enterprise, suggested two things. First, affective wonder at the elephant was being located in the figure of the anthropomorphic, exceptional elephant. Second, admiration for the elephant was most keenly felt in its absence rather than its closeness. The intimacy consequent to killing *an* elephant could engender a motivation for preserving *the species* as a whole.

Theodore Hubback, a big game hunter turned wildlife conservationist in Malaya, embodied this latter paradox. A colonial official in the Public Works Department in Pahang, he spearheaded initiatives to maintain a viable population of large mammals in Malaya and was the first to introduce state measures to protect the elephant, seladang, and rhinoceros through regulation in 1896, even if the measures were toothless in practice. Conservation became a more urgent issue in 1922 when a new law, the Wild Animals and Bird Protection Agreement, came into force in the colony.[96] By the time this law had been passed, there was practically no large game in Perak and Selangor, where forest had been rapidly converted into profit-making tin and rubber enterprises. The law was wielded largely to preserve populations of megafauna in the agricultural states of Pahang, Trengganu, and Kelantan. Hubback and a government assessor were commissioned to gauge attitudes toward wildlife among peasant cultivators in the early 1930s, with a view toward creating a national park in the area. Their report stated that peasant witnesses "were hostile towards any steps for conservation" and recommended distributing propaganda to promote an educated change.[97] This recommendation failed in its aims, as it ignored the issue of risk to peasants as well as planters living in proximity to elephants. In an ironic twist, Hubback, a man with plenty of elephant kills to his name, became known as the colony's biggest advocate for wildlife by fashioning himself as an expert objective observer of what had been lost.

The friction between Hubback and the peasants and planters whom he came up against redefined the relationship between humans and elephants to a point where the former's affection for the latter appeared inversely correlated to how closely they lived together. Live elephants were, on the one hand, complicated and vexing to live with on a daily basis, especially when they were no longer needed for labor. Dead elephants, on the other hand, inspired love. A realignment of affect and wonder toward the elephant from a close-up to a distant lens meant that top-down conservation measures, such as those initiated by

Hubback, kept running into the problem of being perceived as inimical to local interests.[98] Returning to religion as a lens to analyze this change, we can tap religious scholar Lisa Sideris's argument that science consecrates what had previously been religious wonder at the natural world.[99] It was twentieth-century science, driven by conservationist movements of which Hubback was a pioneer, that designated the elephant as a "charismatic species," defined by the animal's ability to be a boundary object holding significant affect for different epistemic communities capable of generating popular support for conservation.[100] This designation is reminiscent of the elephant's past representation as a symbol of life, power, and authority that spread globally across diverse communities. Its ubiquity in the fabric of Malayan life prior to the end of the nineteenth century was woven from threads of animism, Hinduism, Buddhism, and to a certain extent Islam, while rooted to local forests. The term "charismatic megafauna" thus relocated the elephant back into that ecology, but in a scientific manner.

Scientific consecration has its limits; it cannot encompass the diversity of class and culture and its inequalities.[101] Universalizing environmental ethics rooted in science often failed to account for disparities in wealth as well as environmental injustice. Likewise, Hubback was part of a bureaucracy that sought a universal, rationalized approach to conservation when species scarcity was quantifiably proven to be a problem. His efforts failed to connect with human groups who could no longer find enough affection for megafauna to justify the risks of living with them or to deny themselves the opportunity to profit from them. Planters and peasants were seemingly united by a lack of affective restraint toward changing their local forest environment and a turn away from religious wonder at nature. Nevertheless, the two groups remained divided by their relative wealth and power. The planters' lack of wonder, on the one hand, stemmed from their complicity with a rationalized colonial capitalist project. Sedentarized peasants, on the other hand, were corralled by that same project. Displaced to the bottom of the economic hierarchy and bereft of local charismatic leadership, they dis-enchanted a pragmatic, long-running struggle to gain the upper hand over elephants, removed the animals from the domain of religious self, and disavowed the fluidity of human and nonhuman nature, as had been presaged by Raja Bilah's perabun charm.

Emotional motivations served to preserve the elephant in life and in memory. Earlier conceptualizations of the elephant were grounded in religious beliefs that such animals shared the same capacity as humans to be vessels of spirit inhabitation and were crucial to the production and reproduction of life on earth itself. Even when affect for the elephants was being displaced from its former domains, they could still induce wonder at their largeness and recall the royal performances of powers past. Sporadically, elephants would be commemorated for qualities like heroism, kindness, and loyalty. Increasingly, however, these moments became inversely correlated with distance. The motivation to keep elephants alive shifted from being articulated in everyday religious mantras to the abstract responsibility of a rationalized bureaucracy. The supplication for distance and humans' special power over animals invoked in Raja Bilah's perabun charm in the name of the Islamic God were, in a way, answered. In its Malayan postenchantment, the elephant became an Other being.

The simultaneous disenchantment of forests, buy-ins to an anthropocentric, rationalized form of Islam, and declines in elephant populations in Malaya as the twentieth century began are changes that resonated with the processes of mass conversions to Christianity in Sumatra, which had displaced charismatic tribal religious leaders and eroded resistance to environmental change. However, the Malayan side of the story has its own unique features, among which was a fairly swift retreat of animist-inflected everyday practices that had survived in religious life in the peninsula since conversion to Islam five centuries earlier. Here, there was no morphing of syncretism into religious resistance comparable to that of the Parmalim and Parhudamdam in North Sumatra. Rather, migration facilitated by the colonial transition—not just of Chinese, Indians, and Arabs but also of Sumatrans such as the Mandailing Raja Asal and Raja Bilah—encouraged a rationalized practice of religion that centralized divine power and was detached from local landscapes.

The elephant not only experienced but also embodied these changes. Mediated always through human eyes, the elephant is first seen as an enchanted body not so unlike a human. Captive elephants were put to work as royal transport mounts; their importance as vehicles for travel and transport into the wilderness ensured that wild and captive elephants were able to reproduce their own populations as well as mark and perpetuate human authority at the forest's fringes. We see that importance decline as the forest became increasingly legible to humans, thus fatally shrinking the elephants' habitat. We see the elephant's superfluity in the new economy translated into new religious imaginaries with little space to accommodate it. And, in the bodies of dead elephants, we see the fragility and futility of humans' affectionate outreach to them.

Did one decline cause the other? Put another way, would more of Malaya's megafauna have survived if the pawang had not lost their place in the hierarchy of power? Let us be clear that these shamans were not environmentalists. They were simply perceived as having special powers to intercede with the spirits that inhabited beings in nature, human and nonhuman alike. But in those flexible methods of communication, they represented an everyday religion that was invested in local natures as living bodies rather than usable parts. What I wish to stress here are those possibilities that have eroded with this contraction of interlinked religious and ecological imaginations; I have also sought to demonstrate a way in which they might have historically had material effect. This contracted imagination, shaped over a century, remains relevant in contemporary Christian and Muslim efforts to address the environmental crisis.

CONCLUSION Faith-Based Environmentalism in the Anthropocene

In recent years, Christian and Muslim voices raising the pressing need to care for the environment have gained international attention. Pope Francis's 2015 encyclical *Laudato Si'* is one such global clarion call that recognizes that environmental action is not optional. "Although the post-industrial period may well be remembered as one of the most irresponsible in history, nonetheless there is reason to hope that humanity at the dawn of the twenty-first century will be remembered for having generously shouldered its grave responsibilities," he writes.[1] Muslims, too, have increasingly articulated a greater will to take collective action on environmental issues. An Islamic foundation for ecology and environmental sciences was established in the 1980s by British environmentalist Fazlun Khalid, prodding a global reassessment of how Islamic worldviews can be applied to environmental issues.[2] Muslim leaders in Malaysia and Indonesia have regularly issued *fatwa* to condemn actions that led to transborder disasters such as choking hazes and wildlife extinctions. Insofar as it is possible to generalize from a nonmonolithic Islam, Muslim environmentalism emphasizes the accountability of human stewardship in this world, where "precarity, kin and community, ethics of consequence apparent in the natural world, and anticipation of the apocalypse and even what comes after are standard themes."[3] Both Christian and Muslim views of environmentalism leverage the special position of humans as stewards of God-given dominion and the responsibility that this position entails.

In situated contexts, however, faith-based environmentalism faces the challenge of translating environmental concerns into coherent actions that can be enacted on multiple scales: individual, community, and global. Moreover, it faces the challenge of maintaining moral force in a political landscape that is, prima facie at least, secular. The history unfolding through our small, marginalized theater of conversions indicates that Christian and Muslim environmentalist efforts will require more than forceful reminders of moral stewardship. They must also contend with a past in which conversions elevated certain human groups and nonhuman natures at the expense of others. The previous chapters have shown the ways in which the modernist praxis of Islam and Christianity emerged on the back of Dutch and British colonialism to create possibilities for progress through activities that estranged peoples from their local environments—mining, logging, and monocrop agriculture. This praxis translated into an everyday religion that became increasingly anthropocentric and individualistic, and it generated a religious imagination that favored landscapes of human enterprise over forests. Mass conversion occurred apace with endangerment of those nonhumans that did not quite fit into these refashioned spaces, as represented by the camphor tree and the elephant. Islamic ecological thought might at present position itself as an alternative bulwark to modernity's excesses, but in Muslim Southeast Asia modernist Islam has yet to motivate much environmental empathy or inspire large-scale action. As this book has shown, the nineteenth century brought about reformed understandings of Islam through the lens of anthropocentric dominion. Such conversions of understanding conferred responsibility for protecting the nonhuman to faithful individuals while sapping them of the personal motivation and decentralized communal political systems that could have facilitated their doing so. In other words, religious conversions exacerbated inequality in agency to impact local environments, placing such power in peoples estranged from these spaces rather than in those living intimately entangled in them. These conditions governed what I have termed the spiritual Anthropocene.

The limits of faith-based environmentalism partly stemmed from how conversion to monotheism could be, as suggested by the philosopher Marcel Gauchet, a social revolution that shifted societies from immersing themselves in nature to the business of transforming it.[4] The asymmetrical power structures that reduced the investment of local communities in intact forest ecosystems were established when religious and political changes intersected during the long nineteenth century, remaking both peoples and landscapes. Such a renovation involved a constant interplay between fragmentation and unification. Water-based webs of communication, along with the political authority of riverine sultanates, fragmented and were then reunified through the land-based roads and railways constructed by colonial states. Upland forests fragmented under pressure from plantations and mines—developments only constrained by coalescing patchworks of small agricultural holdings at the forest's edge. Migration and conflict fragmented upland identities, and conversions stitched them together once again through new language modalities that articulated ideas of landscapes, peoples, and how they fit together anew. The socio-environmental landscape produced by these processes was amenable to centralized authority, both divine and political, as well as eventual secularization.

It is important to stress that monotheism is not inherently more inimical to nonhuman worlds than animism. Although the latter arguably offered a more expansive ecological imagination and decentralized politics, religious life had centered on charismatic individuals rather than broad-based empowerment to effect change. Moreover, on a material level, animists participated in forest clearings prior to the nineteenth century, and these actions were transformative even though they left a much smaller footprint than those carried out during the Anthropocene.[5] Bearing witness to the experiences of converting landscapes through everyday religion lets us appreciate the insights of scholars who have viewed "power and protection" as continuous themes shaping religious worldviews on the environment across diverse traditions.[6] Nonetheless, mass conversions, including reforms against heterodoxy, implicated modernist Islam and Christianity in the relentless othering of the nonhuman and peoples who related to them as persons; this process was part of colonialism in the Anthropocene and accelerated environmental degradation. This othering is seen today not only through the relegation of indigenous faiths to superstition but also in the heterodoxy assigned to traditional communions with nature in which some Muslims actively participated. Islam and to a smaller extent Christianity both occupy privileged positions in maritime Southeast Asia as influential modern religions. This positioning confers to their faithful a possible platform through which to launch change, articulated through religious thought, that could mitigate the specter of environmental crisis. How and to what extent has this platform been used?

FAITHS, FORESTS, AND FIGHTS

The Anthropocene shaped hierarchies of power that intensified human domination over nonhuman natures, leaving an indelible imprint on today's religious landscape. The legacies of this history are evident in two sites of contestation: in hostility toward forest faiths that cast doubt on whether forest peoples could be effective stewards of their adat land and in monotheistic faith-based environmentalism that does not seriously question the power structures enabling accelerated anthropogenic environmental change. On both sides of the Straits of Malacca, recent reports indicate increasing pressure to convert the small pockets of animist forest peoples remaining outside monotheism. Several news reports showed that the Orang Rimba in Sumatra and the Orang Asli, a loose conglomeration of eighteen ethnic groups recognized as Indigenous in Malaysia, are currently being pushed to convert to Islam through a mix of aggressive religious outreach and state neglect in upholding their rights.[7] These religious contestations are intertwined with environmental struggles over forest ecosystems, as these groups maintain a lifestyle deeply invested in an intact forest currently under threat from capitalist development.

While this book has identified colonialism as a catalyst for change in the long nineteenth century, the impact of these changes trails into the present. In the wake of the colonial period, the rights of forest peoples to lands haunted by the spirits of their ancestors are often challenged on two contradictory fronts: the peoples are either considered not indigenous enough or too indigenous, that is, too backward. In independent Indonesia during the 1950s, some Indigenous peoples, mostly adherents of old faiths, were designated as *masyarakat terasing*, a term that can be translated as "isolated communities," imputing alienation and strangeness. Beginning in 1950, the Indonesian Department for Social Affairs maintained a Dutch-era initiative to resettle these communities. Although mechanisms to recognize customary land were later developed by the Indonesian state, the criteria defined for such recognition were difficult to fulfill. As the anthropologist Tania Li notes, "To qualify for forest licenses, *masyarakat adat* must have both the institutional formality of a colonial-era adat law regime and be embedded in nature, an unlikely combination."[8] In independent Malaysia, the Orang Asli are seen as native "sons of the soil" (*bumiputera*) but remain largely excluded from real political power. The cultural anthropologist Rusaslina Idrus assesses the situation this way: "Malay leaders espouse native rights rhetoric while continuing to sideline the other natives, the Orang Asli."[9] Such exclusion coupled with land dispossession has played out in courts of law. In 1995, the state of Selangor tried to appropriate land from an Orang Asli group, arguing in court that its members no longer practiced a traditional way of life and planted rice rather than root crops. The state further argued the group had no right to claim land under a reservations act for Malays as it was not Malay. After a lengthy legal battle, Malaysia's federal court ruled that the displaced Orang Asli deserved better financial compensation but that the land itself would not be returned to them.[10]

Following mass conversions in North Sumatra, there are now few Batak communities recognized by the state as Indigenous (*masyarakat adat*). As mentioned in this book's introduction, one such group, called the Pandumaan-Sipatihuta, has long struggled to protect their benzoin forests (*tombak haminjon*) against pulp and paper corporation PT Toba Lestari; their fight signifies the difficulties of maintaining forest land stewardship in the face of state-championed development, which is more often than not supported by peoples adhering to more privileged religions. Local Christian leaders have gotten involved in this fight against land appropriation, and Batak Protestant priests were among those arrested for leading protests around this issue.[11] On an official level, though, the Batak Christian Protestant Church's efforts were less confrontational. With support from the World Bank, the church quietly ran a small-scale forestry division comprising tree planting programs and religious-based education on natural resource management targeted at village communities.[12] The scope of these programs appears resolutely local, with little ambition for scaling up. In the latest turnabout by the central government, part of the adat land returned to the Indigenous groups in 2017 was alienated for agricultural use in 2021.[13] The victories of Indigenous peoples were precarious and remained dependent on allyship, which could prove unreliable, especially for an ethnic and religious minority.

As Islam is the religion of the ruling majority in this region, Muslim environmentalism in particular cannot just inculcate moral will for responsible stewardship of the environment among the faithful. It will also have to contend with the question of how to position itself with respect to environmental movements that seek to accord stewardship to peoples *outside* its religious tradition, while reflecting on whether to disentangle itself from the yoke of capitalism to redefine development and, if so, how to accomplish that shift. Thus far, there is little available data on action taken under the loose banner of Muslim environmentalism. Extant analyses suggest that movements identifying with this rubric tend to sidestep the entwined issues of inclusion and progressiveness by focusing on small-scale projects that do not significantly apply pressure to the levers of power installed by the Anthropocene. The anthropologist Kristina Grossmann has surveyed some projects representing "green Islam" in Indonesia, including permaculture farms, a revival of Sufi eco-mysticism, and expansion in biofuel use as a renewable energy source inspired by the Qur'an. In her evaluation, however, "green Islam is still a toothless tiger," as its reach does not even extend to Sumatra and Kalimantan, where the majority of land conversions in the 2010s took place.[14] Furthermore, an empirical study on environmental attitudes among high school students in Yogyakarta and Surabaya studying in "eco-schools" demonstrates a rather blinkered stance toward environmental issues. Despite identifying as environmentalists, most of the one thousand students surveyed saw waste as the country's main environmental problem, consistent with a local urban optic, and were not informed about issues at the national and international levels. The study finds "shallow education" contributes to locals' "failure to identify the complex interactions among environmental problems and human behavior."[15] These findings suggest that broad-based educational efforts are somewhat ineffectual and have yet to be penetrated by a religious environmental consciousness.

The most promising actions taken by religious groups have been interfaith calls. In the face of choking haze in 2016, representatives from eight major religious organizations in Indonesia, including the Indonesian Council of Ulema (MUI), the Indonesian Communion of Churches (PGI), and the Supreme Council of Confucian Religions in Indonesia (Matakin), condemned large-scale forest burnings by corporations as immoral acts.[16] The condemnation was long overdue; regional haze has been a regular problem since the early 1990s. More recently, a group of Muslim clerics, Christian pastors, and representatives from the Syncretic Beliefs Council in Indonesia publicly rejected an omnibus bill passed by the parliament that would relax regulations against rampant deforestation.[17] It remains to be seen whether moral condemnations can compel change without action on a political level; regional Muslim political groups have so far declined to take up an environmental agenda.

Diffuse, marginal, and lacking a radical edge, action under the umbrella of Muslim environmentalism contrasts with environmental protest that allies with the cause of indigeneity. The environmental activist group Indonesian Forum for the Living Environment (Wahana Lingkungan Hidup Indonesia, WALHI) has spearheaded much of this effort since the late 1980s, creating a new network from which the Pan-Indonesian Alliance of Indigenous Peoples (Alliansi Masyarakat Adat Nusantara, AMAN) emerged. Formed a year after the fall of the authoritarian Indonesian New Order, AMAN offered a radical politics signaled through a declaration during its inaugural congress that "if the state does not recognize us [the Indigenous peoples], then we will not recognize the state."[18] In many ways, AMAN poses a challenge to the political status quo by drawing on environmentalism and traditionalism in a bid to reclaim some measure of power sapped by a century of conversions in land, politics, and religion. AMAN's approach may not be *the* answer to environmental issues facing the region, but it revives a view of the world that harks back to those who are stateless and long obscured by a century of conversions that reinforced the centralization of religious and secular power.

WIZARDS AND PROPHETS OF THE ANTHROPOCENE

The North Sumatran uplands are still being made and unmade. During my fieldwork, I was welcomed to Lake Toba by the sight and scent of dead fish. In May 2016, millions of them floated to the surface, and news reports later estimated them to have totaled about fifteen hundred tons. Experts were at a loss to explain this apocalyptic mass die-off, although later it was suggested that volcanic activity or pollution through tourist detritus had cut the oxygen supply for the fish. This was not the first time such an event had occurred; a similar mass die-off had occurred in the 1990s, occasioning unease among the community. A fisherman by the lake conversing with me about these die-offs mentioned that smallholder fish farms in the area would soon be shut down to make way for greater state-led development of tourism in Toba and Samosir. The dead fish presaged further endings—of smallholder fish farms, their fish, and their aspirations. The squeezing of small-scale fishing laborers caused enough dissatisfaction to become an election issue, with one such local laborer named Pak Najib becoming "the representation of the unjustly persecuted *wong cilik* (little people)," in the words of political analyst Iqra Anugrah.[19] Still, many in Toba welcomed the projected increase in tourism, including drivers who praised the new roads out of the town of Prapat leading to a new airport in Medan. These formed yet more new connections, adding to the many constructed over two long centuries of state-led development.

The Anthropocene is distinguished by its far-ranging human impact on the earth as a system. Looking through a historical lens at a local level, we may find that these changes sound like a continuous hum of making and remaking, punctuated by sudden catastrophes. Environmentalist efforts do not and indeed cannot seek to freeze or return the world to one desired endpoint. In a recent influential work, the science writer Charles Mann has argued that there are two general approaches toward managing environmental issues, and he uses a metaphor with religious overtones to define them.[20] One approach is spearheaded by a group he calls the prophets, who believe that the capacity to effect change in the Anthropocene lies in changing human values and character; they see less consumption, less greed, and a restructuring of power relations that incentivizes these behaviors as the necessary measures to address the environmental crisis. The other approach comes from a group he calls the wizards, who promote technology and innovation as propellers for crisis mitigation; they hold that if technological progress proved decisive in breaking through past ecological constraints, then cultivating and funding such expertise can prevent environmental catastrophe.

Starting from the long nineteenth century, on many different levels, wizards have largely eclipsed prophets. The resurgence of faith-based environmentalism in recent years has unveiled the possibilities that still exist along the prophets' line: a rethinking of what it means to be human, humanity's responsibilities, and ecological imagination. Will the most influential religions in the region restrict this reevaluation to those within their own communities and seek change through converting individuals? Or will prophets from various traditions find shared concern for the earth to be a more expansive platform for redressing the power asymmetries that have resulted from the Anthropocene? What new structures, representations, and materialities will result? Through answers and nonanswers, conversions are sure to continue.

GLOSSARY OF MALAY AND BATAK TERMS

adat (Malay/Batak) · Customary norms or system of traditional laws

Angkola · Batak subgroup and its dialect

begoe (Batak) · Ancestral spirits or the soul after death

bomoh (Malay) · A person with spiritual or healing powers but usually regarded as having lower status than a *pawang*

bona hajoe (Batak) · *Datu* who leads a search for camphor in the forest

Bugis · Ethnic group in Sulawesi

Dairi · Batak ethnic subgroup and its dialect

datu (Batak) · Animist priest(s) or spirit-medium(s) in traditional Batak society

Dalihan Na Tolu (Batak) · Literally, "three hearthstones," symbolizing a system of interlinked sociocultural obligations toward one's patriclan, the patriclan of one's spouse, and the patriclan into which one's daughter marries

dulang (Malay) · A wide pan, usually used in traditional tin mining

gajah (Malay) · Elephant

gembala · Elephant handler or herder

Harahap · A Batak clan name

harimau (Malay) · Tiger

hatoban (Batak) · Slave or enslaved class

horja · Loose unit of two to three villages

hulu/hilir (Malay) · Upstream/downstream

huta (Batak) · Village

Karo · A Batak ethnic subgroup

kepala · Head or chief

keramat · Sacred nature sites

lampan (Malay) · Ground sluice

Lauje · Upland ethnic group on Sulawesi

lombong (Malay) · Open-pit mines

Mandailing · A Batak subgroup and its dialect

mantri (Malay) · An official in a Malay royal court

marga (Batak) · Patriclan

marserak (Batak) · To migrate

Minangkabau · An ethnic subgroup

naga (Batak/Malay) · Large, serpent-like creature, localized from South Asian mythology

Naipospos · A Toba Batak clan

Nasution · A Batak clan

Orang Rimba · An ethnic group in Sumatra

pagar (Batak/Malay) · A gate or, in the context of ritual, a reference to defensive spells

Pakpak · A Batak subgroup and dialect

pamena (Batak) · A Karo Batak term for the "original" religion (before conversions to Christianity and Islam)

Pandumaan-Sipatihuta · An Indigenous community

pangulubalang (Batak) · Wood or stone sculpture for protecting the village; associated with human sacrifice, as it is believed to be animated by the ghost of the sacrificed

parbegu (Batak) · A term for the "spirit" religion before Christianity and Islam

Parmalim (Batak) · Adherents of pre-monotheistic religion from the late nineteenth century onward

Parhudamdam (Batak) · A movement of Parmalim who protested Dutch policies in the 1920s

pawang (Malay) · A person regarded as having spiritual and healing powers and the ability to communicate with spirits

penghulu · Village headman under colonial power

perabun (Malay) · A charm to limit the vision of a targeted game animal

pustaha (Batak) · Books made from bark, usually recording ritual knowledge or medical recipes from the datu

raub (Malay) · Handful

Rawa · An ethnic subgroup in Sumatra

sahala (Batak) · Spiritual prowess or charisma

seladang · Extinct species of cattle

siluman (Batak) · Shapeshifter, usually a human who can morph into predatory animals such as tigers

Simalungun · A Batak subgroup

sopo (Batak) · Communal hall in a Batak village

tarekat (Malay) · Muslim Sufi school or order

Toba · A Batak subgroup and dialect

tombak haminjon (Batak) · Forest of benzoin/frankincense trees

tondi (Batak) · Soul of a living human

towkay (Malay) · Colloquial term for Chinese capitalists or entrepreneurs

tunggal panaluan (Batak) · Magic staff of a datu

Yang Dipertuan (Malay) · Honorific for a sultan

NOTES

Foreword

1. See Jenkins, Tucker, and Grim, *Routledge Handbook of Religion and Ecology*.

2. Tsing, *In the Realm of the Diamond Queen*; Laakkonen, Tucker, and Vuorisalo, *Long Shadows*; Tucker and Russell, *Natural Enemy, Natural Ally*.

Introduction

1. "Tiger Brutally Killed in North Sumatra, Hung from Ceiling," *Jakarta Post*, March 4, 2018, www.thejakartapost.com/news/2018/03/04/tiger-brutally-killed-in-north -sumatra-hung-from-ceiling.html. Similar reports appeared in the *Washington Post*, *Independent*, and *South China Morning Post*.

2. Vincent Bevins, "'We'd Rather Die than Lose': Villagers in Indonesia Fight for a Land Rights Revolution," *The Guardian*, September 4, 2017, www.theguardian.com /global-development/2017/sep/04/villagers-in-indonesia-fight-for-a-land-rights -revolution.

3. Forsyth and Walker, *Forest Guardians, Forest Destroyers*.

4. Szerszynski, "Gods of the Anthropocene."

5. Van Leur, *Indonesian Trade and Society*, 95.

6. Reid, "Islamization and Christianization of Southeast Asia," 151–52; Ricklefs, "Six Centuries of Islamization in Java," 100–128.

7. Skeat, *Malay Magic*, 19.

8. Crutzen and Stoermer, "The Anthropocene"; Crutzen, "Geology of Mankind"; Steffen, Crutzen, and MacNeill, "The Anthropocene."

9. Cronon, "Trouble with Wilderness."

10. Steffen et al., "Trajectory of the Anthropocene," 91–92.

11. Davies, *Birth of the Anthropocene*, 2.

12. Chakrabarty, "Climate of History." See also Latour, *Facing Gaia*.

13. Århem, "Southeast Asian Animism in Context," 3–4.

14. Skeat, *Malay Magic*, 321–49; Boomgaard, *Frontiers of Fear*, 186–206.

15. Sprenger, "Dimensions of Animism in Southeast Asia," 41–42.

16. On Islam *mondain* and expert religion, see Soares and Osella, "Islam, Politics, Anthropology." On lived religion, see Hall, *Lived Religion in America*. On high/low and folk Islam, see Grehan, *Twilight of the Saints*.

17. Orsi, *Madonna of 115th Street*.

18. Lofton, *Consuming Religion*.

19. Ammerman, *Everyday Religion*.

20. Reid, "Islamization and Christianization of Southeast Asia," 178–79.

21. An anonymous reviewer of the manuscript for this book perceptively highlighted how this book is "haunted by Weber" and provided sharp advice on how to better engage with Weber's ideas.

22. Szerszynski, "Gods of the Anthropocene," 253.

23. On how official religions could be used to legitimize environmental degradation in Indonesia, see Bagir, "Importance of Religion and Ecology in Indonesia."

24. Reid, "Is There a Batak History?," 1.

25. L. Andaya, *Leaves of the Same Tree*, 146–72; L. Andaya, "Trans-Sumatra Trade."

26. Sibeth, *The Batak*; Maloney, "Possible Early Dry-Land and Wetland Rice Cultivation in Highland North Sumatra"; Maloney, "Pollen Analytical Evidence for Early Forest Clearance in North Sumatra."

27. See Vergouwen, *Social Organisation and Customary Law of the Toba-Batak*; Aritonang, *Mission Schools in Batakland*; Kipp, *Disassociated Identities*; Kipp and Kipp, *Beyond Samosir*; and Van Bemmelen, *Christianity, Colonization and Gender in North Sumatra*.

28. See Singarimbun, *Kinship, Descent and Alliance among the Karo Batak*; Kipp, *Early Years of a Dutch Colonial Mission*; Kushnick, "Resource Competition and Reproduction in Karo Batak Villages"; and Steedly, *Hanging without a Rope*.

29. On Mandailing literature, see Rodgers, *Telling Lives, Telling History*; and Rodgers, "Compromise and Contestation in Colonial Sumatra." On historical linguistics, see Kozok, *Surat Batak*. On textiles, see Niessen, *Batak Cloth and Clothing*. On music, see Byl, *Antiphonal Histories*.

30. See Tugby, *Mandailing Immigrants in West Malaysia*; Lubis and Nasution, *Raja Bilah and the Mandailings of Perak*; A.-R. Lubis, *Sutan Puasa*; and Lees, "Becoming Malay."

31. See, among others, Situmorang, *Toba Na Sae*; Pospos, *Aku dan Toba*; Parlindungan, *Pongkinangolngolan Sinambela gelar Tuanku Rao*; and A.-R. Lubis, *Tarikh Raja Asal dan keluarganya*.

32. Steedly, "Modernity and the Memory Artist," 814.

33. See Harahap, *Si Bulus Bulus*. Titles and copies of the translations of educational materials by Willem Iskander are available from Leiden University Library, National Library in Jakarta, and a private documentation center, Pusat Dokumentasi Mandailing, in Medan, Indonesia. For the full list, see Zakaria, "Sacral Ecologies of the North Sumatran Highlands," 46–47.

34. See Z. Lubis, *Kumpulan catatan lepas*; Z. Lubis, *Asal usul marga-marga di Mandailing*; Sinambela, *Ayahku, Si Singamangaradja XII*; Parlindungan, *Pongkinangolngolan Sinambela gelar Tuanku Rao*; Lumbantobing, *Sejarah Si Singamangaradja*; Sangti, *Sejarah Batak*. Akhir Matua Harahap maintains an online repository of sources on local Mandailing history at http://akhirmh.blogspot.com/p/akhir-matua-harahap .html.

35. Sidjabat, *Ahu Si Singamangaradja*.

36. See A.-R. Lubis, *Tarikh Raja Asal dan keluarganya*.

37. Grove, *Green Imperialism*, 16–34.

38. Tsing, *In the Realm of the Diamond Queen*, 4.

39. See Manickam, *Taming the Wild*; and Sysling, *Racial Science and Human Diversity in Colonial Indonesia*.

ONE A Time before Religion

1. Conversation with tour guide on Samosir Island, June 2015.

2. Nongbri, *Before Religion*, 15–24, 106–31.

3. Cited in Tomich, "Order of Historical Time," 59.

4. Scott, *Art of Not Being Governed*.

5. Li, *Land's End*, 48.

6. Henley, "Conflict, Justice and the Stranger-King."

7. This is known as the Toba catastrophe theory. For details, see Petraglia et al., "Toba Volcanic Super-Eruption."

8. Sibeth, *The Batak*, 151–80.

9. See Knappert, "Why There Is Only One Sun," for an alternative version in which the princess was known as Si Borudea and she landed on earth because of her curiosity when she looked down from the heavens. On sources and varieties of the Boru Daeng Parudjar story, see Zakaria, "Toba Super-Catastrophe as History of the Future," 38–40.

10. Niessen, *Motifs of Life in Batak Texts and Textiles*, 16–17.

11. Byl, *Antiphonal Histories*, 81–83; Van Bemmelen, *Christianity, Colonization and Gender*, 45–46.

12. The Karo, for example, did not share in these origin tales and had neither their own protoreligious origin stories nor a ritual center. See Singarimbun, *Kinship, Descent and Alliance*, 70–72.

13. The three-tiered universe pre-dates the coming of monotheistic religion, and its symbolism persists in the material culture of the Batak.

14. Widianto, "Dawn of Humanity in Sumatra," 29.

15. Byl, *Antiphonal Histories*, 102.

16. Brown, *Sejarah Melayu*, 5–6.

17. L. Andaya, *Leaves of the Same Tree*, 143–72.

18. See De Casparis, *Indonesian Palaeography*, 45; and Perret and Surachman, *History of Padang Lawas*, 355.

19. Perret and Surachman, *History of Padang Lawas*, 108; Schnitger, *Forgotten Kingdoms in Sumatra*, 85–108.

20. Sangti, *Sejarah Batak*, 120–28; L. Andaya, *Leaves of the Same Tree*, 160.

21. Hirth, *Chau Ju-kua*, 62–66.

22. L. Andaya, "Trans-Sumatra Trade."

23. Kozok, *Warisan leluhur*, 65.

24. Kozok, *Surat Batak*, 31–44.

25. Winkler and Voorhoeve, "Pane Na Bolon, ein Kriegsorakel auf Sumatra."

26. Sibeth, *The Batak*, 40. The *naga padoha* is also called Pane Na Bolon in Batak. I use the word *naga* here to make it consistent with Malay mythology of the *naga* discussed in chapter 3.

27. Pogos and Sitanggang, *Batak na marserak*, 11.

28. L. Andaya, *Leaves of the Same Tree*, 166–69. The Batak clans Harahap and Siregar moved from north (Toba) to south, probably in the fifteenth century, as part of a seeming spike in migrations during this period. Andaya speculated that the "Batak" ethnic identity was formed during this time.

29. The Batak preserved the memory of links to the Acehnese state even as they resolutely held to a different form of governance and religious identity, as noted in Reid, *Imperial Alchemy*, 154.

30. Even as late as the 1910s, the majority of the Pardebanam Batak in Asahan, who had migrated from the Karo plateau, identified as *parbegu* rather than Muslim or Christian. See Bartlett, "Batak and Malay Chant"; and Bartlett, *Labors of the Datoe*, 78–79.

31. Sangti, *Sejarah Batak*, 121–27.

32. Sangti, *Sejarah Batak*, 214–15. This story was adopted by a state-appointed committee in the 1970s as an official account that celebrates Medan's founding.

33. Description obtained from my visits to replicas of Batak villages in Toba and Mandailing.

34. Maloney, "Possible Early Dry-Land and Wetland Rice Cultivation"; Maloney, "Pollen Analytical Evidence." The sample cores are mainly from the Toba, Karo, and Dairi regions, and there has been no study done on the rest of the Batak highlands. It is

possible that the evidence of foliage change from tree to grass was indicative of climate change rather than agriculture, but the different rates of change among sites sampled that were geographically close together indicates the latter.

35. Reid, "Humans and Forests in Pre-colonial Southeast Asia," 97.

36. On the limits of rice cultivation geographies, see Maloney, "Possible Early Dry-Land and Wetland Rice Cultivation," 173–86.

37. On this debate, see Henley, "Swidden Farming as an Agent of Environmental Change."

38. Boomgaard, *Southeast Asia*, 220.

39. Henley, "Swidden Farming as an Agent of Environmental Change," 525.

40. Sherman, "What Green Desert?"; Dove, *Southeast Asia Grasslands*, 22–28.

41. Sherman, *Rice, Rupees and Ritual*, 150–53.

42. Reid, "Humans and Forests in Pre-colonial Southeast Asia," 97–103.

43. Anderson, *Acheen and the Ports of Sumatra*, 328–56.

44. Junghuhn, *Die Battälander*, 233.

45. Joustra, *Bataksspiegel*, 286, 303; Tideman, *De Bataklanden*, 118. Michael Dove notes that present data now indicate that two to four harvests are normal for a swidden cycle and not a sign of depleted soil.

46. Reid, *Southeast in the Age of Commerce*, 1:26–27.

47. Skeat, *Malay Magic*, 218; Ypes, *Bijdrage tot de kennis van der stamverwantschap*, 118.

48. Van Hasselt, "Eenige mededelingen omtrent het voorkomen van geophagie," 310–12.

49. Here I give the terms in Toba dialect, also used in Pakpak/Dairi and Angkola. The Karo term for wife-giving clan is *kalimbubu*, while wife-receiving clan is *anak beru*. In Mandailing, the wife-giving clan is *mora* and the wife-taking clan is *anak boru*. These kinship ties were prevalent in all the subgroups despite the different vocabulary.

50. Quoted in Byl, *Antiphonal Histories*, 36.

51. Kipp and Kipp, *Beyond Samosir*, 116.

52. Voorhoeve, "Bataksche buffelwichelarij," 238–48.

53. Sherman, *Rice, Rupees and Ritual*, 107–38. It is possible that other parts of Tapanuli might also have had the same rituals involving pigs, but this changed after the conversion to Islam.

54. Sibeth, *The Batak*, 47–51.

55. Kuiper, "Cosmogony and Conception," 91–138; Sangti, *Sejarah Batak*, 364–400.

56. Rodgers, *Adat, Islam and Christianity*, 137–61. For Toba Batak marriages, see Sherman, *Rice, Rupees and Ritual*, 867–68; for the Mandailing, see Tugby, "Social Function of *Mahr*."

57. Donkin, *Dragon's Brain Perfume*, 11.

58. L. Andaya, "Trans-Sumatra Trade," 367–90.

59. Fuller, *Camphor Flame*, 121.

60. Quoted in Donkin, *Dragon's Brain Perfume*, 73. Donkin adds that the description was probably an exaggeration based on some truth.

61. Macdonald, "On Three Natural Productions of Sumatra," 20–25.

62. Macdonald, "On Three Natural Productions of Sumatra," 20; Marsden, *History of Sumatra*, 149.

63. It is probable that "Si Pagedag Si Pagedog" was not his real name but a reference to the sound he hears. "Nan Tar Tar Nan Tor Tor" is also not a personal name; it simply means "The Dancing One."

64. De Ligny, "Legendarische herkomst de kamfer Baroes," 549–50.

65. De Ligny, "Legendarische herkomst de kamfer Baroes," 551–54.

66. De Ligny, "Legendarische herkomst de kamfer Baroes," 552.

67. Van Vuuren, "De handel van Baroes."

68. Marsden, *History of Sumatra*, 149.

69. Drakard, *Malay Frontier*, 33.

70. Drakard, *Malay Frontier*, 171–84.

71. Cited in Drakard, *Malay Frontier*, 75–76.

72. Pleyte, "Singa Mangaradja," 1–10; Byl, *Antiphonal Histories*, 54–56.

73. Reid, "Merchant Princes and Magic Mediators," 255.

74. Camphor was brought to Barus through Rambe, Kelasan, and Tukka. See Van Vuuren, "De handel van Baroes," 1400; and Ypes, *Bijdrage tot de kennis van der stamverwantschap*, 503.

75. Drakard, *Malay Frontier*, 175.

76. Iskandar, *Hikayat Aceh*, 92, 186–87.

77. Reid, *Imperial Alchemy*, 151; Reid, "Islamization and Christianization," 164.

78. McKinnon, "Ceramics, Cloth, Iron and Salt," 127.

79. Ahmad, *Hikayat Hang Tuah*, 522–23.

80. McKinnon, "Ceramics, Cloth, Iron and Salt," 23–24.

81. Foucault, *History of Sexuality*, 138.

82. Hendri Sihite, interview by author, Samosir, May 24, 2016.

83. Reid, "Why Do the Batak Erect *Tugu*?"

84. Marsden, *History of Sumatra*, 322–23.

85. Pedersen, *Batak Blood, Protestant Soul*, 25–28.

86. See Parkin, *Batak Fruit of Hindu Thought*, 43; and Wolters, *History, Culture and Region in Southeast Asian Perspectives*, 93–96.

87. Pedersen, *Batak Blood, Protestant Soul*, 28; Warneck, *Die Religion der Batak*, 68.

88. L. Andaya, "Ethnicization of the Batak," 394.

89. Winkler, *Die Toba-Batak auf Sumatra*, 23–37; Sibeth, *The Batak*, 109–10.

90. Steedly, *Hanging without a Rope*, 237.

91. Pedersen, *Batak Blood, Protestant Soul*, 30.

92. Reid, *Slavery, Bondage and Dependency*, 131.

93. Kozok, "On Writing the Not-to-Be-Read," 33.

94. Reid, *Bondage and Dependency*, 129–36.

95. Liaw, *Undang-undang Melaka*, 88–93.

96. Reid, *Southeast Asia in the Age of Commerce*, 1:132–33.

97. On Manees, see Document 388, General Protocol Books, India Office Records, R/9/22/52, British Library. For the average price of an enslaved male, see Reid, *Slavery, Bondage and Dependency*, 27.

98. Barrow, *Voyage to Cochin-China*, 240.

99. Data used to compile the figure in the text derived from General Protocol Books, India Office Records, R9/22, British Library. These records contain enclosures to legal deeds that served to provide proof of ownership for merchandise being traded in Malacca before 1824. Among these enclosures of the General Protocol Books were eighty-three sale-of-slave documents. I counted the number of documents that indicated the ethnicity of the persons sold in each transaction to obtain the figure in the text. I exclude English, Dutch, and Chinese sale-of-slave documents, as I am primarily interested in the activity of Malay slave traders. Note that the snapshot provided by these records may not represent the entire volume of trade. On the limitations of these sources, see Teh-Gallop, "Malay Documents in the Melaka Records."

100. Document 639, General Protocol Books, India Office Records, R/9/22/51, British Library.

TWO Rupture and Resilience in Conversion

1. Hamilton, "Anthropocene as Rupture," 100.

2. Ghosh, *Great Derangement*, 22.

3. By modernism in global Islam, I am referring to a broad suite of new Islamic thought that began in the nineteenth century and sought to reinterpret scriptural sources—the Qur'an and Hadith—to suit the modern context. These included the modernist Islam that developed in response to colonialism and Salafism, as well as later Islamic secularism and Islamism.

4. See Steijn-Parvé, "De secte der Padaries"; H.v.D., "Oorsprong der Padaris"; De Stuers, *De vestiging en uitbreiding*.

5. Sangti, *Sejarah Batak*, 102.

6. Byl, *Antiphonal Histories*, 22.

7. On modernist Islam in Indonesia, see Feener, *Muslim Legal Thought*; and Noer, *Modernist Muslim Movement in Indonesia*. Modernist Muslim movements have generally been thought to have started around 1900, but here I view the Padri as forerunners

of those organizations due to their shared emphasis on universal scripture and antipathy toward *adat*.

8. See Voll, "Muhammad Hayya al-Sindi and Muhammad b. Abd al-Wahhab"; and Commins, *Wahhabi Mission*, 3–17.

9. Scholars have puzzled over the origins of the term "Padri." One explanation is that "Padri" derived from the Portuguese word for father (*padre*) and was thus externally imposed, not a self-identification. See Kathirithamby-Wells, "Origin of the Term Padri." An alternative, less persuasive explanation is that the term refers to "men from Pidie/Pedir," a port in Aceh that served as an embarkation point for pilgrims to Mecca. See Dobbin, *Islamic Revivalism*, 128.

10. Richards, *Unending Frontier*.

11. See Dobbin, *Islamic Revivalism*; and Hadler, *Muslims and Matriarchs*.

12. See Steedly, *Rifle Reports*; and Rodgers, *Telling Lives, Telling History*.

13. Aritonang, *Mission Schools in Batakland*, 36.

14. Manik, *Batak-Handschriften*, 7–8.

15. Winkler, *Die Toba-Batak auf Sumatra*, 76–77.

16. Sevea, *Miracles and Material Life*, 180–210.

17. Schreiner, as quoted in Aritonang, *Mission Schools in Batakland*, 40.

18. Kratz and Amir, *Surat keterangan Syeikh Jalaluddin*, 20. This source is a published version of an autobiographical manuscript written by the religious scholar Syeikh Jalaluddin, who studied with Tuanku nan Tuo. It was written in the 1820s at the behest of colonial administrators who were preparing for an intervention when Minangkabau leaders who were losing against the Padri requested aid from the Dutch in their base at Padang.

19. Dobbin, *Islamic Revivalism*, 125–7.

20. Cited in Kratz and Amir, *Surat keterangan Syeikh Jalaluddin*, 22.

21. Steijn-Parvé, "De secte der Padaries," 271–72.

22. Raffles, *Memoir*, 404.

23. Hadler, *Muslims and Matriarchs*, 34; Raffles, *Memoir*, 358–60.

24. Kathirithamby-Wells, "Origin of the Term Padri," 6.

25. Kratz and Amir, *Surat keterangan Syeikh Jalaluddin*, 49.

26. Kratz and Amir, *Surat keterangan Syeikh Jalaluddin*, 49.

27. In Indonesian convention, the place is spelled as Bonjol and the person as Tuanku Imam Bondjol. Here I omit the *d* to avoid confusion.

28. See Syafnir, *Naskah Tuanku Imam Bonjol*. This memoir was brought to West Sumatra by his son, Sutan Saidi, who had followed him into exile. The text was put together with the memoir of Sutan Saidi's brother, Naali Sutan Caniago, who had been granted a position in the Dutch colonial government as one of the terms of Tuanku Imam Bonjol's surrender. These two memoirs were compiled with a third section de-

tailing the minutes of two meetings of Minangkabau highland leaders in 1865 and 1875, and all three were combined into one manuscript, titled "Naskah Tuanku Imam Bonjol." The original has since been lost, but Rusydi Ramli, a professor at the State Institute of Islamic Studies (IAIN) in Padang, had made a full copy before the manuscript's disappearance. This copy was transliterated and published by Syafnir Aboe Nain in 2004.

29. Asnan, "Transportation on the West Coast of Sumatra," 729–30.

30. Syafnir, *Naskah Tuanku Imam Bonjol*, 12.

31. Syafnir, *Naskah Tuanku Imam Bonjol*, 12–38.

32. The importance of Rao in this conflict lived on in the combative reputation of their diaspora at Malaya. Their aggression is associated with Padri leader Tuanku nan Renceh; in Malaya they were nicknamed "orang Renceh." See Watson, "Rawa and Rinchi."

33. Fakih means "student; this was his title rather than his real name. His origins are the subject of much speculation, as the next two sections of the chapter show.

34. Syafnir, *Naskah Tuanku Imam Bonjol*, 16–17.

35. Syafnir, *Naskah Tuanku Imam Bonjol*, 24, 32, 41.

36. On Bonjol's horses, see Clarence-Smith, "Elephants, Horses and the Coming of Islam," 276.

37. Syafnir, *Naskah Tuanku Imam Bonjol*, 76. Half a million people working on one mosque does not seem a likely figure and was probably exaggerated by Tuanku Imam Bonjol.

38. Syafnir, *Naskah Tuanku Imam Bonjol*, 37–39.

39. Syafnir, *Naskah Tuanku Imam Bonjol*, 39. His exact phrase in Malay is "mencari hukum Kitabullah yang adil."

40. Syafnir, *Naskah Tuanku Imam Bonjol*, 44–45.

41. Hadler, *Muslims and Matriarchs*, 27. It is not clear when this public repentance took place, but in Dutch records, Tuanku Imam Bonjol surrendered to Colonel Elout in 1832 after a futile uprising; thus, this event was likely in 1830.

42. Jones, *Hikayat Raja Pasai*, 68–69.

43. "Kedatangan Bondjol," anonymously handwritten notes, dated 1934, preserved on microfilm, Call no. D Or. 435–69, Collectie V. E. Korn, Leiden University Library.

44. Gabriel, "Kriegszug der Bondjol," 157–90.

45. For an overview of Batak family history writing in the 1920s, see Zakaria, "Sacral Ecologies of the North Sumatran Highlands," 337–47.

46. "Kedatangan Bondjol," 7.

47. Gabriel, "Kriegszug der Bondjol," 201; "Kedatangan Bondjol," 6.

48. Gabriel, "Kriegszug der Bondjol," 163–71.

49. Gabriel, "Kriegszug der Bondjol," 178; "Kedatangan Bondjol," 15–16.

50. "Kedatangan Bondjol," 10.

51. According to Dutch military sources, the Padri entered Toba in 1820 and returned briefly in 1824 and 1829. Dobbin suggests that the Padri began encouraging more trade with the Batak but did not seem able to impose a different social order. See Dobbin, *Islamic Revivalism*, 281–83.

52. Raffles, *Memoir*, 429, indirectly corroborated the story of the disease by mentioning an outbreak of "cholera morbus" in the highlands stretching toward Aceh in 1820.

53. "Kedatangan Bondjol," 24.

54. "Kedatangan Bondjol," 46–48.

55. Voorhoeve, "Bataksche buffelwichelarij," 238–48.

56. Wessing, "Symbolic Animals," 219.

57. Burton and Ward, "Report of a Journey into the Batak Country," 487.

58. Dobbin, *Islamic Revivalism*, 218.

59. See Lumbantobing, *Sejarah Si Singamangaradja*; and Sangti, *Sejarah Batak*.

60. Rodgers, "Antic Histories," 261–62.

61. Parlindungan, *Pongkinangolngolan Sinambela gelar Tuanku Rao*, 141, 254, 349.

62. Although Parlindungan's work reads like a parody of academic history, some details agree with those of scholars who worked much later, suggesting he had some sound sources. It is not possible to check them, since he claimed to have burned most of them after writing his epic. One example is his appendix on Chinese Muslims, discussed in Wade, "Southeast Asian Islam and Southern China."

63. Rodgers, "Antic Histories," 257–59.

64. Hamka, *Antara fakta dan Khayal*.

65. Harahap, *Greget Tuanku Rao*.

66. Parlindungan, *Pongkinangolngolan Sinambela gelar Tuanku Rao*, 313–16.

67. Lubis, *Kumpulan catatan lepas tentang Mandailing*, 76.

68. Syafnir, *Naskah Tuanku Imam Bonjol*, 27.

69. Dobbin, *Islamic Revivalism*, 200–201.

70. Radjab, *Perang Paderi*, 31–56; Castles, "Political Life of a Sumatran Residency," 21–22.

71. Radjab, *Perang Paderi*, 31. Radjab referred to the Mandailing somewhat derisively as *umpan peluru* (cannon fodder) for turning against the Padri and allowing themselves to be used by the Dutch on the front lines.

72. Lubis, *Kumpulan catatan lepas tentang Mandailing*, 14. Lubis quotes a Dutch letter from the copy handed down in his family, through his ancestor Raja Junjungan Lubis, a contemporary of Raja Gadombang.

73. De Stuers, *De vestiging en uitbreiding der Nederlanders*, 71–72.

74. Castles, "Political Life of a Sumatran Residency," 22–83.

75. De Stuers, *De vestiging en uitbreiding der Nederlanders*, 66–67.

76. Frazer, *Golden Bough*, 153; Lubis, *Asal usul marga-marga di Mandailing*, 31.

77. Lubis, *Kumpulan catatan lepas tentang Mandailing*, 22–23.

78. Multatuli, *Max Havelaar*, 163–204. Multatuli is the pen name of Douwes Dekker. In this novel, General Michiels protected the Yang Dipertuan when the Dutch controleur in Mandailing (Douwes Dekker himself) charged the Yang Dipertuan with corruption and murder. The Yang Dipertuan was brought to Padang for trial but was acquitted and released.

79. Multatuli, *Max Havelaar*, 164.

80. Aung-Thwin, "Myth of the 'Three Shan Brothers,'" 881.

81. On *adat* and modernism in Minangkabau, see Abdullah, "Adat and Islam."

THREE Secularizing "Literate Cannibals"

1. Brakel-Papenhuyzen, *Dairi Stories*, 112–28.

2. McCarraher, *Enchantments of Mammon*, 48–51.

3. Viner, "Changing Batak," 85.

4. Kozok, "On Writing the Not-to-Be-Read,"

5. Teygeler, "Pustaha."

6. Reid, *Southeast Asia in the Age of Commerce*, 1:220–25; Hijjas, "Not Just Fryers of Bananas."

7. Scott, *Art of Not Being Governed*, 221–37.

8. Harahap, *Si Bulus Bulus*, 19–20. *Si Bulus Bulus, Si Rumbuk Rumbuk* is a collection of poems published in the Mandailing dialect and translated into Indonesian by Harahap, on which my English translation is based.

9. See Willer, "Verzameling der Battasche wetten," 202–96; and Junghuhn, *Die Battälander*.

10. For the many lives of *Si Bulus Bulus*, see Lubis, *Lebih jauh tentang Willem Iskander*, 2–9.

11. Parlindungan, *Pongkinangolngolan Sinambela gelar Tuanku Rao*, 419–23. Parlindungan was one of Sutan Gunung Tua's grandchildren through his daughter, who married a schoolteacher called Sutan Martua Radja. In an interview, Akhir Matua Harahap, a contemporary chronicler of family histories in Mandailing, confirms that Sjarif Anwar/Sutan Gunung Tua was a student in Iskander's school but could not specify any dates. It was probable that Sutan Gunung Tua received some education in Iskander's school, most likely after his conversion to Christianity in 1868, and this schooling prepared him for work at the Assistant Resident's Office in 1875.

12. Willer, "Verzameling der Battasche wetten," 257. Mandailing and Angkola were part of the South Tapanuli Residency, under the authority of the governor-general of West Sumatra in Padang. When the Residency was set up in 1841, the administration comprised an assistant Resident in Panyabungan and two *controleurs*, in Angkola and Ulu Pakantan.

13. "Yang Dipertuan" is the Malay rather than the Batak title for sultan, indicating the transplanting of Malay political structures into Mandailing by the Dutch.

14. Van der Tuuk, *Een vorst onder de taalgeleerden*, 123; Kielstra, "Sumatra's Westkust sedert 1850," 266.

15. Van der Tuuk, *Een vorst onder de taalgeleerden*, 135.

16. Kielstra, "Sumatra's Westkust sedert 1850," 257–58.

17. Van der Tuuk, *Een vorst onder de taalgeleerden*, 123.

18. Van der Tuuk, *Een vorst onder de taalgeleerden*, 133.

19. Van der Tuuk, *Een vorst onder de taalgeleerden*, 118–31.

20. Ota, "Tropical Products Out, British Cotton In," 510.

21. Van Asselt, *Achttien jaren*, 29.

22. Brouwer, "Het gouvernmental inlandsch onderwijs op Sumatra," 2.

23. For history of the *kweekschool* in West Sumatra, see Hadler, *Muslims and Matriarchs*, 92–95.

24. On the futility of proselytizing in Angkola and Mandailing, see Van der Tuuk, *Een vorst onder de taalgeleerden*, 134. This conversion seemed quite rapid: it occurred only one generation after the Padri War. It is probable that the Muslims from Minangkabau had been carrying out their own missionary work in the area, but I am unable to find sufficient documentary sources to assess the extent of this Muslim effort.

25. Van Asselt, *Achttien jaren*, 38.

26. Van Asselt, *Achttien jaren*, 40.

27. Van Asselt, *Achttien jaren*, 36.

28. Van Asselt, *Achttien jaren*, 47–48. The Dutch missionary's reception at these feasts was not always friendly. At another feast, for instance, the crowd waited and waited in vain for the spirit to come and the medium finally blamed Van Asselt for scaring it away through his presence.

29. Aritonang, *Mission Schools in Batakland*, 111–12.

30. Warneck, *50 Jahre Batakmission*, 2.

31. Wellem, *Amir Sjarifoeddin*, 51.

32. Harahap, *Si Bulus Bulus*, 30–31. A *beo* is a type of robin commonly found on Nias Island.

33. Harahap, *Si Bulus Bulus*, 12.

34. The story of Si Baroar is important because toward the end of the nineteenth century, many Mandailing, particularly those who migrated to Medan, began asserting a different identity from that of the Batak. One of their arguments was that they descended from Si Baroar and/or Namora Pande Besi and not Si Raja Batak, whom the Toba identified as their common ancestor.

35. Titles and copies of the translations of educational materials by Willem Iskander are available from Leiden University Library, the National Library in Jakarta, and a pri-

vate documentation center, Pusat Dokumentasi Mandailing, in Medan, Indonesia. For the full list, see Zakaria, "Sacral Ecologies of the North Sumatran Highlands," 46–47.

36. Poeze and Van Dijk, *In het land van de overheersers*, 16–17.

37. Van der Chijs wrote his report as part of a proposal to bring more native teachers to the Netherlands for training, and this possibly influenced his stance on the subject.

38. Brouwer, "Het gouvernmental inlandsch onderwijs op Sumatra," 1–11.

39. *De Locomotief Samarangsch Handels-en-Advertentie Blad* (Semang, Central Java), December 4, 1875, 2.

40. Harahap, *Greget Tuanku Rao*, 187–88.

41. "Varia," *TNI*, 483.

42. Harahap, *Si Bulus Bulus*, 20.

43. Poeze and Van Dijk, *In het land van de overheersers*, 17.

44. Poeze and Van Dijk, *In het land van de overheersers*, 17.

45. "Varia," *TNI*, 483–84; Poeze and Van Dijk, *In het land van de overheersers*, 17.

46. Brouwer, "Het gouvernmental inlandsch onderwijs op Sumatra," 1.

47. Burton and Ward, "Report of a Journey," 27.

48. See, among others, Said, *Dari halaman-halaman terlepas*; Sidjabat, *Ahu Si Singamangaradja*; and Lehmann, *Biographical Study of Ingwer Ludwig Nommensen*. Most sources refer to Nommensen as Ludwig Ingwer Nommensen, but Lehmann's book went with a variant, Ingwer Ludwig, in the title.

49. L. Andaya, *Leaves of the Same Tree*, 163; Pleyte, "Singa Mangaradja."

50. Sidjabat, *Ahu Si Singamangaradja*, 30; Pleyte, "Singa Mangaradja," 35.

51. This staff doubled as a spear and was called Hudjur Sitonggo Mual (Spear That Brings Water).

52. Sidjabat, *Ahu Si Singamangaradja*, 442–43. The text of this bark book is rendered by Sidjabat in Batak and Indonesian, and the English translation provided is mine. Another version of this prayer was published in the newspaper *Soeara Batak* in 1917, as cited in Lumbantobing, *Si Singamangaradja*, 15–17.

53. Warneck, *Die Religion der Batak*, 127.

54. Lumbantobing, *Si Singamangaradja*, 17–18. When a *horja* gathers for a ritual, the gathering was led by Raja Doli in Toba, known as Sibajak in Karo and Dairi and as Tuhan in Simalungun, as well as a designated *horja*-level priest known as Pande Bolon.

55. Sidjabat, *Ahu Si Singamangaradja*, 73.

56. Lumbantobing, *Si Singamangaradja*, 8.

57. Sidjabat, *Ahu Si Singamangaradja*, 77.

58. Van der Tuuk, *Een vorst onder de taalgeleerden*, 157–58.

59. Van der Tuuk, *Een vorst onder de taalgeleerden*, 150–57.

60. "Account of the Camphor Tree of Sumatra," *Philadelphia Recorder*, June 21, 1823, 46.

61. Van der Tuuk, *Een vorst onder de taalgeleerden*, 153.

62. Van der Tuuk, *Een vorst onder de taalgeleerden*, 157.

63. Van der Tuuk, *Een vorst onder de taalgeleerden*, 161.

64. Ota, "Tropical Products Out, British Cotton In," 510.

65. Anderson, *Acheen and the Ports on the North*, 188.

66. Junghuhn, *Die Battälander*, 128–29.

67. Parts of this section are reconstructed from Nommensen's and other missionaries' monthly reports to the Rhenish Missionary Society (Rheinisch Missionsgessellschaft). These monthly reports were compiled and printed annually from 1830 to 1964 under the title *Berichten der Rheinische Missionsgesellschaft* (hereafter *BMG* plus the year).

68. *BMG* 1864, 228–32.

69. Van Bemmelen, *Christianity, Colonization and Gender*, 200–201.

70. *BMG* 1865, 195–97.

71. *BMG* 1865, 203.

72. Lehmann, *Biographical Study of Ingwer Ludwig Nommensen*, 165.

73. Lehmann, *Biographical Study of Ingwer Ludwig Nommensen*, 112.

74. Lehmann, *Biographical Study of Ingwer Ludwig Nommensen*, 133.

75. *BMG* 1866, 66–67.

76. Sidjabat, *Ahu Si Singamangaradja*, 87–89; Lumbantobing, *Si Singamangaradja*, 56. Missionary sources did not corroborate this view, categorizing the Singamangaradja together with other chiefs who accepted slavery.

77. Vergouwen, *Social Organisation and Customary Law*, 113–19.

78. *BMG* 1869, 369–72.

79. Lehmann, *Biographical Study of Ingwer Ludwig Nommensen*, 238.

80. Sidjabat, *Ahu Si Singamangaradja*, 158.

81. Warneck, *50 Jahre Batakmission*, 62; Pedersen, *Batak Blood, Protestant Soul*, 56.

82. *BMG* 1873, 246.

83. *BMG* 1873, 247–48, 257–58.

84. Kozok, "Seals of the Last Singamangaradja," 261.

85. This seal, which Kozok denotes as Seal B, was found in at least five letters sent by Si Singamangaradja XII to Nommensen and others. Kozok, "Seals of the Last Singamangaradja," 257.

FOUR Mountains, Water, Derangement

1. For characterization of early Malay literature, see Van der Putten, "Abdullah Munsyi."

2. Van der Putten, "Abdullah Munsyi," 407.

3. Ghosh, *Great Derangement*, 19–22.

4. On existing work, see Lubis and Nasution, *Raja Bilah*; and Lubis, *Sutan Puasa*.

5. Wallace quoted in Veth, "Dutch Expedition to Central Sumatra," 776.

6. Veth, "Dutch Expedition to Central Sumatra," 776.

7. See Wessing, "Symbolic Animals," 221; Barendregt, "From the Realm of Many Rivers," 51.

8. Kreemer, *De karbouw*, 211.

9. Skeat, *Malay Magic*, 2–6.

10. W. E. Maxwell, "Folklore of the Malays," 26.

11. Kartomi, *Musical Journeys in Sumatra*, 59–60.

12. Salleh, *Sejarah Melayu*, 16–18.

13. "Hikayat Hikamat," 302. ca. 1880, manuscript, SP/5c/13, National Archives of Malaysia.

14. "Hikayat Hikamat," 4–5.

15. Ché Ross, "Hikayat Hikamat: The Malay Memoirs of a Sumatran Christian."

16. Dean, "Missionary Work among the Malays," 132. On Keasberry's missionary work, see Van der Putten, "Abdullah Munsyi," 421–35.

17. Dean, "Missionary Work among the Malays," 153, citing Keasberry's obituary in the same magazine as William Dean's article, the *Baptist Missionary Magazine*.

18. See White, "Historical Roots of Our Ecological Crisis"; Stoll, *Inherit the Holy Mountain*; Jenkins et al., *Routledge Handbook of Religion and Ecology*, 70–79.

19. O'Connor, "Iron Working as Spiritual Inquiry," 180 (emphasis added).

20. Tanjung Padang is a village in the Riau Islands; possibly the sojourn was a seasonal mining trip.

21. "Hikayat Hikamat," 16–20.

22. "Hikayat Hikamat," 29.

23. "Haru" probably refers to Aru, discussed in chapter 1 as a polity ruled by Batak Karo and defeated by Aceh. See L. Andaya, *Leaves of the Same Tree*, 114–17.

24. "Hikayat Hikamat," 41–44.

25. "Hikayat Hikamat," 44–48.

26. "Hikayat Hikamat," 170.

27. Herzog, "Domesticating Labor."

28. "Hikayat Hikamat," 180–84.

29. Dean, "Missionary Work among the Malays," 153.

30. "Hikayat Hikamat," 185.

31. "Hikayat Hikamat," 194.

32. Elvin, "Who Was Responsible for the Weather?"

33. Amrith, *Unruly Waters*, 70.

34. "Hikayat Hikamat," 303–4.

35. I am grateful to Abdur-Razzaq Lubis for allowing me to work with his transliterated and privately held version of Raja Muhammad Yacob's manuscript, "Ini tarikh

Raja Asal dan keluarganya" (henceforth cited simply as "Tarikh Raja Asal"), as the original was not available from the Perak branch of the National Archives of Malaysia, where the rest of the Raja Bilah papers and books were kept. Lubis has since fleshed out this family manuscript by tracing the references, sources, and people mentioned in it. See Lubis, *Tarikh Raja Asal dan Keluarganya*.

36. "Tarikh Raja Asal," 50. Raja Yacob concluded his manuscript on 7 Syawal 1352 Hijri, which is January 23, 1934.

37. On *sejarah* connoting family trees and genealogy, see Al-Attas, *Historical Fact and Fiction*, 120–27. My thanks to Ismail Fajrie Al-Attas for highlighting these shades of meaning.

38. Richardson, *Geology and Mineral Resources of the Neighbourhood of Pahang*, 36.

39. "Tarikh Raja Asal," 4.

40. "Tarikh Raja Asal," 4. The Slim River was at the boundary of what is now the states of Perak and Selangor.

41. Burns, *Journals of J. W. W. Birch*, 148.

42. Burns, *Journals of J. W. W. Birch*, 148.

43. "Tarikh Raja Asal," 13.

44. The *qadi* is a judge in a sharia court. In the Malay world before colonialism, this judge could be formally appointed by the political leadership or establish himself as a learned Muslim authority informally in the community. The Sumatran-born Minangkabau *qadi* established among the Perak Mandailing community seemed a sign of Mandailing migrants' subtle break from the leadership of the Perak Malay sultan, who may have disliked the Sumatran *qadi* but could do little to stop the community from gravitating toward him.

45. Clifford, "Journey through the Malay States," 5–6 (emphasis added). Clifford became the governor of the Straits Settlements in the 1920s.

46. Richardson, *Geology and Mineral Resources of the Neighbourhood of Pahang*, 88–90; Gullick, *Kuala Lumpur*, 10. Seasonal migrants from Sumatra began mining in the Klang area before 1860. Their journey was known as *pai kolang*, although when this enterprise started is still unknown.

47. Wong, *Malayan Tin Industry*, 161–98; Ross, "Tin Frontier," 458.

48. "Tarikh Raja Asal," 19.

49. "Tarikh Raja Asal," 11. For descriptions of similar pits in old gold mines in Pahang, see R. Braddell, "Further Notes upon a Study of Ancient Times," 30–31.

50. Middlebrook, "Yap Ah Loy," 8–9.

51. Middlebrook, "Yap Ah Loy," 8.

52. Ross, "Tin Frontier," 458.

53. Penrose, "Tin Deposits of the Malay Peninsula," 151.

54. "Tarikh Raja Asal," 18.

55. "Tarikh Raja Asal," 30.

56. Ghosh, *Great Derangement*, 62.

57. Ghosh, *Great Derangement*, 56.

58. Beighton, *Betel-Nut Island*, 31.

59. Beighton, *Betel-Nut Island*, 34.

60. Hale, "Mines and Miners in Kinta," 310. See also, among others, De La Croix, *Les mines étain de Perak*; and Pasqual, "Chinese Tin Mining in Selangor," 25–29.

61. Skeat, *Malay Magic*, 265.

62. Hale, "Mines and Miners in Kinta," 304.

63. See T. Braddell, "Notes of a Trip to the Interior from Malacca," 82; Lister, *Mining Laws and Customs*, 15–16; Pasqual, "Chinese Tin Mining in Selangor," 25–29.

64. Sevea, *Miracles and Material Life*, 111.

65. Sevea, *Miracles and Material Life*, 132–34.

66. B. Andaya, "Seas, Oceans and Cosmologies in Southeast Asia," 364.

67. Tong, "Sinicization of Malay Keramats," 38. The person of a Muslim saint is regarded as *keramat*, and the grave of such as saint becomes a sacred site. In the Malay context, *keramat* status also extended to the nonhuman: tigers, trees, rocks, and earth mounds (representing mountains).

68. Winstedt, "Karamat," 271.

69. "Tarikh Raja Asal" did mention Chinese miners but only in the context of them opening new mines in Mandailing areas with the permission of Raja Bilah. Lubis and Nasution have since fleshed out part of this association. See Lubis and Nasution, *Raja Bilah*.

70. Middlebrook, "Yap Ah Loy," 48. Here I follow Middlebrook's transliteration of Chinese names.

71. Yap has long been credited with the founding of what is now Malaysia's capital, Kuala Lumpur. Lubis has called this into question, however, arguing that Sutan Puasa, a Mandailing aristocrat, was the true founder. See Lubis, *Sutan Puasa*.

72. Middlebrook, "Yap Ah Loy," 68–73.

73. Linehan, *History of Pahang*, 98–99.

74. Ross, "Tin Frontier," 460.

75. W. G. Maxwell, *In Malay Forests*, 34.

76. Kratoska, *Honourable Intentions*, 284.

77. "Tarikh Raja Asal," 19–20.

78. "Tarikh Raja Asal," 20. Here, Raja Yacob used the phrase "beratus kuli Melayu belaka," with *belaka* stressing the Malayness of the coolies, implying that the indigeneity of the enterprise was a point of pride.

79. Manap and Voulvoulis, "Data Analysis for Environmental Impact of Dredging," 394–404.

80. Balamurugan, "Tin Mining and Sediment Supply in Peninsular Malaysia," 281–91.

81. Ross, "Tin Frontier," 468.

82. James, "Knockers, Knackers, and Ghosts," 169–71.

FIVE Camphor and Charismatic Retreat

1. Neumann, *Een jaar onder de Karo Batak*, 45–46.

2. M. Barstow and A. Randi, "*Dryobalanops sumatrensis*," IUCN Red List of Threatened Species, 2018, accessed June 16, 2019, www.iucnredlist.org/species/61998024 /61998026.

3. For debate and origins of the term, see Moore et al., "Interrogating the Plantationocene."

4. On this literature, see, for example, Wolf, *Europe and the People without History*; Mintz, *Sweetness and Power*; Stoler, *Capitalism and Confrontation*; and Rood, *Reinvention of Atlantic Slavery*.

5. Gerth and Mills, *From Max Weber*, 245, cited in Fogg, "Reinforcing Charisma," 123.

6. *BMG* 1878, 133; Kozok, *Utusan damai*, 97; Sidjabat, *Ahu Si Singamangaradja*, 375. There is some debate as to whom Si Singamangaradja was primarily opposed: the missionaries or the Dutch colonial government. See Van Bemmelen, *Christianity and Colonization*, 209–39.

7. See, among others, Kielstra, "Sumatra's Westkust van 1819–1825"; Meerwaldt, "Aantekeningen betreffende de Bataklanden"; Coolsma, *De zendingseeuw voor Nederlandsch-Indië*; Sidjabat, *Ahu Si Singamangaradja*; and Sinambela, *Ayahku, Si Singamangaradja XII pahlawan nasional*.

8. Sidjabat, *Ahu Si Singamangaradja*, 90–137.

9. Van den Arend, "De opkomst der landbouwondernemingen."

10. Pelzer, *Planter and Peasant*, 83–110.

11. Dorset, "Cultivation of Tobacco," 5. Dorset was an American administrator who studied tobacco plantations in Deli, as he planned to adopt their techniques for use in the US colony in the Philippines.

12. Dorset, "Cultivation of Tobacco," 6–7.

13. Dove, *Swidden Agriculture in Indonesia*, 30–37.

14. Coppicing allowed benzoin trees to continue growing after the resin was extracted.

15. See Bulbeck et al., *Southeast Asian Exports since the 14th Century*, 144–49; and Anderson, *Acheen and the Ports on the North and East Coasts of Sumatra*, 217.

16. Dove, "Forest Discourses in South and Southeast Asia," 113.

17. Veth, "De oorlog van 1872," 152.

18. De Jong, "Negotiations in Bismarckian Style," 41.

19. Veth, "De bovenlanden."

20. Stoler, *Confrontation and Capitalism*, 87–100.

21. Tsing, *Mushroom at the End of the World*, 63.

22. Veth, "De opkomst van de landbouwondernemingen," 160.

23. Veth, "De oorlog van 1872."

24. Sidjabat, *Ahu Si Singamangaradja*, 182.

25. Van Hoëvell, "Iets over t' oorlogvoeren der Batta's," 112.

26. Sidjabat, *Ahu Si Singamangaradja*, 187.

27. Van Bemmelen, *Christianity, Colonization and Gender*, 211.

28. Sidjabat, *Ahu Si Singamangaradja*, 134–36, 182; Van Bemmelen, *Christianity, Colonization and Gender*, 74–77. Sidjabat obtained information about these marriages from a family history manuscript written by one of Si Singamangaradja XII's children, Raja Buntal, in 1934.

29. E. E. W. C. Schröder, Assistant Resident, *Memorie van overgave 1920* (732), 73, National Archives of the Netherlands; Sidjabat, *Ahu Si Singamangaradja*, 190. The *Memories van overgave* were a collection of reports from the outgoing Residents, assistant Residents, or controleurs to their successors.

30. Van Dijk, "Die excursie naar de westelijke onafhakelijke landschappen," app.

31. Coolsma, *De zendingseeuw*, 403–9.

32. *BMG* 1897, 278–79.

33. Pelzer, *Planter and Peasant*, 52; Steedly, *Hanging without a Rope*, 53.

34. See L. C. Welsink, Resident for Tapanuli, *Memorie van overgave 1908* (171); and G. J. Westenberg, Resident for Tapanuli, *Memorie van overgave 1911* (172).

35. Van Duuren, "Parmalims and Parhudamdams," 60.

36. This exclusion of animist leaders was similar to the sidelining of Muslim leaders in Aceh and Mandailing. For the situation in Mandailing, see Castles, *Political Life of a Sumatran Residency*, 43–49; and for the situation in Aceh, see Reid, *Blood of the People*.

37. Hirosue, "Batak Millenarian Response to Colonial Order," 388. Hirosue cites Guru Somalaing's statement under police interrogation after his arrest in 1896.

38. Modigliani, *Fra i Battachi indipendenti*; Situmorang, *Guru Somalaing dan Modigliani*. Situmorang provides an abridged Indonesian-language translation of Modigliani's account. See Situmorang, *Toba Na Sae*, 217–325.

39. Hirosue, "Prophets and Followers," 87. "Malim" later developed the meaning "pure" in the Toba dialect. See Warneck, *Toba-Batak deutsches Wörterbuchs*, 153.

40. Hirosue, "Prophets and Followers," 104; Van Duuren, "Parmalims and Parhudamdams," 74.

41. De Boer, "De Permalimsekten."

42. Hirosue, "Prophets and Followers," 117; Van Duuren, "Parmalims and Par-hudamdams," 73.

43. Van Duuren, "Parmalims and Parhudamdams," 74.

44. Westenberg, *Memorie van overgave 1911* (172), 237.

45. Bodaan, "Een Bataksche perkara," 117.

46. Bodaan, "Een Bataksche perkara," 117.

47. Pedersen, *Batak Blood, Protestant Soul*, 108; Kipp, *Early Years of a Dutch Colonial Mission*, 223.

48. Steedly, *Hanging without a Rope*, 60.

49. Hirosue, "Prophets and Followers," 188.

50. Janssen et al., *Kort verslag omtrent de verrichtingen van het Bataksch Instituut*, 1–10.

51. These development plans were summarized in the *Memories van overgave*. For the relevant period, refer to the following *Memories* by author and year: Welsink in 1908; Westenberg for 1911; E. Gobée (controleur), 1914; F. R. Monteiro (controleur), 1916; J. P. J. Barth, 1915; and W. K. H. Ypes, 1926. On small-scale agricultural development research by the Batak Institute, see Schadée, *De uitbreiding van ons gezag*; and Joustra, *De toestanden in Tapanoeli*.

52. Middendorp, "Het inwerken van Westersche krachten," 461.

53. Van Kessel, "Reis in de nog onafhankelijke Bataklanden," 88.

54. Boomgaard, *Frontiers of Fear*, 100–101; Harahap, *Greget Tuanku Rao*, 43–47.

55. Ricklefs and Voorhoeve, *Indonesian Manuscripts in Great Britain*, 9.

56. Bartlett, *Labors of the Datoe*, 305–16.

57. Boomgaard, *Frontiers of Fear*, 123.

58. Boomgaard, *Frontiers of Fear*, 55.

59. Boomgaard, *Frontiers of Fear*, 123.

60. Voorhoeve, *Elio Modigliani's Batak Books*, 80. It is worth noting that better guns came from both sides: Si Singamangaradja XII apparently married off his daughter, Rinsan, to a gun merchant, enabling his side to get better weapons as well. See Sidjabat, *Ahu Si Singamangaradja*, 242.

61. Ris, "De onderafdeling klein Mandailing," 464.

62. The plan described here was mainly derived from *Memories van overgave*. From this collection, see the reports of Monteiro from 1916, 17–36; and from Gobée in 1914, 72–73. See also Joustra, *Van Medan naar Padang*, 9–26.

63. Monteiro, *Memorie van overgave 1917* (755), 7.

64. Steedly, *Hanging without a Rope*, 77–80.

65. *BMG* 1896, 235; Rijnsche Zending, "De zending onder de Batta's in 1881," 65–66.

66. Tideman, *Simeloengoen*, 17–20.

67. *BMG* 1893, 115.

68. Hirosue, "Prophets and Followers" 163–79; De Boer, "De Permalimsekten," 326–34; "De sekte de Permalim," in *BMG* 1902, 126–31.

69. Neumann, "De Bataksche Goeroe," 23.

70. De Boer, "De Permalimsekten," 191–92.

71. De Boer, "De Permalimsekten," 193–204; "De Permalims," *Tijdschrift voor het Binnenlandsch Bestuur*, 331–34.

72. Van den Berg, "De Parhoedamdambeweging."

73. Tichelman, "De parhoedamdam beweging," 33; Hirosue, "Prophets and Followers," 308–11; Van Duuren, "Parmalims and Parhudamdams," 80–83. In contrast, acquiescent chiefs would write to missionaries asking for a vaccinator to be sent to their village. For an example of such a letter, see Manik, *Batak-Handschriften*, 71.

74. Wallace, "Revitalization Movements," 264.

75. Adas, *Prophets of Rebellion*.

76. "Sumatra Camphor," *New Remedies*, 331.

77. See "De kamferboom op Sumatra," *Tijdschrift voor Nijverheid en Landbouw*.

78. De Vriese became chief scientist to lead a study on how to liberalize colonial agriculture from forced cultivation in the late nineteenth century. For more on De Vriese, see Goss, *The Floracrats*, 34–37.

79. De Vriese, *Mémoire sur le camphrier*, 31.

80. "The Camphor Tree of Sumatra," *Scientific American*, August 6, 1870, 81.

81. De Vriese, "On the Camphor-Tree of Sumatra," 329.

82. See, for instance, "Account of the Camphor Tree of Sumatra," *Philadelphia Recorder*, June 21, 1823, 46.

83. "Camphor," *American Journal of Pharmacy*, 459.

84. Baekeland, "Invention of Celluloid," 90; Böckmann, *Celluloid*.

85. Quoted in Goss, *The Floracrats*, 57.

86. *Koloniaal Verslag* (1884 and 1885), bijlage C, National Library of the Netherlands (Koninklijke Bibliotheek). *Koloniaal Verslag* was the annual report published in The Hague by the Dutch Ministry of the Colonies (Ministerie van Koloniën). All figures obtained on the camphor trade cited in this section are extracted from appendix C (bijlage C) of the report for the year cited; this appendix lists the level of Dutch East Indies exports each year for important products, including camphor, up to 1924.

87. On forest products being sent to Singapore, see *Koloniaal Verslag* (1890), 221.

88. *Koloniaal Verslag* (1893), bijlage C, 6.

89. *Koloniaal Verslag* (1911), 3–4, reports that traders in Singapore visited Singkel to examine samples of camphor available and noted that the price had then reached 4,500 gulden per pikul.

90. *Koloniaal Verslag* (1884), bijlage D, 5.

91. Van Vuuren, "De handel van Baroes," 871.

92. Dewey, "Camphor Tree," 7.

93. "Domesticating Camphor Trees in the United States," *Scientific American*, June 6, 1891, 353–54.

94. de Ligny, "Legendarische herkomst," 550.

95. Haraway, *Staying with the Trouble*.

96. Quoted in Steedly, *Hanging without a Rope*, 33.

97. Richtmann, "Camphor," 7.

98. Burkill, *Dictionary of Economic Products*, 877.

99. *Koloniaal Verslag* (1908), 291. It is not stated in the report exactly when this experiment started.

100. "Camphor," *Nature*, June 4, 1896, 116.

101. *Koloniaal Verslag* (1909), 275.

102. Burkill, *Dictionary of Economic Products*, 877.

103. Symington, *Malayan Forest Records No. 16*, 45–48; Foxworthy, *Malayan Forest Records No. 3*, 48.

104. Welsink, *Memorie van overgave 1908*, (171), 31.

105. "Opzet N.V. Houthandel Singkel," 3, speech delivered in 1916 on the establishment of the company Nijverheid Houthandel Singkel, call no. KITLV3 M 1996 A 1398, Leiden University Library.

106. Situmorang, *Toba Na Sae*, 12.

107. Djamin Harahap's appointment as *mantri polisi* and assistant *hoofdjaksa* was announced in *De Sumatra Post*, February 27, 1911, and *Bataviaasch Nieuwsblad*, May 12, 1914.

108. See Janssen, "De Batak als exploitanten," 356–58; Tideman, *De Bataklanden*, 12–13; and P. C. A. van Lith, *Memorie van overgave 1911* (750), 165–67.

109. This benzoin tapping method varies little from today's practice. For a description of contemporary benzoin tapping, see Susilowati et al., "Propagation of Valuable North Sumatera Benzoin Trees."

110. Brans, "Sumatra-Benzoë," 21; Van Vuuren, "De handel van Baroes," 1399. Van Vuuren's earlier account differed slightly from that of Brans in terms of land rights allocation. In the former, anyone who planted the trees and marked them could then claim the land, while in the latter, the land was first allocated before the planting. This discrepancy might be due to regional variation between Toba (Brans) and Dairi (Van Vuuren) or could reflect a change in organization when available land became scarcer.

111. Eijkemans, *Profitability or Security*, 41; Pelzer, *Planter and Peasant*, 46.

112. Brans, "Sumatra Benzoë," 46.

113. Steedly, *Hanging without a Rope*, 77–110.

114. Even within a particular species, not all tree varieties were valued unless they could yield salable material in abundance. See Goss, *The Floracrats*, 53–97.

115. The film was produced by a local environmental group, Kelompok Studi dan Perkembangan Prakarsa Masyarakat (KSPPM), and the international organizations Life Mosaic and the Forest Peoples Programme. "Film: Don't Pulp the Pandumaan-Sipatihuta: A David and Goliath Tale," Forest Peoples Programme, accessed June 2, 2018, http://www.forestpeoples.org/en/pulp-paper/video/2013/film-dont-pulp-pandumaan -sipituhuta-david-and-goliath-tale.

116. Van Bemmelen, *Christianity, Colonization and Gender*, 218.

117. Vitebsky, *Living without the Dead*, 233.

118. Barclay, *Outcasts of Empire*, 184–89.

119. Li, *Land's End*, 58–114.

120. Barita N. Lumbanbatu, "For an Indigenous Group in Sumatra, a Forest Regained Is Being Lost Once More," *Mongabay*, July 27, 2021, https://news.mongabay.com /2021/07/for-an-indigenous-group-in-sumatra-a-forest-regained-is-being-lost-once -more/.

SIX Disenchanting Elephants

1. "Tarikh Raja Asal," 10.

2. Aiken and Leigh, "On the Declining Fauna of Peninsula Malaysia," 15–22; Sukamar, *Asia's Elephants*, 219; Trautmann, *Elephants and Kings*, 2.

3. See, among others, Elvin, *Retreat of the Elephants*; Trautmann, *Elephants and Kings*; Allsen, *Royal Hunt*; and Sivasundaram, "Trading Knowledge."

4. Weber, "Science as a Vocation," cited in Gerth and Mills, *From Max Weber*, 129–55.

5. Gauchet, *Disenchantment of the World*, 3–26.

6. Benjamin, *Temiar Religion*, 301.

7. This structure in Perak was based on that of the Malacca sultanate, which was in turn partly based on the Minangkabau in Sumatra. For details, see Gullick, *Indigenous Political Systems*, 44–60; and Winstedt and Wilkinson, "History of Perak," 170–80.

8. W. G. Maxwell, *In Malay Forests*, 3.

9. Birch, "My Trip to Belum," 132.

10. Burns, *Journals of J. W. W. Birch*, 21; W. E. Maxwell, "Perak from Native Sources," 320–21.

11. Winstedt, "Old Minangkabau Legal Digest," 8.

12. For details on the pawang's role in court, see B. Andaya, *Perak, the Abode of Grace*, 58; Wilkinson, "Some Malay Studies," 93–97; and Winstedt, "Perak Genies."

13. Winstedt, "Perak Genies," 460–63. Winstedt's description of the ritual was based on information from Raja Haji Yahya, a relative of the Sultan Muda in the late nineteenth century.

14. According to the colophon, the manuscript was transcribed for W. E. Maxwell on the orders of Raja Dris, later Sultan Idris (1887–1916). See "Kitab perentah pawang," Perak, dated AH 1296/AD 1879, Maxwell Malay 106, Royal Asiatic Society of Great Britain and Ireland (hereafter cited as "Kitab perentah pawang"). On the broader relationship between pawang and elephants, also see Sevea, *Miracles and Material Life*, 152–79.

15. "Kitab perentah pawang," 1–2.

16. A formal procession of elephants gathered to greet a visiting chief in most accounts numbered around fifty. The same number is also estimated as the number of elephants in the Perak sultan's regalia. See Gullick, "Elephants of Syed Zin," 120.

17. Kathirithamby-Wells, "Human Impact on Large Mammal Populations."

18. Olivier, "Conservation of the Asian Elephant," 146.

19. Birch describes the difficulties that an elephant handler faced when three female captive elephants ran off with a wild male. Birch, "My Trip to Belum," 121.

20. "Kitab perentah pawang," 98.

21. "Kitab perentah pawang," 58.

22. Gerth and Mills, *From Max Weber*, 155.

23. "Kitab perentah pawang," 9.

24. Skeat, *Malay Magic*, 151.

25. Locke, "Elephants as Persons," 356. Locke was referring to Nepali elephants.

26. Burns, *Papers on Malay Subjects*, 89–90.

27. Winstedt and Wilkinson, "History of Perak," 78.

28. Burns, *Papers on Malay Subjects*, 96–100.

29. Burns, *Journals of J. W. W. Birch*, 70.

30. Burns and Cowan, *Swettenham Malayan Journals*, 80. For details, see Cowan, "Sir Frank Swettenham's Perak Journals."

31. For the reproduction of the map, see Burns and Cowan, *Swettenham Malayan Journals*, 1.

32. Burns and Cowan, *Swettenham Malayan Journals*, 148.

33. Winstedt and Wilkinson, "History of Perak," 168.

34. W. E. Maxwell, "Journey on Foot," 21.

35. Burns and Cowan, *Swettenham Malayan Journals*, 332.

36. Maxwell, "Journey on Foot," 30–31. *Ninring* refers to a local fruit that elephants particularly liked.

37. Leech, "About Slim and Bernam," 36–37; Swettenham, "From Perak to Slim."

38. Maxwell, "Journey on Foot," 27.

39. Lubis and Nasution, *Kinta Valley*, 48–58. Kinta in the 1870s was a relatively untouched mining frontier. It was so inaccessible from the more settled areas of Perak that it took Raja Bilah's family two months on elephants to get there from Slim.

40. Leech, "About Slim and Bernam," 34.

41. Scott, *Seeing Like a State*.

42. Maxwell, "Journey on Foot," 22.

43. Quoted in Barlow, *Swettenham*, 151.

44. *Buku daftar kes aduan*, ca. 1903–9, 1, Raja Bilah Collection, National Archives of Malaysia, Perak branch. This bound volume contains wood-collection permits signed by Raja Bilah and his son Raja Yacob from the years 1903 to 1909. The title, meaning "Registry of Legal Complaints," is misleading; it might have been miscategorized as belonging to another set of volumes that records the village complaints adjudicated by the village headman in Papan.

45. Sainsbury, *Tin Resources of the World*, 26–27. My statement on tin production is based on the figure of twelve million tons of tin produced in Kinta Valley alone from 1876 to 1950.

46. "Tarikh Raja Asal," 11.

47. Lubis and Nasution, *Raja Bilah*, 102.

48. Potter, "Forest Product Out of Control."

49. Lubis and Nasution, *Raja Bilah*, 100.

50. Potter, "Forest Product Out of Control," 234–35. The decline was greatest in trees such as gutta percha, which provided a valuable natural rubber export.

51. Annual Report of Federated Malay States, 1888, 39, call no. PPMS 31/File 3, School of Oriental and African Studies Library.

52. Wong, *Malayan Tin Industry*, 161. The impact of the ban was cushioned by booming tin prices, according to Lubis and Nasution, *Raja Bilah*, 103.

53. "Tarikh Raja Asal," 12.

54. Serullas, "Rediscovery of Gutta Percha," 230–31.

55. Swettenham, "Annual Report of the British Resident of Perak for the Year 1894," 371.

56. Annual Report of Federated Malay States, 1897, 13.

57. Kathirithamby-Wells, "Human Impact on Large Mammal Populations," 108–9.

58. "Tarikh Raja Asal," 21–22; Lubis and Nasution, *Raja Bilah*, 77.

59. *Buku daftar kes aduan*, 21.

60. For an overview of this scholarship, see Kahn, *Other Malays*, 1–20.

61. "Raja Bila punya ini takwil mimpi," ca. 1890, manuscript, Raja Bilah Collection, National Archives of Malaysia, Perak branch (hereafter cited simply as "Takwil mimpi"). The original manuscript was in the form of loose papers bound together. The first page features a recipe for an herbal concoction whose purpose was not stated. The remainder is devoted to the topic of interpreting dreams.

62. The term "Islamicate" is employed here in the sense pioneered by Marshall Hodgson: as an adjective that describes culture in the Muslim world that is not

necessarily related to Islam's precepts. Unlike "Islamic," the term does not assume that cultural norms in the Muslim world were inherently linked to the religion. See Hodgson, *Venture of Islam*, 59–60.

63. "Takwil mimpi," 10.

64. Clarence-Smith, "Elephants, Horses and the Coming of Islam," 273.

65. The three manuscript texts are "Surat mantra gajah," Perak, dated AH 1296/AD 1879, Maxwell Malay 107, Royal Asiatic Society of Great Britain and Ireland; "Mantra gajah," Perak, undated, MSS. INDIA OCEAN S.49 WH/1184, National Archives of Malaysia, Kuala Lumpur; and "Three Anonymous Manuscripts in Malaya Entitled Elephant Charm Books," Perak, dated 1929, MSS. INDIA OCEAN S.48 WH/11, National Archives of Malaysia, Kuala Lumpur.

66. W. G. Maxwell, "Mantra gajah" (1906), 1–53.

67. Ross, "Tin Frontier," 460.

68. Kathirithamby-Wells, "Human Impact on Large Mammal Populations," 238–40; Sukamar, *Asia's Elephant*, 219.

69. Burns and Cowan, *Sir Frank Swettenham Malayan Journals*, 84–85.

70. MacKenzie, *Empire of Nature*, 278; Kathirithamby-Wells, "Human Impact on Large Mammal Populations," 238.

71. Hornaday, *Experiences of a Hunter*, 99–129.

72. H. C. Syers, "Report on His Tour round the Stations," (1876), 1–5, call no. 1957/0000301, National Archives of Malaysia, Kuala Lumpur.

73. Hornaday, *Experiences of a Hunter*, 125.

74. Burns, "Annexation in the Malay States," 62.

75. Burns, "Annexation in the Malay States," 62.

76. Hornaday, *Experiences of a Hunter*, 321.

77. Wharton, "Man, Fire and Wild Cattle," 153–57.

78. Leech, "About Slim and Bernam," 39.

79. There seemed to be more than one Batu Gajah near the Kinta Valley. For other sites and origins of the name, see Lubis and Nasution, *Kinta Valley*, 113–14.

80. Leech, "About Slim and Bernam," 40.

81. "The First Catch," *Straits Times*, August 5, 1974, 28.

82. Lubis and Nasution, *Raja Bilah*, 143–46.

83. Gullick, "Elephants of Syed Zin," 120.

84. Amoroso, *Traditionalism*, 55–63.

85. Amoroso, *Traditionalism*, 77.

86. Harrison, *Council Minutes Perak*, 225.

87. Koay Su Lyn, "Sitiawan: The Promised Land of the Foochows," *Penang Monthly*, March 2018, https://penangmonthly.com/article/11324/sitiawan-the-promised-land-of-the-foochows-1.

88. It is not clear exactly who raised this plaque and when, but from the newspaper reports referencing it, the memorial must have been established well before the 1920s.

89. Rathborne, *Camping and Tramping in Malaya*, 179.

90. "The Train and the Elephant," *Singapore Free Press and Mercantile Advertiser*, July 21, 1926, 46.

91. "Dying Company of Malaya's Animals," *Straits Times*, November 22, 1965, 13.

92. "Tale of a Day an Elephant Met a Train," *Straits Times*, June 30, 1986, 7. Online mentions of this incident include Stephen Messenger, "The Incredible Story of the Elephant Who Derailed a Train to Defend His Herd," *Treehugger*, October 11, 2018, www.treehugger.com/natural-sciences/story-elephant-who-stood-train.html.

93. The Sakai were said to poison troublesome elephants. See Hornaday, *Experiences of a Hunter*, 123–26.

94. Mayer, *Trapping Wild Animals*, 60–61.

95. "With Reference to the Elephant Killed near Kajang: Memoranda on Correspondence regarding This Matter," 1884, reference no. 1957/0003783, National Archives of Malaysia, Kuala Lumpur.

96. Mackenzie, *Empire of Nature*, 279.

97. Hubback Commission, "Interim Report," 39.

98. Similar problems are faced in conserving Thailand's elephants. See Parreñas, "Materiality of Intimacy."

99. See Sideris, *Consecrating Science*, 1–13.

100. This conceptualization of charismatic megafauna links back to Weber. See Lorimer, "Nonhuman Charisma," 914–17.

101. Sideris, *Consecrating Science*, 190–94.

Conclusion

1. Pope Francis, *Laudato Si'* [On care for our common home], 123, accessed September 26, 2019, http://w2.vatican.va/content/dam/francesco/pdf/encyclicals/documents/papa-francesco_20150524_enciclica-laudato-si_en.pdf.

2. Jenkins, Tucker, and Grim, *Handbook of Religion and Ecology*, 79–84.

3. Gade, *Muslim Environmentalisms*, 4.

4. Gauchet, *Disenchantment of the World*, 67–74.

5. Boomgaard, *Southeast Asia*, 109–67; Reid, *History of Southeast Asia*, 149–52.

6. Tannenbaum, *Who Can Compete against the World?*; Gade, *Muslim Environmentalisms*, 10–12.

7. See, among other reports, Rebecca Henschke, "Indonesia's Orang Rimba: Forced to Renounce Their Faith," *BBC News*, November 17, 2017, www.bbc.com/news/world-asia-41981430; and Vincent Tan, "Malaysia's Indigenous Tribes Fight for Ancestral

Land and Rights in a Modern World," *Channel News Asia*, last updated December 14, 2020, www.channelnewsasia.com/news/asia/malaysia-orang-asli-ancestral-land -rights-11848294.

8. Li, "Masyarakat adat," 675–76.

9. Idrus, "Contesting Indigeneity," 107.

10. Idrus, "Contesting Indigeneity," 117–18; Bunnell and Nah, "Counter-Global Cases for Place."

11. Satria E. Hadinaryanto, "Special Report: Lake Toba Indigenous People Fight for Their Frankincense Forest," *Mongabay*, May 8, 2014, https://news.mongabay.com/2014 /05/special-report-lake-toba-indigenous-people-fight-for-their-frankincense-forest/.

12. World Bank, *Faiths and the Environment*, 19–20.

13. Barita Lumbanbatu, "For an Indigenous Group in Sumatra, a Forest Regained Is Being Lost Once More," *Mongabay*, July 27, 2021, https://news.mongabay.com/2021/07 /for-an-indigenous-group-in-sumatra-a-forest-regained-is-being-lost-once-more/.

14. Kristin Grossmann, "'Green Islam': Islamic Environmentalism in Indonesia," *New Mandala*, August 28, 2019, www.newmandala.org/green-islam/.

15. Parker et al., "How Young People in Indonesia See Themselves as Environmentalists," 267.

16. Francis Chan, "Indonesia Islamic Council Issues Fatwa against Forest-Burning," *Straits Times*, September 13, 2016, www.straitstimes.com/asia/se-asia/haram-to-burn -forest-intentionally-says-indonesian-islamic-council.

17. Tri Indah Oktavianti, "Interfaith Leaders Join Opposition to Jobs Law, Call for Judicial Review," *Jakarta Post*, October 6, 2020, www.thejakartapost.com/news/2020 /10/06/interfaith-leaders-join-opposition-to-jobs-law-call-for-judicial-review.html.

18. Li, "Masyarakat adat," 645.

19. Igra Anugrah, "Fishing for Votes in Indonesia," *New Mandala*, March 12, 2019, www.newmandala.org/fishing-for-votes-in-indonesia/.

20. Mann, *Wizard and the Prophet*, 39–94.

BIBLIOGRAPHY

Abbreviations

BKI . Bijdragen tot de Taal-, Land- en Volkenkunde van Nederlandsch-Indië
JMBRAS . Journal of the Malayan Branch of the Royal Asiatic Society
JSBRAS . Journal of the Straits Branch of the Royal Asiatic Society
TAG . Tijdschrift van het Aardrijkskundig Genootschap (1874–1884); *Tijdschrift van het Nederlandsch Aardrijkskundig Genootschap* (1885 onward)
TIV . Tijdschrift voor Indische Taal-, Land-, en Volkenkunde
TNI . Tijdschrift voor Nederlands-Indiës

Primary Sources

British Library, London, United Kingdom
   General Protocol Books, India Office Records. Documents on microfilm. Series R9/22.
   Malacca Records, India Office Records. Documents on microfilm. Series R9/23/57.
Leiden University Library, Leiden, The Netherlands
   "Kedatangan Bondjol." Anonymously handwritten notes, dated 1934, preserved on microfilm. Call no. D Or. 435–69. Collectie V. E. Korn.
   "Opzet N.V. Houthandel Singkel." Speech delivered in 1916 on the establishment of the company Nijverheid Houthandel Singkel. Call no. KITLV3 M 1996 A 1398.
National Archives of the Netherlands, The Hague, The Netherlands
   Memories van overgave, 1852–1962. Documents on microfiche. Archive no. 2.10.39.
National Library of the Netherlands (Koninklijke Bibliotheek), The Hague, The Netherlands
   Koloniaal Verslag. Bijlagen bij de Handelingen van de Tweede Kamer der Staten Generaal, 1868–1924. Call no. TG 32881.

National Archives of Malaysia, Kuala Lumpur, Malaysia

"Hikayat Hikamat." Manuscript, ca. 1880. Call no. Sp/5c/13.

"Mantra gajah." Perak, undated. MSS. INDIA OCEAN S.49 WH/1184.

Syers, H. C. "Report on His Tour round the Stations." 1876. Call no. 1957/0000301.

"Three Anonymous Manuscripts in Malaya Entitled Elephant Charm Books." Perak, 1929. MSS. INDIA OCEAN S.48 WH/11.

"With Reference to the Elephant Killed near Kajang: Memoranda on Correspondence regarding This Matter." 1884. Call no. 1957/0003783.

National Archives of Malaysia, Perak branch, Ipoh, Malaysia

"Raja Bila punya ini takwil mimpi." Perak, undated. Manuscript. Call no. 1999/0000381.

Buku daftar kes aduan. Perak, ca. 1903–9. Call no. 1999/0000410, Raja Bilah Collection.

Private Holdings

Raja Muhammad Yacob. "Ini tarikh Raja Asal dan keluarganya." Perak, ca. 1934. Courtesy of Abdur-Razzaq Lubis.

Royal Asiatic Society of Great Britain and Ireland, London, United Kingdom

"Kitab perentah pawang." Perak, dated AH 1296/AD 1879, Maxwell Malay 106.

"Surat mantra gajah." Perak, dated AH 1296/AD 1879, Maxwell Malay 107.

School of Oriental and African Studies Library, London, United Kingdom

Annual Reports of Federated Malay States, 1880–1919. Call no. PPMS 31/File 3.

"Rajas and Chiefs of Perak," Perak, 1876. Compiled by W. E. Maxwell. Call no. MS46943A, ff. 1–15.

Secondary Sources

Abdullah, Taufik. "Adat and Islam: An Examination of Conflict in Minangkabau." *Indonesia* 2 (October 1966): 1–24.

Adas, Michael. *Prophets of Rebellion: Millenarian Protest Movements against the European Colonial Order*. Chapel Hill: University of North Carolina Press, 1979.

Ahmad, Kasim, ed. *Hikayat Hang Tuah*. Kuala Lumpur: Dewan Bahasa dan Pustaka, 1975.

Aiken, S. Robert, and Colin H. Leigh. "On the Declining Fauna of Peninsular Malaysia in the Post-colonial Period." *Ambio* 14, no. 1 (1985): 15–22.

Al-Attas, S. M. N. *Historical Fact and Fiction*. Johor Bahru: Penerbit UTM Press, 2011.

Aljunied, K., and M. Mohamed, ed. *Melayu: The Politics, Poetics and Paradoxes of Malayness*. Singapore: NUS Press, 2013.

Allsen, Thomas. *The Royal Hunt in Eurasian History*. Philadelphia: University of Pennsylvania Press, 2008.

Ammerman, Nancy T. *Everyday Religion: Observing Modern Religious Lives*. Oxford: Oxford University Press, 2007.

Amoroso, Donna J. *Traditionalism and the Ascendancy of the Malay Ruling Class*. Singapore: NUS Press and SIRD, 2014.

Amrith, Sunil. *Crossing the Bay of Bengal: The Furies of Nature and the Fortunes of Migrants*. Cambridge, MA: Harvard University Press, 2014.

——. *Unruly Waters: How Rains, Rivers, Coasts and Seas Have Shaped Asia's History*. London: Basic Books, 2018.

Andaya, B. W. *Perak, the Abode of Grace: A Study of an Eighteenth Century Malay State*. Kuala Lumpur: Oxford University Press, 1979.

——. "Rivers, Oceans and Spirits: Water Cosmologies, Gender and Religious Change in Southeast Asia." *Trans-regional and -national Studies of Southeast Asia* 4, no. 2 (2016): 239–63.

——. "Seas, Oceans and Cosmologies in Southeast Asia." *Journal of Southeast Asian Studies* 48, no. 3 (2017): 329–52.

Andaya, Leonard. *Leaves of the Same Tree: Ethnic Change along the Straits of Malacca*. Honolulu: University of Hawai'i Press, 2013.

——. "The Trans-Sumatra Trade and the Ethnicization of the Batak." *BKI* 158, no. 3 (2002): 367–409.

Anderson, John. *Acheen and the Ports on the North and East Coasts of Sumatra: With Incidental Notices of the Trade in the Eastern Seas and the Aggressions of the Dutch*. Kuala Lumpur: Oxford University Press, 1971.

Århem, Kaj. "Southeast Asian Animism in Context." In *Animism in Southeast Asia*, edited by Kaj Århem and Guido Sprenger, 3–30. New York: Routledge, 2016.

Århem, Kaj, and Guido Sprenger, eds. *Animism in Southeast Asia*. New York: Routledge, 2016.

Aritonang, Jan S. *Mission Schools in Batakland (Indonesia), 1861–1940*. Leiden: Brill, 1994.

——. *Beberapa pemikaran menuju teologi Dalihan na Tolu*. Jakarta: Dian Utama, 2006.

Asnan, Gusti. "Transportation on the West Coast of Sumatra in the Nineteenth Century." *BKI* 158, no. 4 (2002): 727–41.

Aung-Thwin, Michael. "The Myth of the 'Three Shan Brothers' and the Ava Period in Burmese History." *Journal of Asian Studies* 55, no. 4 (1996): 881–901.

Balamurugan, Gopal. "Tin Mining and Sediment Supply in Peninsular Malaysia with Special Reference to the Kelang River Basin." *Environmentalist* 11, no. 4 (1991): 281–91.

Baekeland, Leo Hendrik. "The Invention of Celluloid." *Journal of Industrial and Engineering Chemistry* 6 (1914): 90–91.

Bagir, Zainal Abidin. "The Importance of Religion and Ecology in Indonesia." *World-views* 19, no. 2 (2015): 99–102.

Barclay, Paul. *Outcasts of Empire: Japan's Rule on Taiwan's "Savage" Border*. Oakland: University of California Press, 2018.

Barendregt, Bart. "From the Realm of Many Rivers: Memory, Places and Notions of Home in the Southern Sumatran Highlands." PhD diss., Leiden University, 2005.

Barlow, Henry S. *Swettenham*. Kuala Lumpur: Southdene Sdn Bhd, 1995.

Barrow, John. *A Voyage to Cochin-China*. London: Cadell and Davies, 1806.

Bartlett, Harley H. "A Batak and Malay Chant on Rice Cultivation with Introductory Notes on Bilingualism and Acculturation in Indonesia." *Proceedings of the American Philosophical Society* 96, no. 6 (1952): 629–52.

———. *The Labors of the Datoe and Other Essays on the Batak of Asahan*. Ann Arbor: Center for South and Southeast Asian Studies, University of Michigan, 1973.

Beighton, John T. *Betel-Nut Island: Personal Experiences and Adventures in the Eastern Tropics*. London: Religious Tract Society, 1888.

Benjamin, Geoffrey. *Temiar Religion 1964–2012: Enchantment, Disenchantment and Re-enchantment in Malaysia's Uplands*. Singapore: NUS Press, 2014.

Birch, Ernest W. "My Trip to Belum." *JMBRAS* 54, no. 1 (1911): 117–35.

Böckmann, F. R. *Celluloid: Its Raw Material, Manufacture, Properties and Uses*. London: Scott, Greenwood & Son, 1907.

Bodaan, L. "Een Bataksche perkara." *Medelingen Nederlandsch Zending* 61 (1917): 112–18.

Boomgaard, Peter. *Frontiers of Fear: Tigers and People in the Malay World, 1600–1950*. New Haven, CT: Yale University Press, 2001.

———. "Land Rights and the Environment in the Indonesian Archipelago, 800–1950." *Journal of the Economic and Social History of the Orient* 54, no. 4 (2011): 478–96.

———. *Southeast Asia: An Environmental History*. Santa Barbara, CA: ABC-Clio, 2007.

Braddell, Roland. "Further Notes upon a Study of Ancient Times in the Malay Peninsula." *JMBRAS* 15, no. 1 (1937): 25–31.

Braddell, Thomas. "Notes of a Trip to the Interior from Malacca." *Journal of the Indian Archipelago and Eastern Asia* 7 (1853): 73–104.

Brakel-Papenhuyzen, Clara. *Dairi Stories and Pakpak Storytelling: A Storytelling Tradition from the North Sumatran Rainforest*. Leiden: Brill, 2014.

Brans, P. H. "Sumatra-Benzoë." PhD diss., University of Amsterdam, 1935.

Brouwer, J. J. van Limburg. "Het gouvernmental inlandsch onderwijs op Sumatra." *TNI* 5, no. 2 (1876): 1–24.

Brown, C. C. *Sejarah Melayu or Malay Annals: An Annotated Translation*. Kuala Lumpur: Oxford University Press, 1970.

Bulbeck, David, Anthony Reid, Tan Lay Cheng, and Wu Yiqi, eds. *Southeast Asian*

Exports since the 14th Century: Cloves, Pepper, Coffee, and Sugar. Singapore: Institute of Southeast Asian Studies, 1998.

Bunnell, Tim, and Alice M. Nah. "Counter-Global Cases for Place: Contesting Displacement in Globalising Kuala Lumpur Metropolitan Area." *Urban Studies* 41, no. 12 (2004): 2447–67.

Burkill, Ian H. *A Dictionary of Economic Products of the Malay Peninsula*. Singapore: Government of the Straits Settlements, 1935.

Burns, Peter L. "Annexation in the Malay States: The Jervois Papers." *JMBRAS* 72, no. 1 (1999): 1–93.

———, ed. *The Journals of J. W. W. Birch: First British Resident to Perak, 1874–1875*. Kuala Lumpur: Oxford University Press, 1976.

———. *Papers on Malay Subjects*. Edited by R. J. Wilkinson. 1907–16. Kuala Lumpur: Oxford University Press, 1971.

Burns, Peter L., and Charles D. Cowan, eds. *Sir Frank Swettenham Malayan Journals, 1874–1876*. Kuala Lumpur: Oxford University Press, 1975.

Burton, Richard, and Nathaniel Ward. "Report of a Journey into the Batak Country, in the Interior of Sumatra, in the Year 1824." *Transactions of the Royal Asiatic Society* 1, no. 1 (1827): 485–501.

Byl, Julia. *Antiphonal Histories: Resonant Pasts in the Toba Batak Musical Present*. Middletown, CT: Wesleyan University Press, 2014.

"Camphor." *American Journal of Pharmacy* 45, no. 3 (1873): 459–74.

Casparis, Johannes Gijsbertus de. *Indonesian Palaeography: A History of Writing in Indonesia from the Beginnings to c. AD 1500*. Leiden: Brill, 1975.

Castles, Lance. "The Political Life of a Sumatran Residency: Tapanuli 1915–1940." PhD diss., Yale University, 1979.

Chakrabarty, Dipesh. "The Climate of History: Four Theses." *Critical Inquiry* 35, no. 2 (2009): 197–222.

Charney, Michael. *Southeast Asian Warfare, 1300–1800*. Leiden: Brill, 2004.

Ché-Ross, Raimy. "Hikayat Hikamat: The Malay Memoirs of a Sumatran Christian." *JMBRAS* 80, no. 1 (2007): 59–89.

Clarence-Smith, William G. "Elephants, Horses and the Coming of Islam to Northern Sumatra." *Indonesia and the Malay World* 32, no. 93 (2004): 271–84.

Clifford, Hugh. "A Journey through the Malay States of Trengganu and Kelantan." *Geographical Journal* 9, no. 1 (1897): 1–37.

Commins, David. *The Wahhabi Mission and Saudi Arabia*. London: I. B. Tauris, 2009.

Coolsma, Sierk. *De zendingseeuw voor Nederlandsch-Indië*. Utrecht: C. H. E. Breijer, 1902.

Cowan, Charles D., ed. "Sir Frank Swettenham's Perak Journals." *JMBRAS* 24, no. 4 (1951): 1–148.

Cronon, William. "The Trouble with Wilderness." In *Uncommon Ground: Rethinking the Human Place in Nature*, edited by William Cronon, 69–90. New York: Norton, 1993.

Crutzen, Paul J. "Geology of Mankind." *Nature* 415 (2002): 23.

Crutzen, Paul J., and Eugene F. Stoermer. "The Anthropocene." *IGBP Newsletter* 41 (2000): 16–18.

Davies, Jeremy. *The Birth of the Anthropocene*. Oakland: University of California Press, 2016.

Dean, William. "Missionary Work among the Malays." *Baptist Missionary Magazine* 56, no. 5 (1876): 131–35.

De Boer, D. W. N. "De Permalimsekten van Oeloean, Toba en Habinsaran." *Tijdschrift voor het Binnenlandsch Bestuur* 47 (1917): 326–33.

De Jong, Josselin. "Negotiations in Bismarckian Style: The Debate on the Aceh War and Its Legitimacy, 1873–74." *Itinerario* 29, no. 2 (2005): 38–52.

"De kamferboom op Sumatra: Stukken, gewisseld nopens de kwestie of voorziening noodig is tegen de uitroeiing van dien boom." *Tijdschrift voor Nijverheid en Landbouw* 17 (1872): 91–108.

De la Croix, J. Errington. *Les mines étain de Perak*. Paris, 1882.

De Ligny, J. "Legendarische herkomst de kamfer Baroes." *TIV* 23 (1923): 549–55.

De Morgan, J. *Explorations dans la Presqu'ile Malaise Royaumes de Perak et de Patani*. Paris: Imprimerie General A. Lahure, 1896.

"De Permalims." *Tijdschrift voor het Binnenlandsch Bestuur* 45 (1913): 326–34.

De Stuers, H. J. L. L. R. *De vestiging en uitbreiding der Nederlanders ter westkust van Sumatra*. Amsterdam: P. N. van Kampen, 1850.

De Vriese, Willem Hendrik. *Mémoire sur le camphrier de Sumatra et de Bornéo*. Leiden: Brill, 1856.

———. "On the Camphor-Tree of Sumatra." *American Journal of Pharmacy*, n.s., 18, no. 4 (October 1852): 329–43.

Dewey, Lyster H. "The Camphor Tree." Circular no. 12, US Department of Agriculture, Division of Botany, 1897.

Dobbin, Christine. *Islamic Revivalism in a Changing Peasant Economy: Central Sumatra, 1784–1847*. London: Curzon, 1983.

Donkin, Robert Arthur. *Dragon's Brain Perfume: An Historical Geography of Camphor*. Leiden: Brill, 1999.

Dorset, C. W. "Cultivation of Tobacco." *Farmer's Bulletin*. N.p.: Manila Bureau of Public Printing, 1903.

Dove, Michael R. "Forest Discourses in South and Southeast Asia: A Comparison with Global Discourse." In *Nature in the Global South: Environmental Projects in South and Southeast Asia*, edited by Paul Greenough and Anna L. Tsing, 103–23. Durham, NC: Duke University Press, 2003.

————, ed. *Southeast Asian Grasslands: Understanding a Vernacular Landscape; Canonical Readings*. New York: New York Botanical Garden, 2008.

————. *Swidden Agriculture in Indonesia: The Subsistence Strategies of the Kalimantan Kantu*. New York: Mouton, 1985.

Drakard, Jane. *A Malay Frontier: Unity and Duality in a Sumatran Kingdom*. Ithaca, NY: Cornell Southeast Asian Studies Program Publications, 1990.

Eijkemans, C. H. J. F. *Profitability or Security: Decision-Making on Land Use among Toba Batak Peasants in North Sumatra, Indonesia*. Saarbrücken: Verlag für Entwicklungspolitik, 1995.

Elvin, Mark. *The Retreat of the Elephants: An Environmental History of China*. New Haven, CT: Yale University Press, 2004.

————. "Who Was Responsible for the Weather? Moral Meteorology in Late Imperial China." *Osiris* 13 (1998): 213–37.

Feener, Michael. *Muslim Legal Thought in Modern Indonesia*. New York: Cambridge University Press, 2007.

Fogg, Kevin W. "Reinforcing Charisma in the Bureaucratisation of Indonesian Islamic Organisations." *Journal of Current Southeast Asian Affairs* 37, no. 1 (2018): 117–40.

Forsyth, Tim, and Andrew Walker. *Forest Guardians, Forests Destroyers: The Politics of Environmental Knowledge in Northern Thailand*. Seattle: University of Washington Press, 2008.

Foucault, Michel. *The History of Sexuality*. 1976. New York: Vintage Books, 1990.

Foxworthy, F. W. *Malayan Forest Records No. 3: Commercial Timber Trees of the Malayan Peninsula*. Singapore: Fraser & Neave, 1921.

Frazer, James G. *The Golden Bough: A Study of Magic and Religion*. London: Macmillan, 1971.

Fuller, Christopher J. *The Camphor Flame: Popular Hinduism and Society in India*. Princeton, NJ: Princeton University Press, 1992.

Gabriel, C. "Kriegszug der Bondjol unter Anfahrung des Tuanku Rau in die Bataklander, zusammengetragen von Guru Kenan Huta Galung und aus dem Batakschen ins Deutsche ubersetzt." *TIV* 61 (1922): 157–90.

Gade, Anna. *Muslim Environmentalisms: Religious and Social Foundations*. New York: Columbia University Press, 2019.

Gauchet, Marcel. *The Disenchantment of the World: A Political History of Religion*. Princeton, NJ: Princeton University Press, 1985.

Gerth, Hans H., and C. Wright Mills, eds. *From Max Weber: Essays in Sociology*. New York: Routledge, 2009.

Ghosh, Amitav. *The Great Derangement: Climate Change and the Unthinkable*. Chicago: University of Chicago Press, 2016.

Gobée, E. "Dr. Neubronner van der Tuuk's bezoek aan Si Singa Mangaradja in 1853 van Bataksche zijde togelicht." *TAG* 34 (1917): 366–69.

Goss, Andrew. "Building the World's Supply of Quinine: Dutch Colonialism and the Origins of a Global Pharmaceutical Industry." *Endeavour* 38, no. 1 (2013): 8–18.

———. *The Floracrats: State-Sponsored Science and the Failure of the Enlightenment in Indonesia.* Madison: University of Wisconsin Press, 2011.

Grehan, James. *Twilight of the Saints: Everyday Religion in Ottoman Syria and Palestine.* Oxford: Oxford University Press, 2014.

Grove, Richard. *Green Imperialism: Colonial Expansion, Tropical Island Edens and the Origins of Environmentalism, 1600–1860.* Cambridge: Cambridge University Press, 1996.

Gullick, John M. "The Economy of Perak in the Mid-1870s." *JMBRAS* 83, no. 2 (2010): 87–46.

———. "The Elephants of Syed Zin." *JMBRAS* 59, no. 1 (1986): 113–23.

———. *Indigenous Political Systems of Western Malaya.* London: University of London, Athlone Press, 1958.

———. *Kuala Lumpur, 1880–1895: A City in the Making.* Petaling Jaya: Pelanduk Publications, 1988.

Hadler, Jeffrey. "Historiography of Violence and the Secular State in Indonesia: Tuanku Imam Bonjol and the Uses of History." *Journal of Asian Studies* 67, no. 3 (2008): 971–1010.

———. *Muslims and Matriarchs: Cultural Resilience in Indonesia through Jihad and Colonialism.* Ithaca, NY: Cornell University Press, 2010.

Hale, Abraham. "Mines and Miners in Kinta." *JSBRAS* 16, no. 1 (1885): 303–20.

Hall, David. *Lived Religion in America: Toward a History of Practice.* Princeton, NJ: Princeton University Press, 1997.

Hamilton, Clive. "The Anthropocene as Rupture." *Anthropocene Review* 3, no. 2 (2016): 93–106.

Hamka. *Antara fakta dan khayal: Bantahan terhadap tulisan-tulisan ir. Mangaradja Onggang Parlindungan dalam bukunya "Tuanku Rao."* Jakarta: Bulan Bintang, 1974.

Harahap, Basyral H. *Greget Tuanku Rao.* Jakarta: Komunitas Bambu, 2009.

———, trans. *Si Bulus Bulus, Si Rumbuk Rumbuk: Sebuah buku bacaan karangan Willem Iskander.* Jakarta: Campusiana, 1978.

Haraway, Donna. *Staying with the Trouble: Making Kin in the Chthulucene.* Durham, NC: Duke University Press, 2006.

Harrison, Charles W. *Council Minutes Perak, 1877–1879.* Kuala Lumpur: Federated Malay States Press, 1936.

Henley, David. "Conflict, Justice and the Stranger-King Indigenous Roots of Colonial Rule in Indonesia and Elsewhere." *Modern Asian Studies* 38, no. 1 (2004): 85–144.

———. "Swidden Farming as an Agent of Environmental Change in Southeast Asia: Ecological Myth and Historical Reality in Southeast Asia." *Environment and History* 17, no. 4 (2011): 525–44.

Herzog, Shawna. "Domesticating Labor: An Illicit Slave Trade to the British Straits Settlements, 1811–1845." *Journal of World History* 28, no. 3–4 (2017): 341–69.

Hijjas, Mulaika. "Not Just Fryers of Bananas and Sweet Potatoes: Literate and Literary Women in the Nineteenth Century Malay World." *Journal of Southeast Asian Studies* 41, no. 1 (2010): 153–72.

Hirosue, Masashi. "The Batak Millenarian Response to the Colonial Order." *Journal of Southeast Asian Studies* 25, no. 2 (1994): 331–43.

———. "Prophets and Followers in Batak Millenarian Responses to the Colonial Order: Parmalim, Na Siak Bagi and Parhudamdam, 1890–1930." PhD diss., Australian National University, 1988.

Hirth, Friedrich. *Chau Ju-kua: His Work on the Chinese and Arab Trade in the Twelfth and Thirteenth Centuries, Entitled Chu-fan-Chi.* St. Petersburg: Imperial Academy of Science, 1967.

Hodgson, Marshall. *The Venture of Islam: Volume 1, The Classical Age of Islam.* Chicago: University of Chicago Press, 1974.

Hornaday, William T. *The Experiences of a Hunter and Naturalist in the Malay Peninsular and Borneo.* Kuala Lumpur: Oxford University Press, 1993.

Hubback, Theodore. *Elephant and Seladang Hunting in Malaya.* London: Ward, 1905.

Hubback Commission. "Interim Report." *Journal of the Society for the Preservation of the Wild Fauna of the Empire* 19 (1933): 30–42.

H.v.D. "Oorsprong der Padaris (Een secte op de Westkust van Sumatra)." *TNI* 1, no. 2 (1838): 113–32.

Idrus, Rusaslina. "Contesting Indigeneity." In *Melayu: The Politics, Poetics and Paradoxes of Malayness*, edited by Khairudin Aljunied and Maznah Mohamed, 99–118. Singapore: NUS Press, 2011.

Iskandar, Teuku, ed. *Hikayat Aceh.* The Hague: H. L. Smits, 1959.

James, Ronald M. "Knockers, Knackers, and Ghosts: Immigrant Folklore in the Western Mines." *Western Folklore* 51, no. 2 (1992): 153–77.

Janssen, J. W. "De Batak als exploitanten van hun eigen gebied." *Koloniaal Tijdschrift* 12, no. 2 (1924): 353–78.

Janssen, J. W., A. W. Nieuwenhuis, C. A. Van Ophuijsen, C. J. Westenberg, and J. C. Van Eerde. *Kort verslag omtrent de verrichtingen van vet Bataksch Instituut te Leiden.* Leiden: Bataksch Instituut, 1913.

Jenkins, Willis J., Mary E. Tucker, and John Grim, eds. *Routledge Handbook of Religion and Ecology.* New York: Routledge, 2017.

Jones, Russell, ed. *Hikayat Raja Pasai.* Kuala Lumpur: Fajar Bakti, 1999.

Joustra, M. *Batakspiegel.* Leiden: S. C. van Doesburgh, 1926.

———. *De toestanden in Tapanoeli en de regeringscommissie: Nota in opdracht van het Bataksch Instituut.* Amsterdam: Schooneveld & Zoon, 1917.

———. *Van Medan naar Padang en Terug.* Leiden: Bataksch Instituut, 1915.

Junghuhn, Friedrich Franz Wilhelm. *Die Battälander der Sumatra.* Berlin: G. Reimer, 1847.

Kahn, Joel. *Other Malays: Nationalism and Cosmopolitanism in the Modern Malay World.* Copenhagen: NIAS Press, 2006.

Kartomi, Margaret. *Musical Journeys in Sumatra.* Urbana: University of Illinois Press, 2012.

Kathirithamby-Wells, Jeyamalar. "Human Impact on Large Mammal Populations in Peninsular Malaysia from the Nineteenth to the Mid-Twentieth Century." In *Paper Landscapes: Explorations in the Environmental History of Indonesia,* edited by Peter Boomgaard, Freek Colombijn, and David Henley, 215–48. Leiden: KITLV Press, 1997.

———. *Nature and Nation: Forests and Development in Peninsular Malaysia.* Honolulu: University of Hawai'i Press, 2005.

———. "The Origin of the Term Padri: Some Historical Evidence." *Indonesia Circle* 41 (1986): 3–9.

Kielstra, E. B. "Sumatra's Westkust sedert 1850." *BKI* 41 (1892): 254–330.

———. "Sumatra's Westkust sedert 1850 (Vervolg)." *BKI* 41 (1892): 622–706.

Kipp, Rita S. *Disassociated Identities: Ethnicity, Religion and Class in an Indonesian Society.* Ann Arbor: University of Michigan Press, 1993.

———. *The Early Years of a Dutch Colonial Mission: The Karo Field.* Ann Arbor: University of Michigan Press, 1990.

Kipp, Rita S., and Richard D. Kipp, eds. *Beyond Samosir: Recent Studies of the Batak Peoples of Sumatra.* Athens: Ohio Center for International Studies Southeast Asia Program, 1983.

Knappert, Jan. "Why There Is Only One Sun." *World and I* 16, no. 10 (2001): 188–96.

Köhler, H. J. *Habinsaran (Het Land van den Zonnestraal).* Zutphen: W. J. Thime & Cie., 1926.

Kozok, Uli. "On Writing the Not-to-Be-Read: Literature and Literacy in a Pre-colonial 'Tribal' Society." *BKI* 156, no. 1 (2000): 33–55.

———. "The Seals of the Last Singamangaradja." *Indonesia and the Malay World* 28, no. 1 (2000): 244–79.

———. *Surat Batak: Sejarah Perkembangan Tulisan Batak.* Jakarta: Kepustakaan Popular Gramedia, 2009.

———. *Utusan damai di kemelut perang: Peran Zending dalam Perang Toba.* Jakarta: Yayasan Obor Indonesia, 2010.

————. *Warisan leluhur: Sastra lama dan Iksara Batak*. Jakarta: Ecole Française d'Extrême Orient/Kepustakaan Populer Gramedia, 2004.

Kratoska, Paul H. *Honourable Intentions: Talks on the British Empire in Southeast Asia, 1874–1928*. Singapore: Oxford University Press, 1983.

Kratz, E. Ulrich, and Adriyetti Amir. *Surat keterangan Syeikh Jalaluddin karangan Fakih Saghir*. Selangor: Percetakan Dewan Bahasa dan Pustaka Siri Warisan Sastera Klasik, 2002.

Kreemer, J. *De karbouw: Zijn betekenis voor de volken van de Indonesische Archipel*. The Hague and Bandung: W. van Hoeve, 1956.

Kuiper, Franciscus B. J. "Cosmogony and Conception: A Query." *History of Religions* 10, no. 2 (1970): 91–138.

Kushnick, Geoff. "Resource Competition and Reproduction in Karo Batak Villages." *Human Nature* 21, no. 1 (2010): 62–81.

Laakkonen, Simo, Richard Tucker, and Timo Vuorisalo, eds. *The Long Shadows: A Global Environmental History of the Second World War*. Corvallis: Oregon State University Press, 2017.

Latour, Bruno. *Facing Gaia: Eight Lectures on Political Theology*. New York: Polity Press, 2017.

Leech, H. W. C. "About Kinta." *JSBRAS* 4, no. 1 (1879): 21–33.

————. "About Slim and Bernam." *JSBRAS* 4, no. 1 (1875): 34–45.

Lees, Lynn Hollen. "Becoming Malay: The Case of Batak Orphans in 1930s Perak." *JMBRAS* 94, no. 2 (2021): 141–67.

Lefebvre, H. *Critique of Everyday Life, Vol. 1*. London: Verso, 1991.

Lehmann, Martin E. *A Biographical Study of Ingwer Ludwig Nommensen (1834–1918), Pioneer Missionary to the Bataks of Sumatra*. New York: Edwin Mellen Press, 1996.

Li, Tania M. *Land's End: Capitalist Relations in an Indigenous Frontier*. Durham, NC: Duke University Press, 2016.

————. "Masyarakat Adat, Difference and the Limits of Recognition in Indonesia's Forest Zone." *Modern Asian Studies* 35, no. 3 (2001): 645–76.

Liaw Yock Fang, ed. *Undang-undang Melaka: The Laws of Melaka*. The Hague: Martinus Nijhoff, 1976.

Linehan, William. *A History of Pahang*. Kuala Lumpur: Malaysian Branch of the Royal Asiatic Society, 1973.

Lister, Martin. *Mining Laws and Customs in the Malay Peninsula*. Singapore: Government Printing Office, 1889.

Locke, Piers. "Elephants as Persons, Affective Apprenticeship, and Fieldwork and Nonhuman Informants in Nepal." *HAU: Journal of Ethnographic Theory* 7, no. 1 (2017): 353–76.

Lofton, Kathryn. *Consuming Religion*. Chicago: University of Chicago Press, 2017.

Lorimer, Jamie. "Nonhuman Charisma." *Environment and Planning Development: Society and Space* 25, no. 1 (2007): 911–32.

Louys, J. "Limited Effect of the Quaternary's Largest Super Eruption (Toba) on Land Mammals in Southeast Asia." *Quaternary Science Review* 26, no. 25–28 (2007): 3108–17.

Lubis, Abdur-Razzaq. *Sutan Puasa: Founder of Kuala Lumpur*. Penang: Areca Books, 2018.

———. *Tarikh Raja Asal dan keluarganya*. Penang: Areca Books, 2021.

Lubis, Abdur-Razzaq, and K. Salma Nasution. *Kinta Valley: Pioneering Malaysia's Modern Development*. Penang: Areca Books, 2005.

———. *Raja Bilah and the Mandailings of Perak, 1875–1911*. Kuala Lumpur: Monographs of the Malaysian Branch of the Royal Asiatic Society, 2003.

Lubis, Z. Pangaduan. *Asal usul marga-marga di Mandailing*. Medan: Pustaka Widiasarana, 2010.

———. *Kumpulan catatan lepas tentang Mandailing*. Medan: Pustaka Widiasarana, 2012.

———. *Lebih jauh tentang Willem Iskander dan "Si Bulus Bulus, Si Rumbuk Rumbuk."* Medan: Pustaka Widiasarana, 2011.

Lumbantobing, Adniel. *Sejarah Si Singamangaradja I–XII*. Jakarta: Toko Buku, 1951.

Macdonald, John. "On Three Natural Productions of Sumatra." *Asiatick Researches* 4 (1795): 1–30.

Mackenzie, John M. *The Empire of Nature: Hunting, Conservation and British Imperialism*. Manchester: Manchester University Press, 1988.

Maloney, Bernard K. "Pea Bullok: A Preliminary Account of a 30 000 Year Record of Vegetation and Climatic Change from Highland North Sumatra." *Quaternary Newsletter* 73 (1994): 7–10.

———. "Pollen Analytical Evidence for Early Forest Clearance in North Sumatra." *Nature* 280 (1980): 324–44.

———. "Possible Early Dry-Land and Wetland Rice Cultivation in Highland North Sumatra." *Asian Perspectives* 35, no. 2 (1996): 164–92.

Manap, Norpadzlihatun, and Nikolaos Voulvoulis. "Data Analysis for Environmental Impact of Dredging." *Journal of Cleaner Production* 137 (2016): 394–404.

Manickam, Sandra. *Taming the Wild: Aborigines and Racial Knowledge in Colonial Malaya*. Sydney: Asian Studies Association of Australia/Southeast Asia Publications Series, 2015.

Manik, Liberty. *Batak-Handschriften*. Wiesbaden: Steiner, 1973.

Mann, Charles C. *The Wizard and the Prophet: Two Groundbreaking Scientists and Their Conflicting Visions of the Future of Our Planet*. New York: Knopf, 2018.

Marsden, William. *The History of Sumatra*. 1783. Kuala Lumpur: Oxford University Press, 1966.

Maxwell, William E. "The Folklore of the Malays." *JSBRAS* 7, no. 1 (1881): 11–29.

————. "A History of Perak from Native Sources." *JSBRAS* 14, no. 1 (1884): 320–21.

————. "A Journey on Foot to the Patani Frontier in 1876: A Journal Kept during an Expedition Undertaken to Capture Datoh Maharajalela of Perak." *JSBRAS* 9, no. 1 (1882): 1–67.

————."Shamanism in Perak." In *A History of Perak*, edited by Richard O. Winstedt and Richard J. Wilkinson, 181–226. Singapore: Malayan Branch of Royal Asiatic Society, 1934.

Maxwell, W. G. *In Malay Forests*. Singapore: Graham Brash, 1907.

————. "Mantra gajah." *JSBRAS* 45 (1906): 1–53.

————. "Mantra gajah." *JSBRAS* 49 (1907): 71–86.

Mayer, Charles. *Trapping Wild Animals in Malay Jungles*. New York: Nuffield & Co., 1921.

McCarraher, Eugene. *The Enchantments of Mammon: How Capitalism Became the Religion of Modernity*. Cambridge, MA: Harvard University Press, 2019.

McKinnon, E. Edwards. "Ceramics, Cloth, Iron and Salt: Coastal Hinterland Interaction in the Karo Region of Northeastern Sumatra." In *From Distant Tales: Archaeology and Ethnohistory in the Highlands of Sumatra*, edited by Dominik Bonatz et al., 120–42. Newcastle upon Tyne: Cambridge Scholars, 2009.

Meerwaldt J. H. "Aantekeningen betreffende de Bataklanden." *TIV* 37 (1894): 513–50.

Middendorp, Wilhelm. "Het inwerken van Westersche krachten op een Indonesisch volk (de Karo Bataks)." *De Socialistische Gids* 7 (1922): 329–465.

Middlebrook, S. M. "Yap Ah Loy (1837–1855)." *JMBRAS* 24, no. 2 (1951): 1–127.

Milner, A. C. "A Note on the Rawa." *JMBRAS* 51, no. 2 (1978): 147.

Mintz, Sidney. *Sweetness and Power: The Place of Sugar in Modern History*. London: Penguin, 1982.

Modigliani, Elio. *Fra i Battachi indipendenti*. Rome: Società Geografica Italiana, 1892.

Moore, Sophie S., Monique Allewaert, Pablo F. Gómez, and Mitman Gregg. "Interrogating the Plantationocene." *Edge Effects*, 2019. Accessed June 16, 2019. http://edge effects.net/plantation-legacies-plantationocene/.

Multatuli. *Max Havelaar or the Coffee Auctions of a Dutch Trading Company*. Translated by Alphonso Nahuys. New York: Penguin, 1987.

Niessen, Sandra. *Batak Cloth and Clothing: A Dynamic Indonesian Tradition*. Kuala Lumpur: Oxford University Press, 1993.

————. *Motifs of Life in Batak Texts and Textiles*. Dordrecht: Foris, 1985.

Neumann, J. H. "Bijdrage tot de geschiedenis der Karo-stammen." *BKI* 82 (1926): 1–36.

————. "De Bataksche goeroe." *Medelingen Nederlandsch Zending* 54 (1910): 1–18.

————. *Een jaar onder de Karo Bataks*. 2nd ed. Medan: V. H. Varekamp, 1949.

Noer, Deliar. *The Modernist Muslim Movement in Indonesia, 1900–1942*. New York: Oxford University Press, 1973.

Nongbri, Brent. *Before Religion: A History of a Modern Concept.* New Haven, CT: Yale University Press, 2015.

O'Connor, Stanley J. "Iron Working as Spiritual Inquiry in the Indonesian Archipelago." *History of Religions* 14, no. 3 (1975): 173–90.

Olivier, Robert, "Conservation of the Asian Elephant." *Environmental Conservation* 5, no. 1 (1978): 1–17.

Orsi, Robert. *The Madonna of 115th Street: Faith and Community in Italian Harlem, 1880–1950.* New Haven, CT: Yale University Press, 2002.

Ota, Atsushi. "Tropical Products Out, British Cotton In: Trade in the Dutch Outer Island Ports, 1846–1869." *Southeast Asian Studies* 2, no. 3 (2013): 499–526.

Parker Lyn, Kelsie Prabawa-Sear, and Wahyu Kustiningsih. "How Young People in Indonesia See Themselves as Environmentalists." *Indonesia and the Malay World* 46, no. 136 (2019): 263–82.

Parkin, Harry. *Batak Fruit of Hindu Thought.* Madras: Christian Literature Society, 1978.

Parlindungan, Mangaradja O. *Pongkinangolngolan Sinambela gelar Tuanku Rao: Terror Agama Islam Mazhab Hambali di Tanah Batak 1816–1833.* Jakarta: Penerbit Tandjung Pengharapan, 1963.

Parreñas, Juno Salazar. "The Materiality of Intimacy in Wildlife Rehabilitation: Rethinking Ethical Capitalism through Embodied Encounters with Animals in Southeast Asia." *Positions* 24, no. 1 (2016): 97–126.

Pasqual, Joseph C. "Chinese Tin Mining in Selangor." *Selangor Journal* 4 (1896): 25–29.

Pedersen, Paul. *Batak Blood, Protestant Soul: The Development of National Churches in North Sumatra.* Grand Rapids, MI: William B. Eerdmans, 1970.

Pelzer, Karl. *Planter and Peasant: Colonial Policy and the Agrarian Struggle in East Sumatra.* The Hague: Martinus Nijhoff, 1978.

Penrose, Richard Alexander F. "The Tin Deposits of the Malay Peninsula with Special Reference to Those of the Kinta District." *Journal of Geology* 11, no. 2 (1903): 135–54.

Perret, Daniel, and Heddy Surachman. *History of Padang Lawas: The Site of Si Pamutung.* Paris: Cahier d'Archipel, 2014.

Petraglia, M. D., P. Ditchfield, S. Jones, R. Korisettar, and J. N. Pal. "The Toba Volcanic Super-Eruption, Environmental Change and Hominin Occupation History in India over the Last 140,000 Years." In "The Toba Super-Volcanic Eruption of 74,000 Years Ago: Climate Change, Environments, and Evolving Humans," edited by M. D. Petraglia, R. Korisettar, and J. N. Pal. Special issue, *Quaternary International*, no. 258 (2012): 119–34.

Pleyte, Cornelis M. "Singa Mangaradja, de heilige koning der Bataks." *BKI* 55 (1903): 1–48.

Poeze, Harry, and Kees van Dijk. *In het land van de overheersers: Indonesiers in de Nederlands, 1650–1850.* Dordrecht: Foris, 1986.

Pogos, Raja N., and Jan P. Sitanggang. *Batak na marserak: Maradat adat na niadathon.* Jakarta: Pustaka Sinar Harapan, 2014.

Pospos, P. *Aku dan Toba: Tjatatan Dari Masa Kanak-Kanak.* Jakarta: Balai Pustaka, 1950.

Potter, Leslie M. "A Forest Product Out of Control: Gutta Percha in Indonesia and the Wider Malay World." In *Paper Landscapes: Explorations in the Environmental History of Indonesia,* edited by Peter Boomgaard et al., 281–308. Leiden: KITLV Press, 1997.

Radjab, M. *Perang Paderi.* Jakarta: Kampusiana, 1954.

Raffles, Thomas S. *Memoir of the Life and Public Service of Sir Thomas Stamford Raffles F.R.S. & Co.* London: John Murray, 1830.

Rathborne, Ambrose. *Camping and Tramping in Malaya.* Oxford: John Beaufoy, 2015.

Reid, Anthony. *Blood of the People: Revolution and the End of Traditional Rule in Northern Sumatra.* Kuala Lumpur: Oxford University Press, 1979.

———. *A History of Southeast Asia: Critical Crossroads.* Sussex: Wiley Blackwell, 2015.

———. "Humans and Forests in Pre-colonial Southeast Asia." *Environment and History* 1, no. 1 (1995): 93–110.

———. *Imperial Alchemy: National and Political Identity in Southeast Asia.* Cambridge: Cambridge University Press, 2010.

———. "Islamization and Christianization of Southeast Asia: The Critical Phase, 1550–1650." In *Southeast Asia in the Early Modern Era: Trade, Power and Belief,* edited by Anthony Reid, 151–79. Ithaca, NY: Cornell University Press, 1993.

———. "Is There a Batak History?" Asia Research Institute Working Paper No. 78, 2006.

———. "Merchant Princes and Magic Mediators: Outsiders and Power in Sumatra and Beyond." *Indonesia and the Malay World* 36, no. 105 (2008): 253–57.

———. *Slavery, Bondage and Dependency in Southeast Asia.* Ithaca, NY: Cornell University Press, 1983.

———. *Southeast in the Age of Commerce 1450–1680.* 2 vols. New Haven, CT: Yale University Press, 1988.

———. "Why Do the Batak Erect *Tugu?*" In *The Potent Dead: Ancestors, Saints and Heroes in Contemporary Indonesia,* edited by Henri Chambert-Loir and Anthony Reid, 88–102. Honolulu: University of Hawai'i Press, 2002.

Richards, John F. *The Unending Frontier: An Environmental History of the Early Modern World.* Berkeley: University of California Press, 2003.

Richardson, J. A. *The Geology and Mineral Resources of the Neighbourhood of Pahang: Federated Malay States with an Account of the Geology of the Raub Australian Gold Mine.* Kuala Lumpur: Geological Survey Department, 1939.

Richtmann, William O. "Camphor: A Pharmaceutical and Pharmacognostical Study." PhD diss., University of Wisconsin–Madison, 1919.

Ricklefs, Merle C. "Six Centuries of Islamization in Java." In *Conversion to Islam*, edited by Nehemia Levtzion, 100–128. New York: Holmes and Meier, 1979.

Ricklefs, Merle C., and Pieter Voorhoeve. *Indonesian Manuscripts in Great Britain*. Oxford: Oxford University Press, 1977.

Rijnsche Zending. "De zending onder de Batta's in 1881." *De Rijnsche Zending* 12 (1882): 36–66.

Ris, H. "De onderafdeling klein Mandailing en Pakantan en hare bevolking met uitzondering van de Oeloe's." *BKI* 6, no. 2 (1896): 441–534.

Rodgers, Susan. *Adat, Islam and Christianity in a Batak Homeland*. Athens: Ohio University, Center for International Studies, 1981.

———. "Antic Histories: Narrating the Past in a Martinican Novel and a Sumatran Mock Family Memoir." *Anthropological Forum* 16, no. 3 (2006): 257–75.

———. "Compromise and Contestation in Colonial Sumatra: An 1873 Mandailing Schoolbook on the 'Wonders of the West.'" *BKI* 158, no. 3 (2002): 479–512.

———. *Telling Lives, Telling History*. Berkeley: University of California Press, 1995.

Rood, Daniel B. *The Reinvention of Atlantic Slavery: Technology, Labor, Race and Capitalism in the Greater Caribbean*. Oxford: Oxford University Press, 2017.

Ross, Carey. "The Tin Frontier: Mining, Empire, and Environment in Southeast Asia, 1870s–1930s." *Environmental History* 19, no. 2 (2014): 454–79.

Said, Mohammad. *Dari halaman-halaman terlepas dalam tjatatan tentang tokoh Singamangaradja XII*. Medan: Waspada, 1961.

Sainsbury, Cleo Ladell. *Tin Resources of the World*. Geological Survey Bulletin 1301. Washington DC: US Government Printing Office, 1969.

Salleh, Muhammad Haji, ed. *Sejarah Melayu*. Kuala Lumpur: Dewan Bahasa dan Pustaka, 1997.

Sangti, Batara Simanjuntak. *Sejarah Batak*. Balige: K. Sianipar, 1978.

Schadée, W. H. M. *De uitbreiding van ons gezag in de Bataklanden*. Leiden: Van Doesburgh, 1920.

Schnitger, Friedrich M. *Forgotten Kingdoms in Sumatra*. Leiden: Brill, 1939.

Scott, James C. *The Art of Not Being Governed: An Anarchist History of Upland Southeast Asia*. New Haven, CT: Yale University Press, 2009.

———. *Seeing Like a State: How Certain Schemes to Improve the Human Condition Have Failed*. New Haven, CT: Yale University Press, 1998.

Serullas, M. "Rediscovery of Gutta Percha Tree at Singapore." *Bulletin of Miscellaneous Information* (Royal Botanic Gardens at Kew), no. 163 (1891).

Sevea, Teren. *Miracles and Material Life: Rice, Ore, Traps and Guns in Islamic Malaya*. Cambridge: Cambridge University Press, 2020.

Sherman, D. George. *Rice, Rupees and Ritual: Economy and Society among the Samosir Batak of Sumatra*. Stanford, CA: Stanford University Press, 1990.

———. "What Green Desert? The Ecology of Batak Grassland Farming." *Indonesia* 29 (April 1980): 112–48.

Sibeth, Achim. *The Batak: Peoples of the Island of Sumatra.* New York: Thames and Hudson, 1991.

Sideris, Lisa. *Consecrating Science: Wonder, Knowledge and the Natural World.* Oakland: University of California Press, 2017.

Sidjabat, Walter Bonar. *Ahu Si Singamangaradja: Arti politis, ekonomi dan religius Si Singamangaradja XII.* Medan: Penerbit Sinar Harapan, 1982.

Sinambela, Poernama Rea. *Ayahku, Si Singamangaradja XII pahlawan nasional.* Jakarta: Aksara Persada, 1992.

Singarimbun, Masri. *Kinship, Descent and Alliance among the Karo Batak.* Berkeley: University of California Press, 1975.

Situmorang, Sitor. *Guru Somalaing dan Modigliani "Utusan Raja Rom": Sekelumit sejarah lahirnya gerakan Ratu Adik di Toba.* Jakarta: Grafindo Mukti, 1993.

———. *Toba Na Sae: Sejarah lembaga sosial politik abad XIII–XX.* Jakarta: Komunitas Bambu, 2004.

Sivasundaram, Sujit. "Trading Knowledge: The East India Company's Elephants in India and Britain." *Historical Journal* 48, no. 1 (2005): 27–63.

Skeat, Walter. *Malay Magic: An Introduction to the Folklore and Popular Religion of Malaya.* London: Macmillan, 1900.

Soares, Benjamin, and Filippo Osella. "Islam, Politics, Anthropology." Supplement, *Journal of the Royal Anthropological Institute* 15, no. 1 (2009): S1–23.

Sprenger, Guido. "Dimensions of Animism in Southeast Asia." In *Animism in Southeast Asia*, edited by Kai Århem and Guido Sprenger, 31–51. New York: Routledge, 2016.

Steedly, Mary M. *Hanging without a Rope: Narrative Experience in Colonial and Postcolonial Karoland.* Princeton, NJ: Princeton University Press, 1993.

———. "Modernity and the Memory Artist: The Work of Imagination in Highland Sumatra, 1947–1995." *Comparative Studies in Society and History* 42, no. 4 (2000): 811–46.

———. *Rifle Reports: A Story of Indonesian Independence.* Berkeley: University of California Press, 2013.

Steffen, Will, Wendy Broadgate, Ludwig Deutsch, Owen Gaffney, and Cornelia Ludwig. "The Trajectory of the Anthropocene." *Anthropocene Review* 2, no.1 (2015): 81–98.

Steffen, Will, Paul J. Crutzen, and John R. MacNeill. "The Anthropocene: Are Humans Now Overwhelming the Great Forces of Nature?" *Ambio* 36, no. 8 (2007): 614–21.

Steijn-Parvé, H. A. "De secte der Padaries (Padries) in de bovenlanden van Sumatra." *TIV* 2, no. 3 (1854): 249–78.

Stoler, Ann Laura. *Capitalism and Confrontation on Sumatra's Plantation Belt.* Ann Arbor: University of Michigan Press, 1985.

Stoll, Mark. *Inherit the Holy Mountain: Religion and the Rise of American Environmentalism.* New York: Oxford University Press, 2015.

Sukamar, Raman. *The Asian Elephant: Ecology and Management.* Cambridge: Cambridge University Press, 1989.

———. *The Story of Asia's Elephants.* Mumbai: Marg, 2011.

"Sumatra Camphor." *New Remedies* 10, no. 11 (1881): 331.

Susilowati, A., K. S. Hartini, H. H. Rachmat, and A. Alvaroby. "Propagation of Valuable North Sumatera Benzoin Trees (*Styrax* sp.) Using Macrocutting Techniques." *IOP Conference Series Materials Science and Engineering* 180, no. 1 (2017): 1–5.

Swettenham, F. A. "Annual Report of the British Resident of Perak for the Year 1894." *Perak Government Gazette* 8, no. 19 (July 19, 1895): 353–72.

Swettenham, Frank. "From Perak to Slim and down the Slim and Bernam Rivers." *JMBRAS* 5, no. 1 (1880): 51–68.

Syafnir Aboe Nain, ed. *Naskah Tuanku Imam Bonjol.* Padang: Pusat Pengkajian Islam dan Minangkabau, 2004.

Symington, C. F. *Malayan Forest Records No. 16: Foresters Manual of Dipterocarps.* Kuala Lumpur: Penerbit University Malaya, 1974.

Sysling, Fenneke. *Racial Science and Human Diversity in Colonial Indonesia.* Singapore: NUS Press, 2016.

Szerszynski, Bronislaw. "Gods of the Anthropocene: Geo-spiritual Formations in the Earth's New Epoch." *Theory, Culture & Society* 34, no. 2–3 (2017): 253–75.

Tannenbaum, Nicola B. *Who Can Compete against the World? Power-Protection and Buddhism in Shan Worldview.* Ann Arbor, MI: Association for Asian Studies, 1996.

Tavares, Antonio. "Crystals from the Savage Forest: Imperialism and Capitalism in the Taiwan Camphor Industry, 1800–1945." PhD diss., Princeton University, 2004.

Teh-Gallop, Annabel. "Malay Documents in the Melaka Records in the British Library." *Itinerario* 30, no. 2 (2006): 54–77.

Teygeler, René, "Pustaha: A Study into the Production Process of the Batak Book." *BKI* 149, no. 3 (1993): 593–611.

Tichelman G. J. "De parhoedamdam beweging." *Mededeelingen van de Vereeniging van Gezaghebbers de Binnenlandsch Bestuur No. 45*, 1937.

Tideman, J. *De Bataklanden, 1917–1931.* Leiden: Bataksch Instituut, 1932.

———. *Simeloengoen: Het land der Timoer-Bataks im zijn vroegere isolatie en zijn ontwikkeling tot een deel van het cultuurgebied van de Oostkust van Sumatra.* Leiden: L. H. Becherer, 1922.

Tomich, Dale. "The Order of Historical Time: The *Longue Durée* and Micro-history." *Almanack Guarulhos*, no. 2 (2011): 52–65.

Tong, Cheu Hock. "The Sinicization of Malay Keramats in Malaysia." *JMBRAS* 71, no. 2 (1998): 29–61.

Trautmann, Thomas. *Elephants and Kings: An Environmental History*. Chicago: University of Chicago Press, 2015.

Tsing, Anna L. *In the Realm of the Diamond Queen: Marginality in an Out-of-the-Way Place*. 1993. Princeton, NJ: Princeton University Press, 1993.

———. *The Mushroom at the End of the World: On the Possibility of Life in Capitalist Ruins*. Princeton, NJ: Princeton University Press, 2015.

Tucker, Richard, and Edmund Russell, eds. *Natural Enemy, Natural Ally: Toward an Environmental History of War*. Corvallis: Oregon State University Press, 2004.

Tugby, Donald J. *Cultural Identity and Change: Mandailing Immigrants in West Malaysia*. St. Lucia: University of Queensland Press, 1977.

———. "The Social Function of *Mahr* in Upper Mandailing, Sumatra." *American Anthropologist* 61, no. 4 (1959): 631–40.

Van Asselt, Gustav. *Achttien jaren onder der Batak*. Rotterdam: D. A. Daamen, ca. 1905.

Van Bemmelen, Sita. *Christianity, Colonization and Gender in North Sumatra*. Leiden: KITLV/Brill, 2017.

Van den Arend, Pieter. "De opkomst der landbouwondernemingen in Deli (I)." *TAG* 2 (1897): 295–96.

Van den Berg, E. J. "De Parhoedamdambeweging." *Medelingen Nederlandsch Zending* 64 (1920): 22–38.

Van der Putten, Jan. "Abdullah Munsyi and the Missionaries." *BKI* 162, no. 4 (2008): 407–40.

Van der Tuuk, Herman Neubronner, and Kees Groeneboer, eds. *Een vorst onder de taalgeleerden: Herman Neubronner Van Der Tuuk, taalafgevaardigde voor Indië voor Nederlandsch Bijbelgenootschap*. Leiden: KITLV Uitgeverij, 2002.

Van Dijk, Pieter A. L. E. "Die excursie naar de westelijke onafhakelijke landschappen in Toba-landen van het jaar 1889." *TAG* 12 (1895): 1–24.

———. "Een tochtje per prauw Zuid Samosir van Nainggolan to Lottoeng en een korte beschrijving van den oostelijke oever van het het Toba-meer van Si Regar tot Poerba," *TAG* 13 (1896): 419–36.

Van Duuren, D. A. P. "Parmalims and Parhudamdams: Twee profetische bewegingen bij de Bataks rond de eeuwwisseling." PhD diss., Utrecht Instituut voor Culturele Antropologie, Rijksuniversiteit, 1983.

Van Hasselt, Arend L. "Eenige mededelingen omtrent het voorkomen van geophagie in Residentie Tapanoeli." *TIV* 33 (1894): 310–12.

Van Hoëvell, G. W. W. C. "Iets over t' oorlogvoeren der Batta's." *TNI* 40 (1878): 110–78.

Van Kessel, Oscar. "Reis in de Nog Onafhankelijke Bataklanden van Klein-Toba, op Sumatra in 1844." *BKI* 4, no. 1–2 (1855): 55–97.

Van Leur, Jacob Cornelis. *Indonesian Trade and Society*. The Hague: W. Van Hoeve, 1955.

Van Vuuren, Louis. "De handel van Baroes, als oudste haven op Sumatra's Westkust, verklaard and voor de toekomst beschouwd." *TAG* 25 (1908): 1389–1402.

"Varia." *TNI* 2 (1976): 476–84.

Vergouwen, Jacob Cornelis. *The Social Organisation and Customary Law of the Toba-Batak of Northern Sumatra*. The Hague: Martinus Nijhoff, 1964.

Veth, Pieter Johannes. "De bovenlanden." *TAG* 2 (1877): 154–58.

———. "De oorlog van 1872." *TAG* 2 (1877): 165–71.

———. "De opkomst van de landbouwondernemingen." *TAG* 2 (1877): 159–64.

———. "The Dutch Expedition to Central Sumatra." *Proceedings of the Royal Geographical Society and Monthly Record of Geography* 1, no. 12 (1879): 759–77.

Viner, A. C. "The Changing Batak," *Journal of the Malayan Branch of the Royal Asiatic Society* 52, no. 2 (1979): 79–87.

Vitebsky, Piers. *Living without the Dead: Loss and Redemption in a Jungle Cosmos*. Chicago: University of Chicago Press, 2017.

Voll, John. "Muhammad Hayya al-Sindi and Muhammad b. Abd al-Wahhab." *Bulletin of School of Oriental and African Studies* 38 (1975): 32–39.

Voorhoeve, Pieter. *Batak Bark Books*. Manchester: Bulletin of the John Rylands Library, 1951.

———. "Bataksche buffelwichelarij." *BKI* 114, no. 1 (1958): 238–48.

———. *Elio Modigliani's Batak Books*. Florence, 1980.

Wade, Geoff. "Southeast Asian Islam and Southern China in the Second Half of the Fourteenth Century." In *Anthony Reid and the Study of the Southeast Asian Past*, edited by Geoff Wade and Li Tana. Singapore: Institute of Southeast Asian Studies, 2012.

Wallace, Anthony F. C. "Revitalization Movements." *American Anthropologist* 56, no. 2 (1956): 264–81.

Warneck, Johannes. *Die Religion der Batak*. Gottingen: Vandenhoek & Ruprecht, 1909.

———. *Toba-Batak Deutches Wörterbuchs*. Batavia: Landsdrukkerij, 1906.

———. *50 Jahre Batakmission in Sumatra*. Berlin: M. Warneck, 1912.

———. *Von Heiden und Christen in Sumatra*. Barmen: Verlag des Missionshauses, 1920.

Watson, C. W. "Rawa and Rinchi: A Further Note." *JMBRAS* 55, no. 1 (1982): 82–86.

Weber, Max. *The Protestant Ethic and the Spirit of Capitalism*. 1904–5. New York: Penguin Classics, 2002.

Wellem, Frederick D. *Amir Sjarifoeddin: Tempatnya dalam Kekristenan dan perjuangan kemerdekaan Indonesia*. Jakarta: Ut. Omnes Unum Sint Institute, 2009.

Wessing, Robert. "Symbolic Animals in the Land between the Waters: Markers of Place and Transition." *Asian Folklore Studies* 65, no. 2 (2006): 205–39.

Westenberg, C. J. "Aantekeningen omtrent de Godsdienstige begrippen der Karo Bataks." *BKI* 5 no. 7 (1891): 208–53.

Wharton, Charles M. "Man, Fire and Wild Cattle in Southeast Asia." In *Southeast Asian Grasslands: Understanding a Vernacular Landscape; Canonical Readings*, edited by Michael R. Dove. Bronx: New York Botanical Garden Press, 2008.

White, Lynn. "The Historical Roots of Our Ecological Crisis." *Science* 155 (1967): 1203–7.

Widianto, Harry. "The Dawn of Humanity in Sumatra: Arrival and Dispersal from the Human Remains Perspective." In *From Distant Tales: Archaeology and Ethnohistory in the Highlands of Sumatra*, edited by Dominik Bonatz et al., 28–42. Newcastle upon Tyne: Cambridge Scholars, 2009.

Wilkinson, Richard J. "Some Malay Studies." *JMBRAS* 10, no. 1 (1932): 67–137.

Willer, T. I. "Verzameling der Battasche wetten en instellingen in Mandheling en Pertibie." *TNI* 7 (1845): 202–96.

Winkler, Johannes. *Die Toba-Batak auf Sumatra in gesunden und kranken Tagen: Ein Beitrag zur Kenntnis des animistischen Heidentums.* Stuttgart: Belser, 1925.

Winkler, Johannes, and Pieter Voorhoeve. "Pane Na Bolon, ein Kriegsorakel auf Sumatra." *BKI* 112, no. 1 (1956): 25–40.

Winstedt, Richard O. "'Karamat': Sacred Places and Persons in Malaya." *JMBRAS* 2, no. 3 (1924): 264–79.

———. "An Old Minangkabau Legal Digest from Perak." *JMBRAS* 26, no. 1 (1953): 8–15.

———. "Perak Genies." *JMBRAS* 7, no. 3 (1929): 460–66.

Winstedt, Richard O., and Richard J. Wilkinson. "A History of Perak." *JMBRAS* 12, no. 1 (1934): 1–180.

Wolf, Eric. *Europe and the People without History.* Berkeley: University of California Press, 1982.

Wolters, Oliver W. *History, Culture and Region in Southeast Asian Perspectives.* Ithaca, NY: Cornell SEAP Publications, 1999.

Wong, Lin Ken. *The Malayan Tin Industry to 1914: With Special Reference to the States of Perak, Selangor, Negri Sembilan, and Pahang.* Tucson: published for the Association for Asian Studies by the University of Arizona Press, 1965.

World Bank. *Faiths and the Environment: World Bank Support, 2000–5.* Washington, DC: International Bank for Reconstruction and Development, 2006.

Ypes, W. K. H. *Bijdrage tot de kennis van der stamverwantschap, de inheemsche rechtsgemeenschappen en grondenrecht der Toba en Dairibataks.* The Hague: Martinus Nijhoff, 1932.

Zakaria, Faizah. "Sacral Ecologies of the North Sumatran Highlands: An Environmental History of Conversions, 1800 to 1928." PhD diss., Yale University, 2017.

———. "The Toba Super-Catastrophe as History of the Future." *Indonesia* 113 (2022): 33–50.

INDEX

Page numbers in *italics* refer to illustrations

spirits and, 14; trade of, 51–52, 66, 149; writing and, 96

conservation: laws and, 183–84; in North Sumatra, 1–2; swidden and, 28

conversion: camphor trees and, 124–25, 151–52; Christianity and, 2–6, 86, 98, 132–35, 140–41, 185; Dutch power and, 131; environment and, 154; environmentalism and, 187–89, 192–94; of identity, 26; impediments to, 86–87; Indigenous Batak and, 190; the Padri and, 59, 64, 68; writing and, 74, 96–97, 101–5, 111–19

Council of Elders (Namora Natoras), 66

Crutzen, Paul, 4–5

currency, limited flow of, 91–92

Dalihan Na Tolu, 30–32, 38

darshana, 33

datu (priest magician), 24–41; bark books and, 74; Dutch definition of, 131; Nommensen as, 94; sacrifice by, 61; staff of, 31; tondi and, 41; types of magic and, 49–53

Davies, Jeremy, 6

death, sacral ecology of, 39–42

Debata Na Tolu, 24, 133

Dekker, Douwes, 68

djinn (supernatural being), 19

Dutch colonialism: camphor trade and, 89–91; education by, 84–85; forest products trade and, 91; in West Sumatra, 64–67

Dutch East Indies, 10, 58, 82–85, 143, *144*, 147–51

earth system: rupture in, 47; trends in, 5

East India Company, 36, 52, 104

ecology, sociopolitical, 3

edible earth (*bange*), 30

education, upended social order and, 94–95

Eight Tigers (Harimau nan Selapan), 51–52

elephant: the datu and, 136; disenchantment with, 155–57; enchantment with, 157–62, 179–86, *180*; religious perspective on, 172–79, *174*; as status symbol, 16; use of, 162–66; white elephant as, 87

Elvin, Mark, 105

enslavement (*hatoban*), 42–46, *45*, 94

environmentalism: animist religions and, 3; Padri War and, 68–69

faith: agriculture and, 135; animism and, 153–54; Anthropocene and, 187; Batak and, 59, 133; capitalism and, 74; Christianity, Islam, and, 98; environmental change and, 4; environmentalism and, 187–94; forest faiths and, 16, 189; Hinduism, 23–24, 159, 172; the individual and, 118; material impact of, 15; monotheism and, 7; Padri and, 68–69; Parmalim as, 132, 139–40

folklore, 6, 21–27, 34, 73, 99

forest frontier, 2, 145, 156

Francis (pope), 187

frankincense. *See* benzoin

Fuller, Christopher, 34

Gabriel, C., 57–58

Gadombang, Radja, 65

Ghosh, Amitav, 47, 98–99, 112, 120

Godon, Alexander, 77, 85

Great Derangement, 98

Grove, Richard, 15

Hadler, Jeff, 56

Hale, Abraham, 113–14

Hamilton, Clive, 47

Harahap, Basyral Hamidy, 12, 63

Harahap, Ephraim Sutan Gunung Tua, 74, 81, 83

Harahap, Sjarif Anwar (Sutan Gunung Tua), 76–81

Henley, David, 20

Hikamat (Marjan), 100–106, 112–13, 116, 119

Hikayat Hikamat, 101–4, 112, 116

Hindu: conversion and, 152; influence in North Sumatra of, 23–24; mythology of, 99, 112, 115; puja and, 33–34; ritual and, 159, 172

Hislop, Jim, 182

Hoabinhian culture, 23

Hobsbawm, Eric, 68

horja, 88, 90

Hornaday, William, 177

Hubback, Theodore, 183–84

Hulumbujati, 22

huta: conversion in, 64; physical and spiritual boundaries of, 89; as settlement area, 25; violent conflict in, 49

Huta Dame, 93–96

Indigenous people: as *masyarakat terasing*, 190; recognition of customary rights of, 1

Industrial Revolution, 5, 48, 68

interfaith community, 119, 192

Iskander, Willem (Sati), 12, 74–77, 81–85, 148

Islam: animism and, 16, 20–21, 153; Batak and, 2; conversion and, 5, 8–9, 26, 37–39, 98, 113, 185; the Dutch and, 14; economic interests and, 51; entry into Sumatra of, 26–27; environment and, 115, 187–92; imagery of, 172–73;

monotheism and, 156–57; Padri and, 52–57, 62–69; technological power and, 120; transition in, 4; wood and, 171. *See also* Muslim

Jailani, Syeikh Abdul Qadir al-, 51

Jalaluddin, Syeikh, 52

Jervois, William, 176–77

Joustra, Meint, 29

Judaism, agency of humans in, 6–7

Junghuhn, Franz Wilhellm, 29, 92, 141

Keasberry, Benjamin, 100–105

Kedatangan Bondjol, 57–60

Khalid, Fazlun, 187

Kitab perentah pawang, 172–75, *174*

Korn, Victor Emanuel, 57–58

Lawh Mahfuz, 173

Leech, H. W. C., 165, 177–78

Lelo, Tuanku, 62–63

Li, Tania, 20, 190

literacy, 73–75, 92–97

Lofton, Kathryn, 7

Lumbantobing, Radja Pontas, 86, 95

Malacca, Straits of, 2, 10, 15, 45, 100, 108, 179

Malay Peninsula: camphor trade and, 38, 147–48; charismatic authority in, 15, 156; conflict in, 127–28, 164–65; elephants in, 155, 157–66, 172–86, *174*, *180*; enslavement in, 44; environmentalism in, 187–90; farming in, 127; folklore of, 6, 132–34, 161; forestry in, 168–72, *169*, *170*; history of, 2–21, 38, 106–9; literature from, 98, 106; migration to, 99, *107*, 119, 106–9; Pahang, *107*, 108, 116, 176–77, 183; Pakpak, 11, *11*, 19, 21, 29, 43,

149–51; *pawang* in, 158–60; Perak, elephants and, 157–69, *180*, 181; tin mining in, 110–14; water and, 109–11, 158

Malaysia: adat communities in, 16, 19; elephants in, 178; environmentalism in, 187; geography of, 2; history of, 10–11; religion in, 19, 190

Mandailing: as Batak subgroup, 10–11, *11*; conquest of, 55; development of writing and, 24, 98; dialect of, 75–76; the Dutch in, 64–68, 77–78; Padri War and, 47, *54*, 55, 61–62; school in, 82–85

Mangalabulan, 22

Mangkutur, Sutan, 67

Manik, Liberty, 49

Mann, Charles, 193–94

Marjan. *See* Hikamat

Marsden, William, 36, 40–41, 141

masyarakat adat, 190–91

Max Havelaar, 68

Maxwell, W. E., 164, 175

Maxwell, W. G., 158, 175

Mbuyuk, Si Mbuyuk, 73

McCarraher, Eugene, 97

migration (*marserak*): Batak to Malay Peninsula, 99–100, *107*; new village formation by, 25–27; from Toba, 23

Minangkabau: buffalo and, 57; Dutch intervention with, 14, 64–65; the Padri and, 47–54, *54*

mining: Chinese migrants and, 111; Malay magician and, 114; of tin, 108–17, 162, 166; water and, 110–11, 117–18, 176

Ministry for the Environment and Forestry, Indonesian, 1

Miskin, Haji, 51

missionary, in North Tapanuli, 92–97

Modigliani, Elio, 132–36

monotheistic religion, 4, 6–8, 15, 19

Mount Zion, 101, 104–5

Mula Jadi Nabolon, 22, 24, 41, 133, 137

Muslim: as adat-inflected, 47; as animist-influenced convert, 4; Batak and, 37–39; bureaucrat as, 172; coastal polities of, 20; conversions to, 111, 113; Eight Tigers and, 51; in environmental movements, 2, 16, 118, 186–92; folklore of, 115; Malay literature and, 98, 106–9; Mandailing as, 169; modernist societies of, 9, 47; Padri War and, 48, 68

naga padoha (*naga*), in mythology, 25, 99–100, 117–18

Najib, Pak, 193

Nan Tar Tar Nan Tor, 34

Nasution clan, 26, 75

Navarrete, Fernández, 34

Nommensen, Ludwig Ingwer, 13, 86, 92–97

nonhuman being, the Anthropocene and, 6, 61

North Sumatra: camphor trade in, 33; Hindu influences in, 24

North Sumatra uplands: camphor, benzoin, and, 33–39; death and sacrifice in, 39–40; enslavement in, 41–45, *45*; history of, 9–16, *11*, 20–26; rice and, 27–32

North Tapanuli. *See* South Tapanuli; Tapanuli

O'Connor, Stanley J., 102

Orang Asli, 190–91

Orang Rimba, 190

Orsi, Robert, 7

Padang Lawas, 24, 28, 54, 76

Padri, 47–52, *54*, 57–69, 77

Van Leur, J. C., 3
volcano, 21, 76, 99

Wahhab, Muhammad Ibn Abd al-, 51, 56
Wallace, Alfred Russell, 99
warfare, 29–30, 48–50, 62, 68. *See also*
    Padri War
water: Hindu mythology and, 98–100;
    mining and, 109–12, 117
Weber, Max, 8–9, 97, 156

Wharton, Charles, 177
White, Lynn, 102
Widodo, Joko, land restoration and, 1
Winkler, Johannes, 50
women, during war, 63–64
writing, 24–25, 73–74, 96, 98

Yacob, Raja, 106–17, 168, *169*, 178
Yang Dipertuan, 66–67, 77

Culture, Place, and Nature
Studies in Anthropology and Environment

*The Camphor Tree and the Elephant: Religion and Ecological Change
in Maritime Southeast Asia*, by Faizah Zakaria

*Turning Land into Capital: Development and Dispossession in the Mekong
Region*, edited by Philip Hirsch, Kevin Woods, Natalia Scurrah,
and Michael B. Dwyer

*Spawning Modern Fish: Transnational Comparison in the Making
of Japanese Salmon*, by Heather Anne Swanson

Upland Geopolitics: Postwar Laos and the Global Land Rush,
by Michael B. Dwyer

*Misreading the Bengal Delta: Climate Change, Development, and Livelihoods
in Coastal Bangladesh*, by Camelia Dewan

*Ordering the Myriad Things: From Traditional Knowledge to Scientific
Botany in China*, by Nicholas K. Menzies

Timber and Forestry in Qing China: Sustaining the Market, by Meng Zhang

Consuming Ivory: Mercantile Legacies of East Africa and New England,
by Alexandra Celia Kelly

*Mapping Water in Dominica: Enslavement and Environment under
Colonialism*, by Mark W. Hauser

Mountains of Blame: Climate and Culpability in the Philippine Uplands,
by Will Smith

*Sacred Cows and Chicken Manchurian: The Everyday Politics of Eating
Meat in India*, by James Staples

Gardens of Gold: Place-Making in Papua New Guinea,
by Jamon Alex Halvaksz

www.ingramcontent.com/pod-product-compliance
Lightning Source LLC
Chambersburg PA
CBHW031415270326
41929CB00010BA/1460